ROCHESTER

American Historical Press
Sun Valley, California

ROCHESTER

A Panoramic History

Blake McKelvey
& Ruth Rosenberg-Naparsteck

© 2001 American Historical Press
All Rights Reserved
Published 2001
Printed in the United States of America

Library of Congress Catalogue Card Number: 2001096023

ISBN: 1-892724- 24-3

Bibliography: p. 298
Includes Index

Foreword

Few cities have been as diligent as Rochester in the development of their historical and visual records. The first village *Directory*, issued in 1827, devoted nearly half of its 157 pages to an account of the town's fifteen formative years; and a decade later, when Henry O'Reilly, editor of its first daily, produced his 468-page *Sketches of Rochester*, the first major study of an inland city, he engaged the assistance of skilled artists in preparing a series of forty-five engravings that comprise today an unrivaled record of the town's early mills, taverns, churches and other structures. O'Reilly's successors in due time commemorated the city's 50th and 100th birthdays; and in recent years historians have again supplied Rochester with comprehensive accounts of its development. Yet Rochester's accomplishments in making and preserving visual records have been even more dramatic. Local Daguerrian studios, rivalling those of New York and Paris, made Rochester a photographic center two full decades before George Eastman developed it into the world's leading producer of photographic equipment.

Rochester's special interests in historical and visual records appear in retrospect a natural outgrowth and expression of its essential character as a people's city. Although its location at the falls of the Genesee gave it an initial advantage, that site, undeveloped by its Seneca predecessors, had awaited the arrival of settlers able to exploit its water power and transport facilities. Fortunately, Colonel Rochester, its founder and early leader, was astute enough to harmonize its milling and mercantile interests with those of its more numerous artisans, for, after the potentialities of its mills had been fully developed, the city's continued growth depended on the talents and skills of its artisans.

Attracted in increasing numbers from abroad, Rochester's artisans developed diversified industries and gave the city in its middle years a cosmopolitan character. Although some of their enterprises faltered in the depression of the mid-1890s, others, buttressed by patents and quality standards, prospered and transformed Rochester in the early 1900s into a technological city. Its new specialty required educational proficiency and quality services, and Rochester relied increasingly on expert leadership to attain its goals in the Eastman period.

Although again challenged by the Great Depression of the 1930s, the city's technological industries and bureaucratic institutions achieved a remarkable recovery during the Second World War and opened new and broader horizons. The resultant growth and regional expansion brought new demographic shifts and civic decentralization. These trends, while perplexing and often disturbing, have supplied scope and vitality to a number of neighborhood, ethnic, and group expressions that have transformed Rochester into what may best be described as a grass roots metropolis.

I hope that the following, somewhat anecdotal account, supported by a generous selection of choice documentary views and early and contemporary photographs, will recapture some of the human flavor and animation that from the start characterized the history of Rochester.

June 20, 1979   Blake McKelvey

Only a few months before this update, Dr. McKelvey passed away. Up to the time of his death he was actively researching, writing and asking penetrating questions about our region's history and its impact on us and the nation. He was a wonderful man to study with. As a founding member and first chairman of the Urban History Group, he helped to establish urban history as a legitimate area of study. I am pleased to have been asked to update Dr. McKelvey's *Rochester A Panoramic History*. I have brought this book forward, but have not found it necessary to change his own interpretation of our city's history prior to 1979. I believe he would have been pleased. I hope that you enjoy this book and learn from it.

September, 2001   Ruth Rosenberg-Naparsteck

Contents

Seneca in the costume of the Iroquois. Reproduced from the frontispiece of Lewis H. Morgan, League of the Iroquois *(Rochester, 1851)*

Chapter

1

The Seneca "Time of Troubles"

A community's history properly begins with the origins of that community. But when, as in Rochester's case, its antecedents retain a special fascination, as the Senecas most certainly do, it is almost mandatory to pay them a respectful salute. Why, we must ask, did these proud people, who occupied the broad Genesee Country for some four hundred years, finally cede most of their lands and withdraw into limited reservations?

The question is easier to pose than to answer. The records of the negotiation at Buffalo Creek in 1788, which resulted in the Phelps and Gorham Purchase, shroud some inglorious inequities, to put it mildly. A review of the background of that treaty, however, will help to place our city in its historical setting. Perhaps we may also gain some insight relevant to the future of Greater Rochester by a consideration of the dilemma that confronted our predecessors.

The League of the Iroquois

The fortunes of the Senecas were linked closely with the League of the Iroquois, which they helped to found around 1570. Conceived as a peace league, it brought an end to the internecine raids that plagued the area for a century or more. The league bound together five, later six, neighboring Iroquois tribes in upstate New York in a "chain of friendship" that made them the strongest native bulwark confronting the invading Europeans in the 1600s.

With a self-sufficient economy, enduring traditions, and a stable leadership supported by a large body of hardy and fearless warriors, the Iroquois were supremely self-confident. The Mohawks, who guarded the league's "eastern door," were more impressed than terrified when, at their first encounter with the French under Champlain, a few of their braves fell before his guns. Intrigued by the startling power of the white man's "thunder sticks," the Iroquois soon learned from the French traders, who closely followed Champlain, that gifts of furs, which they could supply in abundance, would secure in return gifts of guns, blankets, gaudy trinkets, and sometimes a swig of "firewater" that added to the merriment of the exchange.

The Senecas, who guarded the league's "western door" and possessed the largest expanse of territory for hunting and trapping, quickly became the chief suppliers of beaver skins. They learned how to dicker with the French at Quebec and the British at Albany for the best bargains. They sheltered a succession of Jesuit missionaries, among them Father Julien Garnier who spent several winters in their villages. They hosted LaSalle at Totiakton, their principal town, on two occasions and dissuaded him from pushing farther south in search of a route to the Ohio Valley. Their efforts to control the fur trade of the upper lakes brought them into violent conflict with the Hurons and the Eries in Canada, prompting the Marquis de Denonville, governor of New France, to lead an army of nearly two thousand French and Indians to the Genesee in 1687 to chastise them. The Senecas quickly rebuilt their longhouse villages, however, and carried their furs to Albany.

The French, eager to resume the lucrative fur trade, soon agreed to an exchange of prisoners and dispatched missionaries, traders, and smiths to reside in the Genesee villages. When the British protested such dealings with their rivals, the Senecas extended their "chain of friendship" to Albany, professed a willingness to shelter English missionaries, too, and urgently requested the location of resident smiths in their villages.

The Dilemma of the Iroquois

It is this request, repeated at several "council fires" with the British, that provides the key to an understanding of their problem. The Senecas and other Iroquois had adopted the firearms, knives, and kettles of the Europeans, but they had not acquired the skills needed to keep them in repair. Their dependence on resident smiths, and on a frequent replenishment of their stores of powder and rum, had

Father Isaac Jogues, S.J., considered the founder of the Iroquois missions, was murdered October 18, 1646. The relentless efforts of the French Jesuits to Christianize American natives during the 17th century in the face of incredible hardships forms the earliest chapter of the recorded history of western New York. Courtesy of City Historian's Office

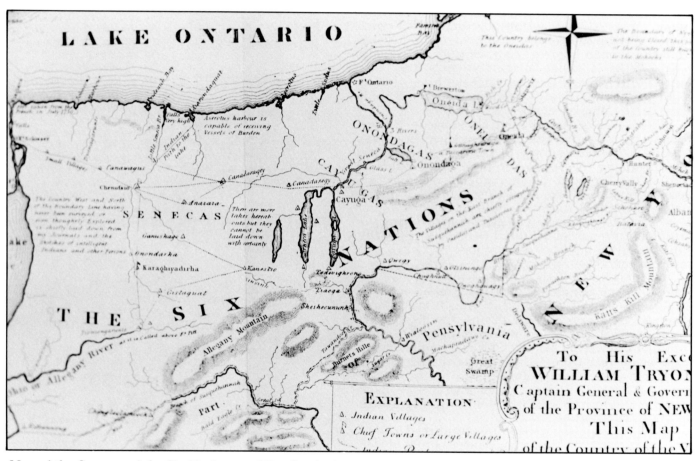

*Map of the Country of the Six Nations...1771. (Section)
drawn by Guy Johnson (ms in State Library) and
reproduced from an engraving in E.B. O'Callaghan,
Documentary History of the State of New York, Vol. IV
(Albany, 1851). Courtesy of City Historian's Office*

undermined their self-sufficient economy and made them more vulnerable to the expanding French and British empires.

Thus in the early 1700s, when the British complained of the establishment of a French trading post on Irondequoit Bay, the Senecas invited them to come and destroy it and replace it with one of their own. The British did develop a post at Oswego, which prompted the French officer, Louis T. de Joncaire, who as a captive of the Senecas had lived several years in their villages and had won adoption into the tribe, to remove his post from Irondequoit to Niagara. In 1722 the British sent Captain Peter Schuyler, Jr., with Laurence Classe to open a post on the bay, but their efforts to maintain it faltered. When the British again protested the continued presence of French traders among the Senecas, their chiefs promised to send the French home *as soon as* the English supplied smiths to reside in their villages; they also agreed to welcome Protestant missionaries *as soon as* the prices at Albany were low enough to enable them to buy Sunday clothes!

There was a hint of their old spirit in this response, but already their earlier independence was waning. The local supply of beaver had been depleted, forcing the Senecas to press their efforts to control the fur trade on the upper lakes, and this activity involved them more closely in the imperial struggles of the British and the French. Their young braves found employment as mercenaries during the protracted French and Indian wars, but the ready supply of guns and powder dropped off sharply in recurrent periods of peace.

Iroquois braves fought on both sides in the final contest. Some Senecas joined the French in their attack on Fort Pitt and in other raids into Pennsylvania where Mary Jemison, destined to become the legendary "White Woman of the Genesee," had been captured a few years before and was now an adopted member of their tribe. Others joined the British expedition led by General John Prideaux in the relief of besieged Oswego, and advanced with his troops along the southern shore of Lake Ontario for an attack on the French fort at Niagara.

It was during their encampment at Irondequoit Bay, on July 3, 1759, that a few Senecas probably led Captain Thomas Davies on a sight-seeing trip through the lower Genesee gorge and watched with curiosity as he made the first sketches of the Genesee falls.

Most of the Iroquois were on the winning side when the British army pushed west and captured Fort Niagara. But that victory and the collapse of the French in Canada left them more dependent on the British for supplies and linked them closely to that side during the Revolution.

It was during the American Revolution that the divisions within the Iroquois league finally sapped its strength. While some of its tribes remained neutral, the Mohawks and the Senecas sided with the British. Several Seneca raids on the colonial settlements in the Wyoming and Cherry valleys provoked General Washington to send Sullivan's army into the

Mary Jemison, the "White Woman of the Genesee," was among the most famous of the early figures in the Genesee country. Born to Irish immigrant parents aboard ship en route to America in 1743, she was captured by a raiding party of Senecas from the family farm in Pennsylvania in 1758. Most of the family were slain. Mary Jemison was adopted by the Senecas and lived among them for the rest of her life. She was provided with land for a farm on the Gardeau flats in what is now Letchworth Park. Even before her death, in 1833, three editions of James E. Seaver's "A narrative of the life of Mrs. Mary Jemison..." had been published. The story proved so popular that eventually more than twenty editions were published. Courtesy of Local History Division, Rochester Public Library

Upper right, "South East View of the Great Cataract..." [1755 to 1763] by Captain Lieutenant Thomas Davies. This, and two other views of the Genesee falls by Davies within what is now the City of Rochester represent the falls as they appeared before the interference of settlement and development. Davies' sketches, which included views of the falls at Cohoes, Passaic, and Niagara, as well as the Main (Great Cataract), Middle (Second Falls), and Lower (Lower Cataract) Falls of the Genesee were originally published in copperplate engravings [London, 1768], now considered rare collectors' items. The steel engravings copied from that edition and published in E. B. O'Callaghan, The Documentary History of New York State, Vol. II, (Albany, 1850) are the source for this illustration. Courtesy of City Historian's Office

Lower right, "South East View of the Lower Cataract..." [1755-1763] by Thomas Davies. In the 1760s the name "Genesee River" had by no means as yet been fixed. Davies called the river "Casconchiagon or Little Seneca's River on Lake Ontario." Courtesy of Historian's Office

Finger Lakes and Genesee region, where it destroyed forty-two Indian villages and laid waste to their orchards and corn fields. The final blow came when the British signed peace terms that ceded the territory south of the Great Lakes to the United States.

To restore order and assure peace on the frontier, the United States signed a treaty with the Iroquois at Fort Stanwix in 1784. It recognized the Iroquois title to the lands west of Cayuga Lake and stipulated that future sales could be made only under governmental supervision.

The Senecas, now equipped with axes, used logs to rebuild their villages, including several in the upper Genesee Valley and around Niagara. But with their supplies of guns and powder curtailed by the end of the war, their major resource was their land, for which venturesome pioneers from the East and old friends from Canada were eagerly bidding.

While a group of speculators in New England, under the leadership of Oliver Phelps, was preparing to negotiate a proper purchase, another group of speculators, mostly former Loyalists who hoped to establish an Indian buffer state south of the Great Lakes, assembled some of the Seneca chiefs at Geneva and negotiated a 999-year lease to all of their lands in western New York. Still another group of speculators in Canada, jealous of the advantage gained by their rivals, protested the illegality of the lease and hastened to join with Phelps in calling a new council fire at Buffalo Creek in July 1788.

The new council fire was duly convened, including official representatives of New York State and of the United States, as well as chiefs of five Iroquois tribes, of which the Senecas—always the strongest tribe—supplied the largest delegation. Oliver Phelps pressed his negotiations. Having promised the rival groups of speculators a share in the estate, he secured their aid in persuading the Indians to sell a major portion of their lands. The Senecas were determined at first to make the Genesee the western boundary, but Phelps induced them to add a sawmill and gristmill at the falls to supply boards and flour for their use.

For a tract of nearly 2.6 million acres Phelps agreed to pay £2,100 in New York currency and, in a separate bond, promised a bonus of £200 in the same currency "annually forever." When the Indians gathered at Canandaigua a year later to receive the final portion of the down payment they discovered that a pound in New York currency was worth only 50 percent of its five-dollar value in Canadian currency. The disgruntled Senecas finally accepted the pouch, although it contained scarcely enough silver pieces to provide one for each brave, but they refused to sign an endorsement of final payment.

The only generous feature of the Buffalo Creek treaty was the size of the mill lot, which encompassed most of the western half of present day Monroe County! Ebenezer Allan, a former Tory who had married a Seneca girl and had acquired in her name a farm tract near what is now Scottsville, had helped to negotiate the mill-lot provision and undertook to build the mill at the falls in return for a clear title to a 100-acre tract at that location.

Allan's Mills at the Falls

A hardy frontiersman, "Indian Allan," as he was known, had cast his lot with the pioneers by marrying Lucy Chapman and drawing her several relatives into his settlement. With her brother-in-law, a millwright, he assembled a dozen men from throughout the valley and raised the frame of his gristmill early in November 1788. By spring he was able to move down to become the first resident of the site of present-day Rochester.

But Allan, a restless trader, not a developer, soon found his new post too isolated. It was too far from the disgruntled Senecas in the upper valley or around Niagara to be of any service to them, and the expected inrush of pioneers from the East was checked by the refusal of the British in Canada to relinquish their posts at Oswego and Niagara. Their restraint on Lake Ontario's shipping forced the early settlers to cluster around Canandaigua and Bath, where they had access to interior trade routes connecting with the Mohawk and Susquehanna valleys. Before the English agreed, in Jay's Treaty of 1794, to abandon their frontier posts, Allan, who had left the mill in charge of his brother-in-law Christopher Dugan in 1791, had found a buyer for the 100-acre tract in

Oliver Phelps, from an oil painting in the court house at Canandaigua. Phelps, the younger and more active partner of Nathaniel Gorham, was responsible for concluding a treaty with the Indians at Buffalo Creek following Phelps' and Gorham's purchase of the preemption rights to western New York from Massachusetts. Phelps died in Canandaigua in 1809. Courtesy of City Historian's Office

Red Jacket, a leader of the Senecas, was called by his people Sa-go-ye-nat-ha, a name which translated as "He Keeps Them Awake." Red Jacket was among the conferees at Buffalo Creek. An all-night session helped pave the way for the treaty sale with Oliver Phelps, but Red Jacket later renounced the deal. Courtesy of City Historian's Office

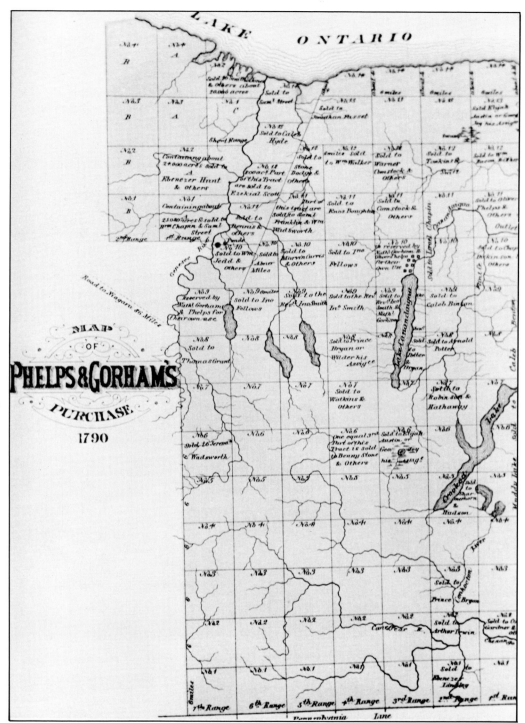

The map labeled:

MAP OF PHELPS & GORHAM'S PURCHASE 1790

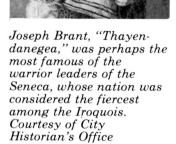

Joseph Brant, "Thayen-danegea," was perhaps the most famous of the warrior leaders of the Seneca, whose nation was considered the fiercest among the Iroquois. Courtesy of City Historian's Office

The Phelps and Gorham Purchase, which extinguished the Indian claims to a large portion of the Genesee country as well as the territory later encompassing Monroe County, set the stage for rapid settlement. Courtesy of City Historian's Office

"THE PIONEER SETTLER UPON THE HOLLAND PURCHASE AND HIS PROGRESS" was a series of four engravings prepared for O. Turner's history of the Holland Purchase, a little further west of the Phelps and Gorham Purchase; but the story they depict of the stages in the making of a farm applies as well to all of western New York. In "view No. 1" the farm is an "opening in the woods...only." Courtesy of City Historian's Office

"THE PIONEER SETTLER...AND HIS PROGRESS" In view No. 2 the pioneer has cleared some acres, built a snake fence, provided space for a small garden, added a stick chimney to his cabin, and has enjoyed an addition to his family. The clearing of primeval timber (both a nuisance and a source of revenue as ashes) continues. Turner observes, "It is a rugged home in the wilderness as yet, but we have already the earnest of progress and improvement. Courtesy of City Historian's Office

16

"THE PIONEER SETTLER...AND HIS PROGRESS." In Turner's *"Third Sketch of the Pioneer"* ten years have passed. The pioneer *"adventurer...has not been idle; thirty or forty acres are cleared and enclosed. Various crops are growing, and the whole premises begin to have the appearance of careful management, of thrift, comfort, and even plenty."* A block house has been added to the cabin; the improvements of neighbors have reached the pioneer, so that *"he can look out, without looking up."* Courtesy of City Historian's Office

"THE PIONEER SETTLER...AND HIS PROGRESS." In Turner's *"Fourth Sketch..."* it is supposed that forty-five years have passed. The land is fully *"improved"* and long since paid for. The pioneer *"has added to his primitive possessions; and ten to one...has secured lands for his sons in some of the western states...."* If Turner's imaginary yeoman is an idealized figure, nevertheless it is true that rapid agricultural settlement throughout the Genesee Valley region underpinned the rapid growth of Rochester and other towns in the first decades after 1800. Courtesy of City Historian's Office

Philadelphia, where his wide-ranging trading ventures had led him.

Allan's repute would fall under a cloud as a result of an event that occurred three decades after his departure. It was in 1822, ten years after the permanent settlement of Rochester, that Seneca Allan, son of Indian and Lucy Allan, returned to the falls to assert a claim to his mother's dowry rights to the 100-acre tract. In a frantic effort to disprove the claim, members of the Rochester family interviewed the few remaining pioneers, including the aged Mary Jemison, to document the tales about the long-forgotten Allan. What had happened to Sally, his Indian wife? Was he legally married to Lucy? Had he pushed her father over the falls in a drunken rage? Did he have a second (and a third?) white wife, and, if so, who had dowry claims? Nobody seemed to know for sure, but the death of Lucy at this crucial point abolished Seneca's dowry claim, and everybody else relaxed. A year later, however, when James E. Seaver began to compile his *Narrative of the Life of Mary Jemison*, the rumors of Allan's misdeeds were fresh in mind and accepted as fact.

Early Visitors

Although the mill continued to languish under Allan's successors, occasional visitors to the falls recognized the value of the site he had chosen. Charles Williamson, agent for a group of Scottish investors who in 1792 had acquired title to a major portion of the vast Phelps and Gorham Purchase, renaming it after their principal leader, Sir William Pulteney, hastened in 1794 to buy Allan's 100-acre tract for the Pulteney estate. After extended journeys by horseback through his virgin domain, Williamson penned "A Series of Letters from a Gentlemen to His Friend," describing the natural beauty and assets of the Genesee Country. Published as a promotional tract at Albany in 1798, it was the first comprehensive appraisal of the region's geographical character.

Many advantageous sites attracted Williamson's attention, among them the four successive falls on the lower Genesee. These, as he reported, dropped the river in giant steps a total of 300 feet through a gorge cut across the same geological ridge that the Niagara River had breached with one tumultuous plunge some seventy miles to the west. Like other early visitors, Williamson noted the grandeur of the falls, but he was chiefly interested in the millsites they afforded and in the commercial accessibility provided by the river below and above the falls. Lake ships could sail six miles up the river to the lower falls, and, after a portage of three miles around the tumbling cataracts, traders could carry supplies and produce by riverboat another sixty miles to the south; moreover, after another ten-mile portage, they could link with other rivercraft on the Susquehanna and its tributaries, developing a transport artery that held great promise for the entire Genesee Country.

Few early observers saw the potentialities of the region as clearly as Charles Williamson. Some, journeying to Niagara, paused to admire and sometimes to sketch the Genesee falls as well, but most of those who published journals commented at length on the poor accommodations encountered on the lower Genesee, where for several years Allan's mill provided the only shelter. John Maude, an Englishman who stopped there briefly in 1800, criticized its dilapidated state and crude facilities, but noted its potential value if relocated on higher ground a few feet to the south, out of the path of springtime ice flows. Nine years later, Thomas Cooper of Pennsylvania found the millsite abandoned and the mill "fallen down in perfect ruin," but pronounced the rapids that adjoined it "the best site for a mill I ever saw." Three prospecting visitors from Maryland—Nathaniel Rochester, William Fitzhugh, and Charles Carroll—had previously reached the same conclusion. They had agreed in 1803 to purchase the 100-acre tract for $1,750.

Col. Charles Williamson in 1791 was made agent and promoter for the sale of lands in the Genesee country by the Pulteney Association, a partnership of English speculators who acquired the bulk of the Phelps and Gorham Purchase from Robert Morris. For ten years Williamson vigorously promoted settlement and widely propagandized the merits of the Genesee country. In 1800 he personally guided Rochester, Fitzhugh, and Carroll on their "prospecting" expedition in the north. Courtesy of City Historian's Office

Western New York in 1799. Section from the map prepared to accompany Charles Williamson's promotional pamphlet, "Description of the Settlement of the Genesee Country..." (New York, 1799). The future site of Rochester, coded "X" on Williamson's map, was then occupied only by Indian Allan's crumbling mill. Courtesy of City Historian's Office

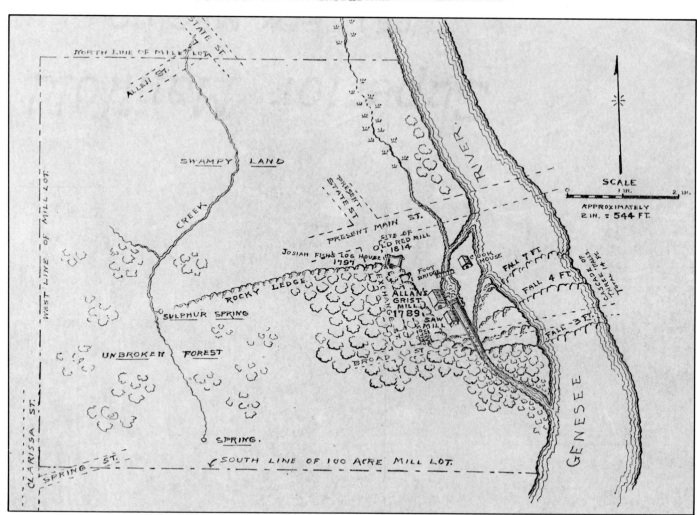

Site of Allan's Mill on the One Hundred Acre Tract. Courtesy of Local History Division, Rochester Public Library

Col. Nathaniel Rochester. Courtesy of Local History Division, Rochester Public Library

Chapter 2

The Mill Town at the Genesee Falls

Colonel Nathaniel Rochester, the eldest of the three Maryland partners, brought new leadership to the falls settlement. Their purchase in 1803 was speculative, but Rochester would soon transform it into an active venture. Years of experience in community affairs in North Carolina, where he rose to colonel in the militia, and in Maryland, as a businessman and legislator, had prepared him for new town developments on the frontier. When the Embargo and Nonintercourse Acts, restricting trade with embattled France and England, blighted prospects at Hagerstown, Maryland, just as his older sons were approaching maturity, Rochester determined in 1810 to remove to the Genesee Country. He located at first in Dansville, a hamlet on the southern rim of the valley that seemed to offer suitable opportunities. However, on a horseback journey down the valley to inspect his tract at the falls, Rochester quickly sensed its more attractive prospects. Observing a number of rafts tied up along the banks above the rapids, awaiting oxcarts to portage their sacks of grain and potash to the lake or bay, he saw that the time was ripe for the development of a mill town at the falls.

Colonel Rochester's Leadership

Several incidental decisions exemplified Colonel Rochester's leadership. When he rode down early in 1811 with surveyor's instruments to stake out a town plat on the 100-acre tract, he found a bridge already under construction a few rods below the rapids and lined up his principal street to extend west from the bridge. He named it Buffalo Street, not to honor that town some sixty miles west, but to assure migrants from the East that the falls settlement was not the last outpost on an exposed frontier. Enos Stone, a settler on the east bank who had initiated the bridge project, was a potential rival, but Rochester promptly engaged him as agent for the sale of town lots, thus linking him with the enterprise. To assure rapid development he placed a modest price of fifty dollars on quarter-acre lots along the two principal streets, and thirty dollars on back streets, but stipulated that buyers would have to erect buildings within a year to clinch their titles. He reserved mill lots on a projected raceway for the proprietors and a central square for a courthouse, thus indicating his conception of the town's future importance.

Unexpected hazards soon appeared, but Colonel Rochester met them with tact as well as resolution. On a return visit to the falls a few months later, he discovered that work on the bridge had been suspended because, as Stone explained, the township's pathmasters had blazed a route for the road from Pittsford so that it would reach the river farther north, just above the main falls, thus bypassing his settlement. Apparently the Brown brothers, who had acquired a 200-acre plot at that site, had sought a

James Wadsworth (1768-1844) was among the first settlers of the Genesee Valley. By amassing a great landed estate in the vicinity of Geneseo he founded a dynasty that produced military and political leaders from western New York for several generations. During Rochester's early years, Wadsworth was among those who subdivided tracts in the growing village. He envied the Rochester, Fitzhugh, and Carroll purchase of the One-Hundred Acre Tract. Courtesy of City Historian's Office

Western New York in 1809. Reproduced from Thomas Cooper, A Ride to Niagara in 1809. *Principal settlements were those located along the Turnpike Road (now route 20), an enlargement of ancient Indian trails. Hartford (now Avon) was the site of the only Genesee River bridge. Courtesy of City Historian's Office*

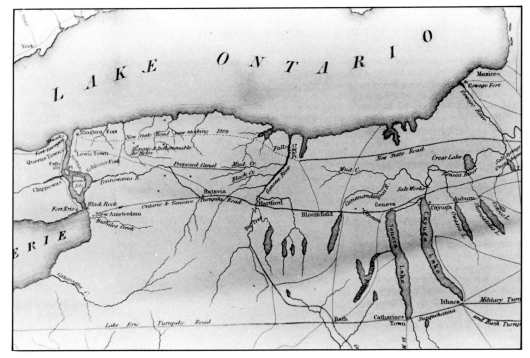

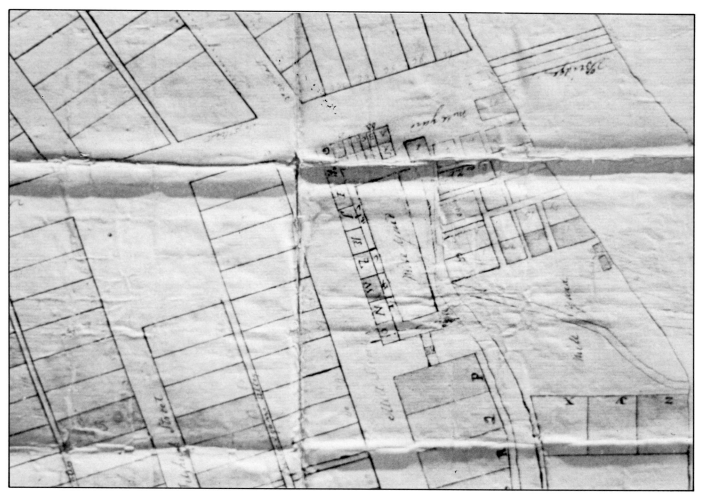

*Section of a Manuscript Survey Map of the One
Hundred Acre Tract, attributed to Nathaniel Rochester,
1811. The badly worn and creased map in the Local
History Division of the Rochester Public Library is
thought to have been prepared by Rochester himself
during his visit to the One Hundred Acre Tract in 1811.
At the lower left in this section Main Street Bridge is
visible; Fitzhugh Street is labeled at the upper right; and
Rochester's (unlabeled) courthouse square is at right
center. Courtesy of Local History Division, Rochester
Public Library*

relocation of the bridge to make their projected settlement of Frankfort the road's destination. Instead of engaging in a direct confrontation, Colonel Rochester made use of his experiences as an assemblyman in Maryland to push a resolution through the legislature at Albany accepting the road as a state project and directing that it be turned to make a proper approach to the bridge below the rapids. (The Liberty Pole at the junction of East Avenue and Main Street marks that turning point today.)

To promote harmony with the Browns, Rochester revised his plat map to link his north-south streets with comparable streets in adjoining Frankfort. He also deferred efforts to extend Buffalo Street westward, so that the principal highway from the east would turn north at his Four Corners to pass through Frankfort and proceed to Falltown at the lower falls turning west along the ridge road already in use.

These accommodations brought a sense of unity to the lower Genesee that proved crucial a year later, when the War of 1812 broke out just as the first settlers were arriving at the falls. The newly opened roads permitted the Americans to assemble forces for a raid into Canada, but when the British made a counter drive that overran Buffalo and Niagara, a wave of terror spread through the settlements along the lake. To dispel alarm and assure firm leadership, Colonel Rochester decided to sell his properties in Dansville and remove to the falls.

Rochester's canny advertisement of the Dansville properties in the Ontario *Messenger and Repository*, the area's leading weekly published at Canandaigua, accomplished his two objectives. Thus before a satisfactory bid on the properties had been secured, two more venturesome migrants, Hervey Ely and Josiah Bissell, had been attracted to the falls and had secured permission to build mills on the Rochester raceway. Fearing that the new settlement could not support two mills, Colonel Rochester moved to a farm in Bloomfield some twenty miles to the south, but still within easy reach of his falls settlement.

The Raising of the Red Mill

The planting of a successful village was more than a one-man job. The location at the upper falls was advantageous, and the timing, with trade down the river increasing, was right, as Rochester had sensed. But the skills and energies of many settlers were needed to build a town. Several of the first arrivals had versatile talents—Hamlet Scrantom as a miller and merchant, Abelard Reynolds as a saddler and developer, Matthew Brown as a doctor and civic leader—and their growing number soon encouraged each to find his specialty. But on occasion the cooperative energies of all were required, as in the raising of the Red Mill late in 1814.

Hamlet Scrantom (1773-1851) became, in 1812, the first permanent settler of the One Hundred Acre Tract. Courtesy of Local History Division, Rochester Public Library

Abelard Reynolds (1785-1878) was Rochester's second permanent settler and the town's first postmaster. In 1828 he constructed the original Reynolds Arcade on the north side of Main Street east of the Four Corners, said to be the grandest commercial structure west of Albany. His sons, William A. and Mortimer F., likewise made contributions to the community's economic and cultural life. Courtesy of Local History Division, Rochester Public Library

Main Street Bridge, as it appeared in 1812. This view is an artist's later (1877) conception. The view depicted is toward the northwest. The cabin of first settler Hamlet Scrantom occupies the future site of the Powers Block. Courtesy of Local History Division, Rochester Public Library

VALUABLE MILLS AND LANDS FOR SALE.

THE subscriber, wishing to remove to the village of Rochester, at the Falls of Genesee River, offers for sale his MILLS and FARM, at Dansville, in the county of Steuben.

The Farm contains about 450 acres of LAND, and the following improvements, to wit:—About fifty acres cleared and under good fence, fifteen acres of Meadow, an apple and peach Orchard, a convenient Dwelling House, with two good dry Cellars, and six rooms on the first floor, a large new merchant Mill and Saw-Mill, Still-House, Store-House, Blacksmith's Shop, Miller's House, house and machinery for carding wool, a good new Barn and Sheds, with all other necessary Out-Houses. The Land is remarkably well timbered, particularly with white and yellow Pine, and white and black Oak. There are on the Land at least six good Seats for Mills, or any other kind of water-works, on a stream that never fails in the dryest seasons.— It is situated in a good wheat country, and in dry seasons grain is brought upwards of 30 miles to be ground. He also offers for sale 325 acres of as good LAND as any in Ontario county, lying on the Canascruga, in the town of Groveland, (late Sparta.) This tract would divide to advantage into two or three Farms. The above mentioned property is to be sold on reasonable terms and easy payments.

N. Rochester.

Dansville, 6 Aug. 1813.   3w17

☞ A good SAW-MILLER wanted.

When Nathaniel Rochester at last determined to move to his new village site, this advertisement for the sale of his other Genesee Country holdings, placed in the Canandaigua weekly, announced his seriousness of purpose to everyone in the region. Courtesy of City Historian's Office

Edwin Scrantom, third son of the town's first permanent resident, would describe that event some fifty years later in his "Old Citizen's Letters":

> I distinctly remember the raising of the Red Mill, when every man and boy in the village, with a majority of the women, were present.... The southern bent and the next one were got up with much difficulty the first day, and many of the cross timbers and girders had been placed and pinned in to make it strong and to form a support in the raising of the remaining two. To raise these with less trouble and strength, tackle-blocks with ropes were fastened to the raised parts...and rigged to the posts of the lying bent; some [men] manned the "fall" while others...lifted the heavy framework. The bent moved up as "Yo, heave" sounded at intervals from the boss workman. A little way up and the great weight proved too heavy. "Every man and boy take hold," shouted the boss, and all obeyed. "Now, now, Yo heave," was the order. At this awful moment I felt the bent sink on my shoulder and jumped away....The tackle rope had broken and but for a strong skid placed under the post...the disaster would have been dreadful. One man suffered an injury to his spine [which later proved fatal], but a renewal with fresh forces completed the first great raising, which was celebrated by...the liberal distribution of cakes made by the women and washed down by "black strap" and water.

Similar "bees" occurred at the raising of the frames for other early mills and taverns, but the arrival of numerous carpenters and builders soon dispensed with these exciting events. Boys and girls found their time absorbed in household chores or as apprentices, and increasingly by attendance at the district and private schools that made their appearance in the village. The women, perhaps, retained their homespun functions the longest, as we learn from the diary of Esther Maria Chapin, who celebrated the second anniversary of her marriage to a young attorney by tabulating her accomplishments of the previous year. In addition to keeping a large vegetable garden, with a corner for flowers, she had made fifteen shirts, three corsets, seven nightcaps, eight nightgowns, three petticoats, ten slips, six gowns, two Vandykes, one greatcoat, one vest, and one pair of pantalettes. During the occasional meetings of a quilting bee with fifteen ladies, she had finished one bed quilt.

It was not all work, of course, for the gowns found display at occasional concerts or dancing parties in the longroom of the Christopher or Ensworth taverns, as well as at church and charity society meetings. A visitor from New England expressed his gratitude for unexpected hospitality in a letter to the recently established Rochester *Gazette* in January 1820:

> The evening after I arrived there was a *Cotillion* party. I was invited...and never have I beheld a more brilliant assemblage of ladies ....Soon...the dance exhibited the female form moving light as zephyrs with grace and dignity in every motion....The room was splendidly illuminated and fancifully decorated with evergreens.

Village Quarrels

The thriving village quickly developed aspirations for a village charter and for the establishment of a new county with Rochester as its seat. Colonel Rochester carried petitions, drawn up by Matthew Brown, to Albany in 1817. The jealous opposition of Canandaigua and Batavia, seats respectively of Ontario and Genesee, the large counties east and west of the Genesee, defeated the bid for a new county. The village charter passed without difficulty, but it limited the size of the new village to 655 acres on the river's west bank—thus locating it firmly within Genesee County.

Proud of attaining the status previously accorded to older Canandaigua, Geneva, and Bath, the seven hundred residents of Rochesterville, as it was officially named, hastened to organize. When a few merchants prepared a list of candidates for trustees and other offices that included no mechanics—as workmen of the day were called—several craftsmen drew up a rival slate, which won the election. Disgruntled by the outcome, some merchants threatened to "proscribe" the leading mechanics, but Colonel Rochester, hearing of the squabble, wrote a hasty note to Matthew Brown pleading for harmony. "I would rather," he wrote, "have sacrificed $50 than that such an event should have happened....I must entreat that you and Esquire Mastick will endeavor to heal the wound before it becomes an ulcer."

Stone Tavern. One of the oldest structures in Monroe County, it was built (c1792-1811) by Orringh Stone on the pioneer road from Pittsford to Rochester. The house is presently maintained as the Stone-Tolan House by the Landmark Society of Western New York. Courtesy of Joseph W. Barnes

Sur Genesee river at a fall

"Town on Genesee River at the falls." A sketch drawn in 1816 by the Frenchman Charles A. Leseur, it is the earliest authentic picture of Rochester. Courtesy of Local History Division, Rochester Public Library; original in the Museum of Natural History, Havre, France

That wound healed more quickly than another occasioned by a flood later that year. Colonel Rochester had readily consented when Elisha Johnson, who had undertaken the development of Enos Stone's tract on the east bank, proposed the construction of a new dam above the rapids to supply water to an east-side as well as a west-side raceway. But Johnson raised the dam a few inches higher than its predecessor in order to insure an adequate flow into his more elevated race. When heavy November rains up the valley sent a rushing torrent over the dam, ripping it apart, lowlands on the west side suffered inundation. Many villagers rallied to build an embankment that saved the west end of the bridge, but several buildings were carried off by the current, which damaged the Red Mill of Ely and Bissell and undermined the sawmill recently built by John C. Rochester, the Colonel's second son, on Allan's old site.

News of the flood spread rapidly, and Colonel Rochester soon received a letter from Charles Carroll, his partner now residing at Williamsburg up the valley. "We have," he complained, "already in public estimation sustained irreparable injury....And the more we suffer in the eyes of the Public, the better for Brighton. I have learnt enough of Yankees to dread and fear their wiles & offers. You are too honest and unsuspicious." The damage, however, had been less than at first reported, and Colonel Rochester approved a reconstruction of the dam and obligingly signed a note enabling the Ely brothers to raise funds for expansion. But when a suit by the Elys against Johnson for damages was widened, on the advice of Elisha B. Strong, a Canandaigua friend of Johnson's, to include Rochester and his partners, the aged colonel's forbearance snapped, as an exchange of letters between the two men, now close neighbors, demonstrated.

That suit continued to rankle men on both sides of the river and would complicate the struggle for control of the first Bank of Rochester in the early twenties. Meanwhile the village survived a challenge posed by Elisha Strong's project for a new town on the east bank at the lower falls. With a dock for steamboats at the head of navigation on the river and with access to waterpower from the lower falls, the prospects of Carthage, as it was named, appeared bright. The key to the project was a single-arch bridge over the gorge to link the ridge road from Niagara with a new road to Canandaigua, thus bypassing Rochester.

The incredible bridge was successfully constructed in nine months—714 feet in length, 190 feet above the river, and supported by a timber arch with a chord of 352 feet. It won exclamations of admiration and astonishment from numerous visitors, including Captain Roger James, who pronounced it a "splendid specimen of American ingenuity," one that "seems to vie with the works of nature" in the view below it. The lower falls, however, proved more enduring, for the great bridge, guaranteed to stand for a year, buckled and collapsed from its own weight after fifteen months and carried the fortunes of Carthage with it into the gorge.

The high bridge built in 1819 over the deep Genesee gorge at the lower falls was the key element in the plans for the rival settlement known as Carthage. This view is reproduced from a watercolor by the obscure American landscapist F.S. Belton. Courtesy of Pittsford Picture Framing Company

The Battle for the County and the Courthouse

The fall of Carthage dealt a severe blow to Canandaigua, the source of its inspiration and support. That town, still in 1820 the largest in central and western New York and openly jealous of Rochester's rapid advance, had successfully blocked a second move for a separate county led by Matthew Brown in 1818 and a third move two years later led by Charles H. Carroll. Yet the mounting population of settlements in the Genesee Valley and eastward along the Ontario shore, tabulated in the 1820 census as totaling 68,000, already comprised more than half the total of Ontario and Genesee counties and made the formation of new counties inevitable. Federalist leaders in Canandaigua had met the challenge by prompting Federalist friends in Avon and Palmyra to enter bids for new counties, one straddling the river from Dansville north, and the other bordering the lake from Irondequoit Bay east. That maneuver had divided the new-county advocates and produced a stalemate.

But the Canandaigua tactic suggested a new strategy to Colonel Rochester, who had finally taken up his residence at the falls. He agreed late in 1820 to lead a new delegation to Albany as soon as snow arrived for good sleighing. First, however, he alerted his friends in Geneseo to push for a second new county in the central part of the valley, and men in Lyons to push for a third county farther east along the lake. He even suppressed his bitter feelings towards Elisha B. Strong and invited him to join the Rochester delegation. The new strategy proved successful. With endorsing resolutions from eleven townships on the lower Genesee and with support from up the river and to the east, Colonel Rochester was able to engineer the passage of new-county bills in February 1821.

This triumph, which gave the lower Genesee county, named after President Monroe, a territory of 607 square miles and an initial population of 27,000, posed a new contest over the location of the courthouse. Two new sites were offered, one by Matthew Brown on Brown's square, and one by Elisha Johnson east of the river on Court Street. But the square still reserved by Colonel Rochester for that purpose was most central and, as a free gift, quickly won approval. Elisha Strong was named First Judge and convened his first session in the newly added loft of the Ensworth tavern at the Four Corners. Colonel Rochester, as county clerk, called the town supervisors together in Christopher's Mansion House, where they elected Matthew Brown as chairman and approved a contract for the building of a modest stone courthouse. When completed and occupied in October 1822, it boasted a belfry and cupola as well as two Ionic porticoes and brought a sense of dignity and permanence to the bustling town.

Elisha Johnson prepared this map of the subdivision he shared with Orson Seymour on the east side of the Genesee River in 1817. "Court Street" and the "Public Square" were laid out in the same hopeful anticipation that motivated Brown's Square in the Frankfort Tract. But when it came time to choose a site for the Court House, Nathaniel Rochester's original public square was the one selected. Johnson and Seymour's Public Square became today's Washington Square. Courtesy of Local History Division, Rochester Public Library

Southeast view of the central part of Canandaigua in 1841. Earlier views of Canandaigua or of Batavia have not come to light. As the county seats of Ontario and Genesee Counties, respectively, it was to these two places that Rochesterians were forced to travel to conduct legal affairs until the erection of Monroe County in 1821. Courtesy of City Historian's Office

Western view of the central part of Batavia. Courtesy of City Historian's Office

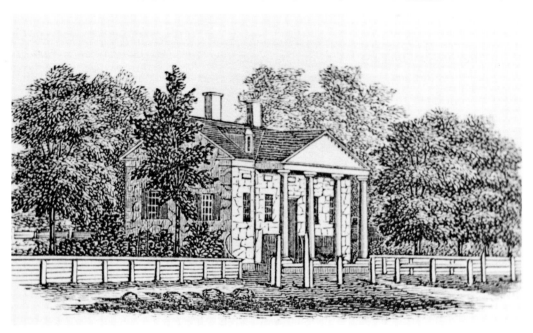

Office of the Holland Land Company. Located in Batavia, this office corresponded roughly to the land offices of Phelps and Gorham and of the Pulteney estate in the Genesee Region. The Holland Company, successors to Robert Morris as chief landholders in the region west of the Phelps and Gorham Purchase, controlled vast holdings. Courtesy of City Historian's Office

The Building of the Aqueduct

But the fortunes of Rochester had been even more firmly assured by another action in that crucial year—the letting of a contract for the Genesee aqueduct in June 1821. The location of the canal, designed to divert the trade of western settlements from Montreal to Albany, had long been a subject of heated controversy across the state. Colonel Rochester, while a resident in Bloomfield, had chaired a convention at Canandaigua advocating a southern route along the state road that traversed several settled towns. When that route was finally rejected as impractical because of the terrain, some Canandaiguans had thrown support to Oswego's bid to be made the western terminus. Indeed, the Carthage venture had been designed in part to take advantage of the increased lake trade that such a canal terminus would stimulate. Advocates of a route through Rochester originally had planned to cross the river in a pond behind a state dam above the rapids, but the flood of November 1817 had convinced the canal engineers of the hazards of such a plan and led to the decision for an aqueduct.

When pressure for a canal across the state to Lake Erie, led by DeWitt Clinton who had traveled that route in 1810, finally triumphed, the engineers located the aqueduct to carry the canal across the Genesee eighty rods (440 yards) south of the Rochester bridge. That decision would route the canal westward along the northern edge of the homestead Colonel Rochester had occupied on the west bank overlooking the river since 1818. As he watched the construction of the aqueduct from his veranda in the early twenties and saw lumbermen building boats to be ready to carry flour and other products eastward, he gradually realized that the pear orchard he had planted along the river bank would have to be uprooted and his house demolished to make way for a boat dock and basin to accommodate the trade the canal would bring.

The First Churches

Most residents were only partially aware of their thriving village's potentialities. Since many were New Yorkers and Southerners with an Episcopal heritage, they had hastened, under Colonel Rochester's leadership, to erect a church on the lot set aside by the proprietors. Their frame building, topped with a steeple and painted white, was completed in 1820. Overlooking the square where the courthouse would soon be built, St. Luke's Church boasted the first bell in the village and added a note of charm to the town. When the more numerous Presbyterians hailing from New England acquired the lot back of the courthouse across the street and began to

haul in stone, members of St. Luke's assumed it was for a foundation; but when the stone piles increased in size, an inquiry was made, and the plan of the Presbyterians to build a stone church was revealed. In a hastily called session, the Episcopalians, determined not to be outdone, decided to move their frame building to the rear of their lot and erect a stone church in its place.

Stonemasons, assembled to build the aqueduct, found ready jobs on its completion in 1823, as the rival churches raced to complete construction. When the Presbyterians, who had enjoyed a head start, finished their building first, the Reverend Francis Cuming, pastor at St. Luke's, could not refuse an invitation to the dedication. But when he heard the Reverend Joseph Penney, the Presbyterian clergyman, declare, "Thank God we are not like some churchmen" who hope to get into Heaven by good works, he could not sit still. As the Reverend Cuming bolted for the door, the words "Our way is by grace through faith" caused him to pause as if to reply, but he thought better of it and strode across the street to write and deliver a sermon in reply. Little did they dream, coming as they had from hamlets and villages in the East and the South, that the mill town at the falls was a different kind of settlement—that it would soon have room and need for many men and women both of faith and of good works.

Rev. Joseph Penney (1793-1860). Educated at Trinity College, Dublin, and at the University of Glasgow, Penney was among the most distingushed of Rochester's early clergymen. He was minister to the First Presbyterian Church, 1822-1832, and later became president of Hamilton College. Courtesy of Local History Division, Rochester Public Library

View of the First Aqueduct from the East. Reproduced from Cadwallader D. Colden, Memoir . . . of the New York Canals (New York, 1825). The first Erie Canal Aqueduct in Rochester, built just north of present-day Broad Street Bridge, was constructed of sandstone which disintegrated within a few winters. Courtesy of City Historian's Office

St. Luke's Church as it appeared in 1830; the older wooden church may be seen behind the stone church, which still occupies a place on Fitzhugh Street and on the National Register of Historic Places. Courtesy of City Historian's Office

Captain Basil Hall's 1827 sketch of the first Court House (and Presbyterian Church behind it) was produced with a camera lucida, a box-like arrangement of lenses, mirrors, and field of ground glass upon which the artist traced a photographic image. Courtesy of Local History Division, Rochester Public Library

The "Young Lion of the West" and the Erie Canal

The mid-twenties brought a dramatic change in Rochester's conception of its prospects. From a burgeoning village vying with Canandaigua for recognition, it had suddenly emerged as America's first boomtown. Enterprising men from nearby hamlets—Dr. Levi Ward from Bergen, for example—jostled for place with aspiring migrants from more distant places—Thurlow Weed from Manlius and Vincent Matthews from Canandaigua, among many others. Rochester's population trebled in five years, surpassing all rivals west of Albany, and reached 5,273 by 1825. The chartering of the Bank of Rochester in 1824 had attracted investors from as far away as New York City and, with other developments, had made Rochester, as Mrs. Basil Hall would write three years later, "the best place we have yet seen for giving strangers an idea of the newness of this country."

Like numerous other British visitors, the Halls reached Rochester by way of Canandaigua, but now Gideon Granger, who had entertained them at his mansion in that "pretty village," accompanied them to the falls "to show us the lions," as Mrs. Hall put it.

They visited the main falls, of course, paused on the bridge to watch boats moving magically on a Roman aqueduct over the river, drove past Colonel Rochester's and Everard Peck's charming homes on Spring Street, and marveled at the number of rumbling mills and bustling taverns and shops encountered on all sides. The sight and sound of workmen busy with hammers, saws, and stone chisels, erecting new commercial blocks, churches, and homes, further impressed them. But the real "lion," as the first village *Directory* boasted, was the town itself, and Captain Hall set his camera lucida in an open window on the second floor of the Ensworth tavern and captured a memorable view of its central feature, the courthouse square.

Dr. Levi Ward, Jr. (1771-1861), native of Killingsworth, Connecticut, was among the foremost village fathers and helped establish both the Bank of Rochester and the Athenaeum. Courtesy of Local History Division, Rochester Public Library

The Opening of the Canal

The canal, of course, was the triggering agent of Rochester's boom; yet nowhere else along its route was a comparable explosion felt. With a fertile valley filling with settlers above it, drained by a natural trade artery, and with abundant waterpower from its falls, Rochester enjoyed a special advantage and hastened to exploit the new commercial outlet.

Gala celebration marked the completion of the aqueduct in 1823. The workmen held a boisterous demonstration on September 10, when the contractors delivered their final wage payments. The community delayed its celebration until a heavy rain up the valley enabled the canal officials to fill the completed ditch on the level stretch west to Brockport and to test and prove the aqueduct as a water carrier. Finally, on October 6, a flotilla of packet and freight boats, active for a year on the stretch east of the Genesee, gathered with a blare of horns for a slow procession across the aqueduct. A salute fired by Captain Whitney's militia company as the first boat reached the west side gave the signal for the village band to strike up the Masonic tune "The Temple's Completed." After swinging about in a large basin on the west edge of town, the flotilla returned to Child's basin near the Red Mill for ceremonies followed by a banquet at Christopher's Mansion House presided over by the venerable Colonel Rochester.

That was but the start of the festivities occasioned by the canal. A boatload of oysters that arrived a week later prompted celebrations among the transplanted New Englanders who thronged the town. The curious onlookers who had formerly congregated near the watering trough in front of the Ensworth tavern to watch the arrival of stagecoaches now lined the bridge over the canal at Exchange Street to view the endless stream of boats passing beneath. No crowds rivaled those at the reception accorded General Lafayette, who reached Rochester on June 7, 1825, in the course of his memorial tour of the nation. Residents from up the valley swelled the throng to an estimated ten thousand

Everard Peck (1791-1854), one of Rochester's first printers, also became a bookseller, paper manufacturer, and banker. He was among Rochester's most public-spirited citizens, a leader of the Female Charitable Society and frequent office holder during village days. Courtesy of Local History Division, Rochester Public Library

The First Erie Canal Aqueduct Over the Genesee, From a Sketch Made in 1826. Originally published in A. Duttenhofer, Study Journey through the United States of North America *(Stuttgart, 1835). Courtesy of City Historian's Office*

Granger Homestead, Canandaigua, N.Y. Gideon Granger (1767-1824) was among western New York's most influential political leaders. Prominent in Connecticut affairs, Granger served as Postmaster General (1801-1814) before moving to Canandaigua where he built this house. He served as a State Senator during debates over the Erie Canal and the formation of new counties. Courtesy of Joseph W. Barnes

Nathaniel Rochester's house, on the corner of Spring Street and South Washington Street, as it appeared late in the 19th century. Courtesy of Local History Division, Rochester Public Library

cheering citizens, double the town's population, as Rochester welcomed the "Nation's Honored Guest."

The weather was not so favorable nor the crowd so large when Governor Clinton arrived on October 27 that year at the head of a flotilla of packets that marked the official opening of the Erie Canal. But the cermonies, if dampened by a steady rain, were more elaborate and culminated in a banquet chaired this time by Vincent Matthews. When Governor Clinton and his party resumed the trip eastward, an elaborately decorated boat, named *The Young Lion of the West*, joined the flotilla.

Rumbling Millstones and Buzzing Saws

By cutting the shipping costs to the east approximately 90 percent, the canal was a great boon to the flour millers and to all the merchants of Rochester. The sawmillers received a more immediate benefit from the increased demand for boats. A dozen enterprising lumbermen built boats at scattered sites along the river and the canal in the mid-twenties. By the end of the decade, six boatyards were each turning out a score or more of freight and packet boats worth from $800 to $1200 apiece.

To supply them with adequate timber, lumbermen brought great rafts of logs bound in cribs down the river each spring and fall. Numerous cribs frequently could be seen tied up along the banks above the new feeder dam for the canal; it was always a thrilling sight to watch a skilled pilot guide a huge raft through the chute when a freshet arrived to help float the heavy logs over the dam to the lumberyards above Johnson's dam. The nine sawmills of 1827 employed only twenty sawyers, plus numerous unskilled workers, yet their products supplied not only the boatyards but also the 304 carpenters and joiners, the town's most numerous group of craftsmen, who were busily engaged in the construction of some three hundred new houses a year. In addition, ninety-five masons shared in that unending task, according to the first *Directory*.

There were nine flour mills in operation at the official opening of the canal; within two years, these had increased to a dozen. By processing the increasing supplies of wheat and other grains from up the valley, already bidding for recognition as New York's grainery, they had doubled their output and would soon quadruple it. Energetic new millers were flocking to Rochester, including Warham Whitney, Benjamin Campbell, and E.S. Beach in 1826. General Beach engaged Robert M. Dalzell, the leading millwright, to construct his six-story mill of stone at the northwest corner of the aqueduct. Its location adjoining Child's basin prompted Dalzell to install a bucket elevator to lift grain out of the boats at its base and carry it to the top floor, whence it passed by gravity and belts through successive separators and grinders until it reached the barrels on the loading platform. This ingenious device captured the attention of

Governor DeWitt Clinton (1769-1828), New York's pre-eminent political figure in the first quarter of the nineteenth century, was so influential in marshalling support for the first Erie Canal that it came to be known as "Clinton's Ditch." Courtesy of City Historian's Office

Canal Packet Boat
Fare Reduced.

The *FARE* in the regular line of *Packet Boats* running between Schenectady and Rochester, is now reduced to the following rates:

From Schenectady to Utica, and from Utica to Schenectady, ⎱ $1 75

From Utica to Rochester, and from Rochester to Utica, ⎱ $3 25

The public are assured that the accommodations furnished in the Packet Boats will continue to be in no wise inferior to what they have been during the season, notwithstanding the reduction of fare.

Utica, October 5, 1824.

No sooner had the canal been finished—in fact, in 1824 it was not yet complete state-wide—than line operators began vigorous competition for the public's trade. Courtesy of Rochester Historical Society Publications

Rochester in 1827. This map was prepared by Elisha Johnson to accompany the village directory published the same year. Courtesy of City Historian's Office

38

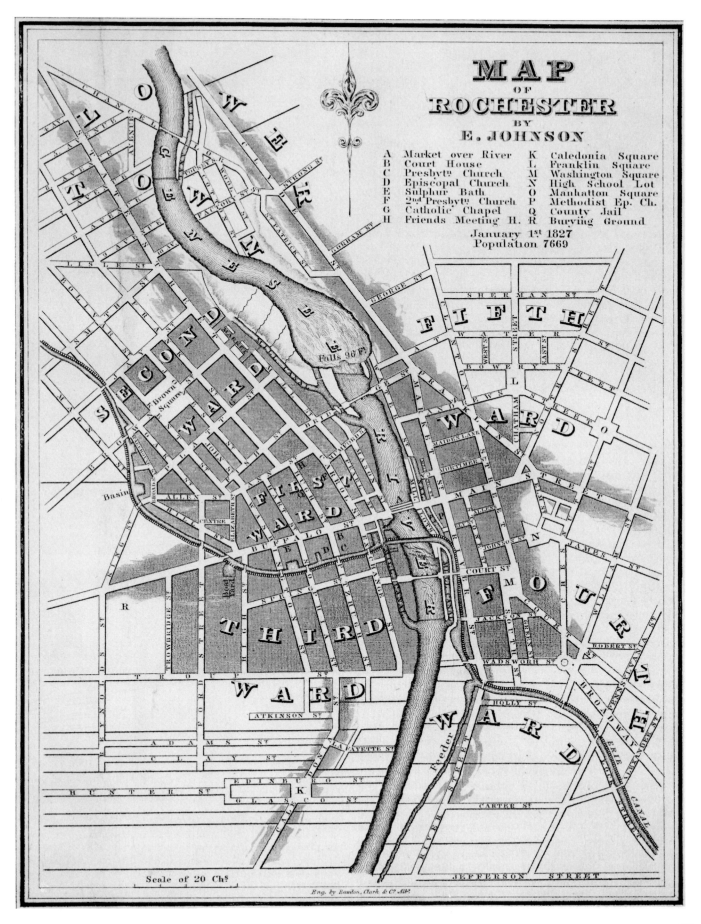

MAP
OF
ROCHESTER
BY
E. JOHNSON

A	Market over River	K	Caledonia Square
B	Court House	L	Franklin Square
C	Presbytᵉ Church	M	Washington Square
D	Episcopal Church	N	High School Lot
E	Sulphur Bath	O	Manhatton Square
F	2ᵈ Presbyᵗᵉ Church	P	Methodist Ep. Ch.
G	Catholic Chapel	Q	County Jail
H	Friends Meeting H.	R	Burying Ground

January 1ˢᵗ 1827
Population 7669

Falls 96 F.

Scale of 20 Chˢ

Eng. by Rawdon, Clark & Cº Albᵞ

numerous visitors, including William L. Stone, owner of the New York *Commercial Advertiser*. Stone, in fact, was so captivated by what he saw in 1829 that he visited the Beach mill and the new Ely mill across the river, equipped with a similar chain of buckets, on a second trip a decade later. He would then describe the Ely mill as "almost as full of machinery as the case of a watch," a model for mills in the west as its bucket chain was for grain elevators.

A special note is perhaps due to Benjamin Campbell's mill, which stood on the island south of the aqueduct. Although destroyed and forgotten after a bolt of lightning set it afire in 1831, its unusual construction would come to light 120 years later when the ruins, long buried in river sediment and fill and covered for decades by the Kimball tobacco factory, were discovered during the excavation of that site for the War Memorial. That archaeological dig revealed two rows of stone arches that had held the frame mill high above the surface of the island to permit floodwaters to pass through below without damage. This precaution had not saved it from fire, however, which also leveled five of the original frame mills, including Ely's Red Mill, within the first decade.

Civic Concerns and the Public Market

Fire, the most persistent problem facing the town, was only one of its civic concerns. The village authorities had created a night watch as well as a bucket brigade early in 1817 and soon expanded and organized them under a warden and fire chief. The village purchased first one, then a second, and finally a third hand-pump fire engine to equip its volunteer companies for recurrent battles with the flames. It erected oil lamps at the central Four Corners and at both ends of the bridge, and authorized a subsidy for the digging of private wells made available to neighborhood use. The condition of the streets presented .a baffling problem, since funds for their improvement were lacking, but an ordinance requiring property holders on certain streets to build sidewalks and erect hitching posts brought a measure of order. It also revealed a problem of congestion, as merchants and shop owners tried to prevent hucksters and farmers with loads of hay from tying up in front of their doors.

The need for a public market was evident, and Elisha Johnson, who had replaced the old bridge with a second and more substantial bridge on stone piers in 1824, proposed an extension of the western pier to support a market platform at its northwest corner. The location seemed ideal, and the village negotiated with Charles H. Carroll for permission to lay beams from the pier to a stone wall he was building along the bank. When a suit arose over the payments due, and Carroll won, the trustees resolved to change the name of Carroll Street, named for his father, to State Street!

This photograph, taken in the early 1950s during excavation for the Community War Memorial, reveals the arched foundations of long-forgotten mills that occupied the island adjacent to the Rochester-Fitzhugh-Carroll Race. Courtesy of Local History Division, Rochester Public Library.

40

Child's Basin, "siding" of the Erie Canal just to the west of the aqueduct over the Genesee, permitted easy access to several mills on the Rochester-Fitzhugh-Carroll race. Courtesy of Local History Division, Rochester Public Library

The Hervey Ely Mill, located on the east side of the river just south of the old aqueduct, was "almost as full of machinery as the case of a watch." Courtesy of City Historian's Office

When the construction of the market proved more costly than expected, it became necessary to sell market stock to meet the bills. Fortunately, the stall rentals soon liquidated the burden, introducing Rochester to the fiscal policy of borrowing. The sight of the market suspended over the river soon prompted east-side property holders to extend similar frame buildings out over the river along the northern edge of the bridge, until it was completely bordered by a line of shops linking the east and west sides of Rochester into one thriving town.

The Rochester Journalists and Their Politics

The appearance in 1816 of the Rochester *Gazette*, the first weekly newspaper, backed by Colonel Rochester, had prompted the launching of the *Telegraph* two years later by Everard Peck. The *Gazette*, soon renamed the Monroe *Republican*, supported Jeffersonian policies, while Peck's editor, Thurlow Weed, was an outspoken leader of the Clintonian faction which had absorbed most of the old Federalists. Several other contentious weeklies appeared, including the Rochester *Observer*, a vigorous advocate of evangelical causes, and the *Liberal Advocate*, a voice for minorities and free thought. The launching of the Rochester *Advertiser* in 1826, the first daily west of Albany, marked a new advance. Henry O'Reilly, its young Irish-born editor and an ardent Jackson supporter, arrived to find the village torn by a new controversy over the disappearance of William Morgan, a disgruntled Mason who had written a book disclosing the secrets of that order.

The abduction and rumored drowning of Morgan stirred an anti-Masonic furor that had many facets. When Weed, alert to the hostility many citizens felt toward secret societies and the influence they exerted, championed the anti-Masonic cause in the *Telegraph*—which had since absorbed the *Republican* and become a daily—local Masonic chapters surrendered their charters, and many of their members rallied to the support of Clinton, whose popularity as the promoter of the canal had mushroomed. Weed, eager to exploit the case, hastened to identify a body found in the Niagara as a "good enough Morgan until after the election," as O'Reilly reported in the *Advertiser*, thus intensifying the conflict.

Although he denied the charge, Weed vigorously promoted the anti-Masonic campaign. He took the lead in organizing an independent Anti-Masonic party with clubs in every ward to counter the Hickory clubs—for "Old Hickory," as Andrew Jackson was called—supported by his rival O'Reilly. Weed's backers carried the county in 1828, supporting John Quincy Adams for President, and sent Weed to the assembly a year later. But Jackson had carried the country, and O'Reilly, who became his chief local representative, made Rochester the base for his blos-

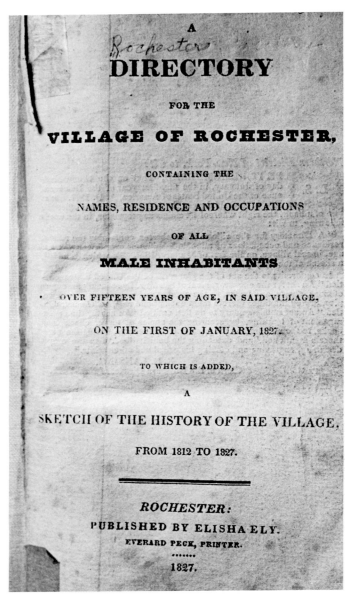

A

DIRECTORY

FOR THE

VILLAGE OF ROCHESTER,

CONTAINING THE

NAMES, RESIDENCE AND OCCUPATIONS

OF ALL

MALE INHABITANTS

OVER FIFTEEN YEARS OF AGE, IN SAID VILLAGE,

ON THE FIRST OF JANUARY, 1827,

TO WHICH IS ADDED,

A

SKETCH OF THE HISTORY OF THE VILLAGE,

FROM 1812 TO 1827.

ROCHESTER:
PUBLISHED BY ELISHA ELY.
EVERARD PECK, PRINTER.
....
1827.

Rochester's single Village Directory was published in 1827, ten years after legal formation of the village and seven years before the first City Charter. Courtesy of City Historian's Office

Thurlow Weed (1797-1882), arrived in Rochester in 1822. His origins were humble, but he had learned the printing trade and went to work as printer-junior editor on the Rochester Telegraph. The Antimasonic enthusiasm helped send him as an Assemblyman to Albany, where he remained a leader of the Whig and Republican parties. Courtesy of City Historian's Office

Henry O'Reilly (1806-1886): newspaperman, politician, and early telegraph promoter. O'Reilly, who emigrated from Ireland at the age of ten, was an untiring booster of Rochester and is perhaps best remembered for his pioneer history, Sketches of Rochester... (1838). Courtesy of Local History Division, Rochester Public Library

Cover from the Anti-Masonic Almanac...1830 issued in Rochester; arguments for and against Freemasonry raged in books, pamphlets, broadsides, and in the daily press. Antimasonry became a significant political force. Courtesy of City Historian's Office

soming career, while Weed transferred to Albany. Peck, who had sold the *Telegraph*, used his presses to publish books and brought out the first *Directory*, in which he included many historical and statistical details.

Sam Patch
and His Motto

Rochester's booming growth as a canal port, and now as the center of anti-Masonry, had made it, as one observer declared, "the bright spot in western New York." A move in 1826 to establish a theater prompted its opening in a circus building on Mill (Exchange) Street, where a museum of wax figures had appeared the year before. The Bishop museum, which had been located at Canandaigua for several years, had displayed its wares in Buffalo as well as Rochester, but had chosen the latter for its permanent home. Among the visiting actors who played at Rochester in its first short-lived theater was Edwin Dean, manager of a theater in Buffalo, who would return some years later to establish a more permanent theater in Rochester.

But the event destined to win the boomtown its widest renown was the daring jump of Sam Patch over the main falls. A New England millhand who had won fame for outjumping all rivals in the East, Sam was returning after a display of his skill at Niagara, where he had survived a jump of 100 feet from the bottom end of Jacob's ladder into the pool behind the falls. Welcoming the challenge of the Genesee falls, he announced a last jump of the season for Friday, November 13, 1829. The widely publicized event attracted a great crowd of onlookers, who gathered around the rim of the gorge. A platform erected on Brown's island overlooking the falls increased the distance to the pool below to 120 feet. The vast throng applauded as Sam climbed up and declaimed his famous motto: "Some things can be done as well as others." The shouting ceased, however, when he made his leap and "alighted in the other world," as Nathaniel Hawthorne would put it a few years later after a visit to the falls. Disagreeing with most commentators, Hawthorne asked, "Why do we call him a madman when he has left his memory more prominently around the falls of the Genesee" than any man of his day—and, he might have added, put Rochester on the map!

"Refreshing
Showers" of
Spirit and Learning

Josiah Bissell took a more somber view of the Sam Patch episode. A zealous believer, staunch backer of the *Observer* and the Bible Society, founder of the six-day stage and packet lines that suspended

Charles G. Finney, at the age of 80, from his Memoirs...(1876). Finney's numerous visits to Rochester between 1830 and 1855 had profound impact. The revival of 1830 was, perhaps, the most efficacious: a local clergyman opined that "...even the courts had little to do and the jail was nearly empty for years thereafter. The only theater in the city was converted into a livery stable and the circus into a soap factory." Courtesy of City Historian's Office

View of the Main Falls and Rochester, looking south, 1830. Visible are buildings on Main Street Bridge near the center of the picture. On the extreme right can be seen the platform, built precariously on an island ledge, from which Sam Patch took his fatal leap. Reproduced from the Rochester Gem and Ladies' Amulet, November 13, 1830. Courtesy of Local History Division, Rochester Public Library

First Presbyterian Church, from a photograph taken later in the 19th century. Here, during Charles G. Finney's first Rochester revival in 1830, a crowd packed the building so tightly that the weight of the balconies pulled a rafter loose. There was considerable panic but no injuries. Courtesy of Local History Division, Rochester Public Library

operation on the Sabbath, Bissell was not one to view the spectacle at the falls lightly. As superintendent of the Third Presbyterian Sunday School, he admonished its members on November 15, "Any who by their presence had encouraged that soul to leap into Eternity will be held accountable on the Judgment Day!" The shivers that flashed up and down the spines of some of his hearers forecast a warm welcome, a few months later, for Charles G. Finney, the great evangelist.

A series of "concerts of prayer" in the courthouse square, deploring licentiousness and prompting temperance and Sabbath observance, helped to set the stage. Possibly some mundane developments also conditioned the response, for the boomtown's great surge, generated by the building and opening of the canal, had subsided as the impetus for new growth moved farther west. A slump in real estate values and other inflated ventures brought a recession in 1829 that created an atmosphere favorable to an otherworldly awakening. Finney's grave manner and reasoned address disarmed many skeptics and brought a "refreshing shower" of spirit.

The Finney revival, featuring three sermons in different churches each Sunday and four or more services during the week, continued for several months. Assisted by a "Holy Band" of cooperating clergymen who labored earnestly with all who found their way to the "anxious seat," Finney won many converts and gave new vitality to the temperance and Bible societies as well as to most Protestant churches. The *Observer* rejoiced to note that the value of tavern sites was declining, as a number of liquor dealers dumped their stock and signed the pledge. A Moral Reform Society made its appearance, and Everard Peck published the first of a series of *Temperance Almanacks*.

Of course, the intensity of the revival could not last. As a countermove, "Obediah Dogberry," as an anonymous freethinker styled himself, brought his *Liberal Advocate* to Rochester in 1832 and hastened to report with glee that "backsliding is becoming the order of the day." But the increased "tranquillity" he applauded would soon bring the demise of Dogberry's paper as well as the *Observer*.

Sure proof that Rochester had survived its recession was the continued solvency of the Reynolds Arcade. Erected in 1828, this four-story brick building was the pride of the town, and all rejoiced when, despite many fears, Abelard Reynolds was able to meet the annual payments on his $30,000 mortgage to John Jacob Astor in New York. His office as Rochester postmaster attracted a stream of people into the Arcade every day and prompted several to locate their shops there, thus making it the town's business center. Reynolds promoted other functions as well. Thus, when Dr. Levi Ward, patron of a short-lived debating society named after Benjamin Franklin, organized the Athenaeum to replace it in 1829, a hall on the second floor of the Arcade was made available for its meetings, lectures, and library. The

The original Reynolds Arcade, built of brick in 1828, was four and one-half stories tall and nearly one hundred feet long. It was said to be the largest commercial structure west of Albany. Inside, the "arcade proper" was a lofty corridor dividing the building through the middle onto which shops opened. The observatory was eighty-nine feet tall. Courtesy of Local History Division, Rochester Public Library

The Rochester "High School," the result of an ambitious cooperative effort by two school districts, was constructed in 1827 and opened its doors in 1828. It soon evolved into the Rochester Seminary and, later, the Rochester Collegiate Institute. Courtesy of City Historian's Office

TEMPERANCE

ALMANAC,

FOR THE YEAR OF OUR LORD

1832:

BEING LEAP-YEAR AND THE 56th—57th OF AMERICAN INDEPENDENCE.

CALCULATED FOR THE MERIDIAN OF ROCHESTER,
And will serve for the western part of New-York and Pennsylvania northern part of Ohio, and Upper Canada.

CONTAINING, BESIDES THE ASTRONOMICAL MATTER,

MANY USEFUL HINTS, FRIENDLY ADMONITIONS

AND

SOLEMN WARNINGS,

ON THE SUBJECT OF

INTEMPERANCE.

ROCHESTER:
PUBLISHED BY HOYT, PORTER & CO.

1832.

Inside cover illustration from the Temperance Almanac. . .*for 1832; graphic and unsubtle. Courtesy of City Historian's Office* plea of the village *Directory* for an "academic grove" had already inspired two school districts to join in erecting a high school, and now the provision of facilities for adults broadened that response.

From Village to City

The prestige of the Arcade was soon challenged by the erection of the Eagle Hotel at the Four Corners. Built of stone and rising to five floors in back, it displaced the Ensworth tavern on Scrantom's old site and won acclaim as the best hostlery west of Albany. Even the new Rochester House overlooking the canal on Exchange Street could not match the Eagle, but together they afforded travelers a choice of accommodations unrivaled by many cities and spurred the drive for city status.

Recurrent moves for a city charter had been blocked by residents who feared increased taxes. But the mounting demands for street improvements, for the digging of sewers and the construction of a waterworks, as well as for a more adequate supervision of taverns and places of entertainment, presented problems the village trustees, even with increased powers acquired in 1826, could not handle. A frightening outbreak of cholera in 1832 prompted inspections by a physician on the board of trustees that revealed unsuspected pockets of poverty and a desperate need for sanitary facilities. Finally, two disastrous fires, one consuming the new market and most of the frame structures on the bridge, with losses estimated at $100,000, silenced most objections.

With concerted backing, the city charter finally won legislative approval in April 1834. It incorporated a greatly expanded area, encompassing 4,819 acres on both sides of the river, and gave the city a population of 12,252. Although local backers of Jackson had been the most active supporters of the charter, the opposing Clay and anti-Masonic factions, drawn together as Whigs by the temperance issue and by their desire to keep the fiscal outlays well below the prescribed limit of $8,000, carried the city election. At their first meeting in June, the aldermen chose Jonathan Child, son-in-law of Colonel Rochester, as mayor. Then they promptly adjourned for a celebration on Brown's island overlooking the falls where, as reported by the *Liberal Advocate* in one of its last issues, they consumed many cold hams and much hot coffee.

The Eagle Tavern at the Four Corners, as it appeared in 1838, when this engraving was published with Henry O'Reilly's Sketches of Rochester. *Courtesy of Local History Division, Rochester Public Library*

Jonathan Child (1785-1860) was Rochester's first mayor in 1834; he resigned the job after a year because of the council's insistence on issuing liquor licenses. Courtesy of Local History Division, Rochester Public Library

J. Hills

CHARTER AND DIRECTORY

OF THE

CITY OF ROCHESTER:

—ALSO—

STATISTICKS, POPULATION, CITY OFFICERS, PUBLICK BUILDINGS, INSTITUTIONS, FIRE DEPARTMENT, &c. &c.

C. & M. MORSE, PUBLISHERS.

Rochester:

MARSHALL & DEAN PRINTERS.

::::::::::::::::::

1834.

Title page from Rochester's first city directory, published in 1834 with the achievement of a city charter (a single village directory had appeared in 1827). The first city directory measured less than 5" x 7" and contained some 200 pages; half the space was taken up by the Charter and advertising.

The Genesee Falls, Rochester, Lithograph by J. Cousen, London. Published by George Virtue, 26 Ivy Lane, 1838. Courtesy of Joseph W. Barnes

Chapter 4

The Flour City: 1834-1854

Rochester's reluctance to accept city status persisted even after the adoption of its charter. Visitors continued to marvel at its sudden growth and to exclaim over its spectacular setting astride the Genesee with its Roman aqueduct and successive waterfalls. Many admired its massive mills, commodious hotels, numerous churches, and fine residences. Willis G. Clark from Philadelphia, for example, compared it favorably with other cities. "The entrance to Rochester from the west is impressive," he reported in an article for the *Knickerbocker* in 1837, "and when you are rattling over its pavements...you fancy yourself in New York or eke in Philadelphia." But Horace Greeley, who two years later spent "a long day...inspecting some of the lions of this place," found only one local civic lion to praise, the beautiful Mount Hope cemetery.

Indeed, except on election days, most civic officials maintained a low profile. All the early mayors and most of the aldermen were prominent citizens, but few could give much attention to municipal affairs. Mayor Child's chief administrative effort was to curb the liquor trade, and when his policy of high license fees prompted a popular reaction that brought the election of a Democratic council, which submitted a batch of new licenses for his signature, Child promptly resigned. Jacob Gould, the merchant shoemaker who succeeded him, rebuilt the public market, constructed a stone-lined sewer on Buffalo Street, and purchased fifty acres for Mount Hope cemetery. But his outlays, though funded by the banks on the expectation of adequate rentals and local assessments, appeared so extravagant that the Whigs recaptured control and chose as mayor Jacob Schermerhorn, the town's leading banker, who resigned after three months. His successor, Thomas Kempshall, an English-born miller, pressed ahead with street improvements but welcomed a nomination to Congress before the end of his term.

Only Elisha Johnson, the east-side developer and engineer who became mayor in 1838, had a firm grasp of Rochester's civic needs. The persistent fire hazards and mounting sanitary problems prompted him to prepare a detailed plan for a public waterworks. Its construction, he argued, would bring an abundance of water from the upper river to cleanse and safeguard the city, and its cost would be offset by reduced insurance rates; moreover, it would provide useful employment in the hard times of that dark year. But the depression of the late thirties had gripped even the Democratic aldermen, who rejected his proposal, and Johnson, too, left with relief at the end of his term.

Thomas Kempshall (1796-1865) was Rochester's fourth mayor in 1837 and the first foreign-born mayor. He was a successful miller and businessman who served a single term (1839-1841) in Congress. Courtesy of City Historian's Office

Commercial Improvements

But if Rochester's business leaders were hesitant in assuming civic responsibilities, they were forthright in promoting commercial improvements. Two of the early mayors—Child, owner of the largest line of canalboats, and Schermerhorn, treasurer of the company that had built a horsecar line to Carthage in 1832—took the lead in organizing the Tonawanda Railroad. They engaged Elisha Johnson to design and build the pioneer line in the mid-thirties. Finally, on May 11, 1837, a steam engine, brought by canalboat from Philadelphia, was fired up for the official opening. "Panting like an impatient war-horse," as one of the several hundred excited onlookers reported, it steamed west from its terminus near the United States Hotel on Buffalo Street and in forty minutes reached Churchville. After ceremonies there and at two other hamlets, it reached Batavia for a boisterous celebration, including a banquet at the Eagle Hotel, before returning triumphantly and without accident to Rochester that evening.

Rochester merchants had from the beginning supported the pleas of lake shippers for federal improvements at the mouth of the Genesee. The building of a lighthouse at Charlotte in 1824 and the construction of piers into the lake to breach the sandbar in the early thirties had improved access to the

Elisha Johnson, early land promoter and surveyor, served as Mayor of Rochester in 1838. Courtesy of Local History Division, Rochester Public Library

Rochester's "New Market" as it appeared in Henry O'Reilly's Sketches...*(1838). This public building enjoyed a useful career, not only as the "Centre Market" but as the sometime headquarters for militia companies, the police department, fire companies, and the poor and street departments. It was demolished in 1865. Courtesy of Local History Division, Rochester Public Library*

Entrance to Mt. Hope Cemetery, as it appeared at mid-century. Land for the cemetery was purchased in 1837, and it was dedicated in 1838, shortly before this "Egyptian" gateway was built. Throughout the century Mt. Hope remained Rochester's most popular and least controversial municipal enterprise. Courtesy of Local History Division, Rochester Public Library

docks at Carthage, which had been absorbed in the expanded city of 1834. Local investors likewise backed the efforts of merchants in Canandaigua and Geneva in building the Auburn & Rochester Railroad and rejoiced on its completion to Canandaigua in 1840 and to Geneva and Auburn a year later. Rochester supported the demands of towns up the valley for the construction of the Genesee Valley Canal, and on his retirement as mayor, Johnson assumed charge of construction on the difficult section south of Mt. Morris.

But Rochester merchants were primarily interested in an enlargement of the overloaded Erie Canal. Jonathan Child and Henry O'Reilly had taken the lead early in the campaign for canal improvements. They had attracted wide support, for congestion had developed at both ends of each of the many single locks scattered along the canal. Rochester, however, had a special concern because of defects that had appeared in its famed aqueduct. Its seventeen-foot width and the right-angle turn at its eastern end made it the worst bottleneck on the canal—a site for many bruising battles between rival boat crews contending for the right-of-way. The brown sandstone of which it was constructed was rapidly deteriorating from exposure to water and air, and despite extensive repairs each spring, the aqueduct continued to crumble and threatened a disastrous breach in the canal. Forthright action was clearly called for, and after some debate the legislature authorized the construction of a large and more substantial aqueduct over the Genesee and of double locks throughout the length of the canal.

These projects, approved before the onset of the depression, provided much new employment across the state and particularly at Rochester, where an expenditure of $445,347 on the second aqueduct—five times the cost of its predecessor—considerably relieved the hard times. The second aqueduct, built of limestone from a quarry near Syracuse, crossed the Genesee on a slant in order to eliminate the right-angle turn at its eastern end. Completed early in 1842, with a trough almost three times the size of its predecessor (which had partially collapsed that winter), it stimulated an increased flow of commerce.

Local boatyards doubled in number, boosted their output to 210 large freight boats valued at $1300 apiece by 1846, and raised Rochester's shipments of flour and other products to over 100,000 tons annually during the next several years. Averaging more than $5 million in value, these exports paid for imports that spurred the city's economy and brought its population to a total of 43,877 in 1855.

Industrial Promotions

Few saw as clearly as O'Reilly in 1835 that "the flouring business for which Rochester is at present most celebrated, is by no means of such importance ...as the other branches of manufactures." The

Old Charlotte Lighthouse. Courtesy of Local History Division, Rochester Public Library

Engine houses in Rochester at mid-century. Few authentic pictures of the earliest local railroads have survived. Courtesy of Local History Division, Rochester Public Library

The First Aqueduct, c 1822-23, from a drawing originally printed by Everard Peck. The first aqueduct, constructed of local sandstone, carried a channel less than half the standard Erie Canal width of forty feet. Courtesy of Local History Division, Rochester Public Library

Views of the Erie Canal Aqueducts. The crossing of the Erie Canal over the Genesee at Rochester was widely regarded as remarkable. The comments of Anne Royall, a travel writer who visited in 1826, are typical: "the canal crosses the river by an aqueduct 758 feet in length, and of great height above the river...we are lost in wonder to see boats and horses, with men on them, passing at such a vast height above the surface of a bold river. The aqueduct is built on arches of hewn stone, and for beauty, symmetry and proportion is unrivalled."

"Plan of the New Aqueduct," published by O'Reilly in 1838, was a hopeful sketch; in that year work on the new aqueduct began in earnest. Main Street Bridge is indicated in the foreground. Courtesy of Local History Division, Rochester Public Library

The Second Aqueduct, with ruins of the first aqueduct visible north of it, from an engraving published in Ballou's Pictorial...Companion in 1855. The second aqueduct, completed in 1842 before the final collapse of its sandstone predecessor, was more massive in every respect. In the twentieth century it serves as the lower level of Broad Street Bridge. Courtesy of Local History Division, Rochester Public Library

Buffalo (West Main) Street, looking east, in 1841. The Four Corners intersection is in the middle distance. The old court house with its cupola is visible in the right side of the picture behind the trees in the court house square. Courtesy of Local History Division, Rochester Public Library

town's most articulate promoter, he called for greater emphasis on other industries. Some utilized raw materials from the valley, including Jacob Graves' tannery, which supplied the thriving shoemakers, and Everard Peck's paper mill, which endeavored to fill the demands of an increasing number of printers. The Cunningham carriage factory relied at the start chiefly on Genesee lumber, but soon it began to import rarer woods by lake boat.

Metalworkers were more completely dependent on imports. The canal had made it possible for Lewis Selye to develop a large machine shop in which he manufactured fire engines, railroad cars, and other metal products. David Barton's Hydraulic building —so called because it supplied waterpower to numerous shops on its several floors—was situated at the southwestern corner of the bridge. Here, Barton and other edge-tool makers supplied implements and tools to meet the diversified needs of the growing city and its agricultural hinterland. Several score of enterprising craftsmen—tailors, shoemakers, woodworkers, and the like—were developing specialized shops that, in many cases, would expand into busy factories as Rochester emerged by mid-century as an industrial rival to Troy, formerly the leader in the state.

Yet few of the rising industrialists vied with the millers, the merchants, and the bankers for community leadership or distinction. The profits reaped by the millers were sometimes quite large, especially in 1836 and 1837 when flour prices soared, and several of them—notably Benjamin Campbell and Hervey Ely—built imposing mansions. Only the most prosperous merchants, such as Jonathan Child and Silas O. Smith, could match them in the late thirties. Several other men built mansions in the next decade, among them Josiah W. Bissell. A canal engineer charged with the task of dismantling the old aqueduct, Bissell salvaged enough brownstone to erect the city's first stone mansion on the old road to Pittsford, which he promptly renamed East Avenue and graced with a double row of young trees.

Unfortunately for the millers, high flour prices could tumble even while their products were en route to market, dragging down their fortunes with them. Both Campbell and Ely lost their mills and their mansions in the early forties; while both recouped their fortunes and acquired new mansions, the toll was severe, and by 1850 only two of the millers of 1835 were still engaged in that trade. It was not surprising that O'Reilly, who became a promoter of telegraph lines after his departure from Rochester, found many backers among its millers, who were eager for the latest price information. Meanwhile, O'Reilly, who never built a mansion, left a more enduring monument in his *Sketches of Rochester; with Incidental Notices of Western New York*, published in 1838, the first considerable history of any interior city in America.

The Cunningham Carriage Factory, one of Rochester's early woodworking industries, gained national recognition for its fine coachwork. The company survived into the twentieth century as a deluxe automobile manufacturer. Courtesy of City Historian's Office

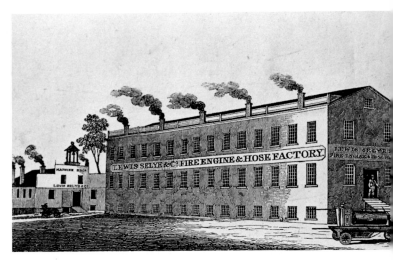

Among the most technically sophisticated of early Rochester manufactures was the fire engine factory of Lewis Selye. His buildings were located between Mill Street and the river, on both sides of Brown's Race. Selye, a blacksmith turned industrialist, served a variety of roles in community leadership: he was an alderman, a country treasurer, congressman, and an original director of Monroe Savings Bank. Courtesy of City Historian's Office.

Three of the water-powered mills of the Flour City, as depicted in O'Reilly's Sketches... (1838). Richard Richardson's mill, and Henry Achilles' "City Grist-Mill" were on Brown's Race, and drew power from the Main Falls. The "Crescent Mills" of Thomas Emerson were built between South Water Street and river, and used the Johnson and Seymour Race. Courtesy of Local History Division, Rochester Public Library

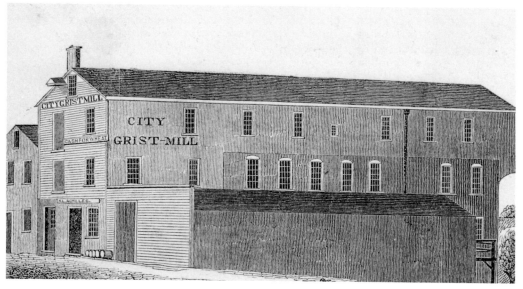

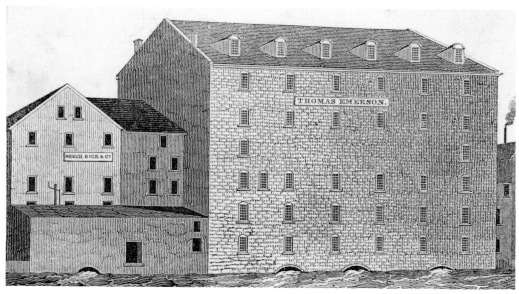

The Other Side of Urban Growth

The millers were not the chief sufferers from hard times. Work on the aqueduct reduced but did not eliminate unemployment and approximately 60 percent of a sample of names in the 1838 *Directory* failed to reappear in the 1844 list. But if many moved on, more arrived, and in the hectic search for jobs and shelter an increasing number of destitute waifs appeared in the streets. With the county almshouse already overcrowded, a group of charitable women opened the Rochester Orphan Asylum in temporary quarters in 1837 and erected a permanent home six years later. The Catholics provided a separate institution in 1842, and the state established the Western House of Refuge at Rochester in 1849 to house youngsters adjudged unruly or delinquent.

The hardships of the poor were graphically revealed during a second cholera epidemic in 1849. Alarmed by the report of several cholera deaths in June, a reorganized board of health endeavored to clear up the many neglected drains and cesspools, but the city's failure to construct a waterworks limited their effectiveness. When the plague struck with a vengeance in July, the officials declared one tenement on Main Street, where five deaths had occurred in six days, unfit for human habitation and set it afire. They inspected several other unsanitary and infected hovels and evacuated the surviving inhabitants; lacking any provision for their shelter, many poor persons joined the more affluent in fleeing the city. Fortunately, a cold spell late in September brought a subsidence of the plague, and the city rejoiced that only 161 had been fatally stricken.

Some of the plague's victims had been found in grog shops, where other poor men also congregated, and the temperance forces, dormant since the midforties, determined to clear up this evil. A Women's Temperance Society was organized in 1851, but when its efforts to work with a new statewide Temperance Alliance were rebuffed, some of the women—notably, young Susan B. Anthony—espoused the new cause of women's rights. The women's movement had its start in Seneca Falls in 1848; by the mid-fifties, Miss Anthony would make Rochester its vital center.

Rochester had a propensity for focusing movements that sprang up in the surrounding area. Joseph Smith, in nearby Palmyra, had attracted some followers from Rochester in the thirties, and his Mormon cause still commanded attention in local journals. William Miller's prediction of an approaching "Second Coming" drew a group of excited followers in white robes to the top of Cobbs Hill on the evening of March 21, 1844. When the next day dawned nevertheless, a new date was set for Judgment Day. A crowd assembled in Talman Hall on October 21 that year, and again for a third ascension date in 1847.

Time continued to march on, and word arrived a year later that the Fox sisters in nearby Hydesville had established contact with the spirit world. The

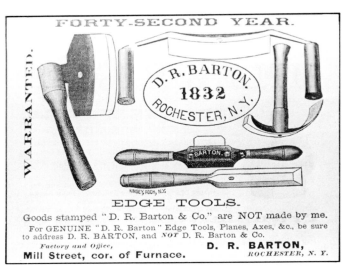

D.R. Barton became Rochester's best-known tool manufacturer. The oval imprint "D.R. BARTON 1832 ROCHESTER, N.Y." (depicted here in an advertisement in the 1874 Directory) was stamped on thousands of implements—many now in the hands of collectors. Courtesy of City Historian's Office

Two Third Ward Mansions: the Greek Revival homes of Hervey Ely and Benjamin Campbell, constructed in the mid-1830s. Courtesy of Local History Division, Rochester Public Library

REPORT.

AFTER an interval of three years, it has become the duty of the Board of Health to give to their fellow-citizens, a brief history of the epidemic which has once more swept over our city, leaving in its train, its usual marks of sadness and mourning.

The crisis, now happily past, has been one of unparalleled severity in the history of this city, and has imposed upon the members of this Board an amount of labor and anxiety, which can be fully appreciated by those only, who have passed through similar scenes of conflict and suffering.

Since its prevalence in this city three years ago, Cholera has lost none of its potency. The same rapid march from its onset to its fatal conclusion, which characterized it in 1849, has marked its progress in 1852. The same subtle, unseen agent, which singled out its victims with such fearful exactness in the former year, has acted with equal energy and precision in the latter. No age or sex, and but few conditions in life have been wholly exempt from its attacks. The temperate and the intemperate—the virtous and the vicious—the laboring man in his strength—the professional man in the midst of his toils—the robust youth—the feeble child—and the veteran, borne down by the weight of four score years—have, each in his turn, yielded to the destroyer.

The amount of mortality, as will hereafter be seen, although less than has been represented in some quarters—has been sufficiently appalling to awaken in the minds of the members of this Board, the deepest solicitude, and the most anxious inquiries.

That their official acts prior to, and during the late trying season, have given satisfaction to all, or even a major part of their fellow-citizens, is more than they had reason to expect at the outset: but that they have endeavored honestly and faithfully to discharge their onerous duties

The Board of Health's painstaking Report *published in 1852, following Rochester's last cholera epidemic, contained over sixty closely printed pages. The actual cause of the dreaded disease was as yet unknown, but the Board's vigorous recommendations for improved sanitation and sewerage were aimed in a worthwhile direction. Courtesy of City Historian's Office*

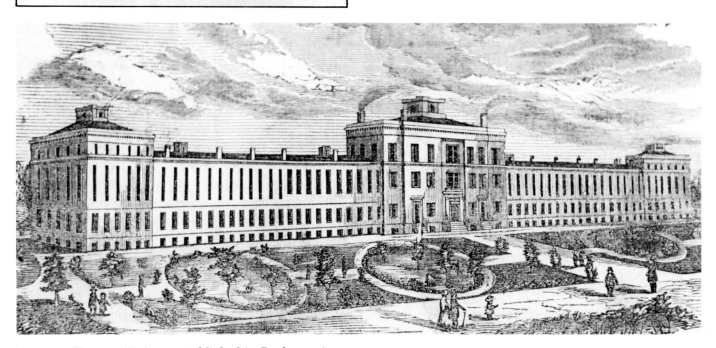

Western House of Refuge, established in Rochester in 1849, contained some 42 acres about one mile northwest of the central city. The main building, by 1851, was 382 feet in length, and before the Civil War the institution housed nearly 400 delinquents. Disciplined study, argriculture, and industry were all emphasized. Courtesy of City Historian's Office

first public demonstration of their power to converse with departed souls was held in the new Corinthian Hall erected by William A. Reynolds in back of the Arcade in 1849. The Spirit Rappers, as they were called, created a sensation that proved convincing to some, including the now aging Abelard Reynolds. Their movement would leave its mark on Rochester in the form of an obelisk, erected following a world-wide subscription drive among believers in 1927, which stands today at Troup and Plymouth in commemoration of the birthplace of modern Spiritualism.

New Educational Perspectives

When Isaac Butts, the caustic new editor of the *Advertiser*, dismissed the Spirit Rappers as another of Rochester's recurrent "humbugs," most residents agreed. Denominational differences had grouped the city's thirty-five churches of 1850 into a half dozen Protestant sects that seldom came together except in opposition to the four Catholic churches, the dissident Unitarians, and the recently organized Jewish temple, B'rith Kodesh. Yet while the activities of the Bible Society continued to agitate some of these hostilities, the Sabbath schools that all maintained provided a common ground of experience and endeavor. Despite renewed visits by Finney and other evangelists, the emphasis was shifting in most churches, as in the city at large, to education as the best preparation for a good life.

In addition to the Sabbath schools, a few Protestant denominations and the Catholic churches maintained day or parochial schools. Several private seminaries for girls made their appearance with social, as well as religious backing, along with two boys' academies. But these schools served only a fraction of the four thousand children between five and sixteen who thronged Rochester in 1840, when the district schools reported fifteen hundred registrants. In an effort to correct this situation, O'Reilly headed a campaign for a revision of the charter that called for the election of a board of education empowered to name a superintendent and to maintain a unified system of free public schools. Within three years, the board and Superintendent Isaac Mack, formerly a custom miller, erected nine new schools, thereby increasing the total to fifteen, and boosted total enrollment to 4,246.

The attempt of two Brighton districts in the late twenties to maintain a high school had proved too ambitious, and its principal's efforts to carry on in the same building as a privately operated seminary soon faltered. Fortunately, Dr. Chester Dewey arrived to take charge in 1836, and, by adding courses in elementary science and accounting, attracted support that enabled him to reorganize the school in 1839 as the Rochester Collegiate Institute. Dewey had eagerly collaborated with O'Reilly in scheduling the annual series of Athenaeum lectures for adults, and he had backed the drive for a school board. When

The Fox Sisters. From left to right: Margaretta Fox, Catharine Fox, and Leah (Fox) Fish, in 1852. The Fox sisters' professed clairvoyance—demonstrated at sessions widely known as the "Rochester Rappings"— began a movement which developed into modern Spiritualism. Courtesy of Local History Division, Rochester Public Library

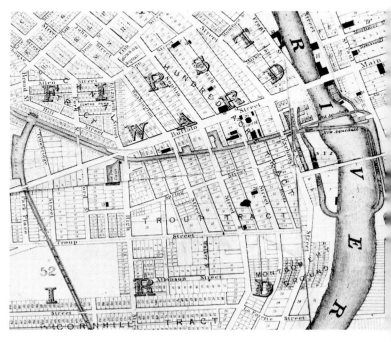

Section of the Silas Cornell Map of Rochester, 1839. Rochester contained, in 1839, nearly 20,000 persons. Courtesy of City Historian's Office

Isaac Butts (1816-1874) took control of the Daily Advertiser *at the age of thirty. In 1856 he helped merge the* Advertiser *with the* Daily Union, *forming the* Union & Advertiser; *that paper, now known as the* Times-Union, *is regarded as the oldest daily newspaper west of the Hudson because of the antecedent* Advertiser. *Courtesy of Local History Division, Rochester Public Library*

Dr. Chester Dewey (1784-1867), first professor of chemistry and natural science at the University, came to Rochester in the late 1830s and was Director of the Collegiate Institute. Dewey took an active part in the intellectual life of the city —and compiled its first weather statistics. Courtesy of Local History Division, Rochester Public Library

SKETCHES OF ROCHESTER;

WITH

INCIDENTAL NOTICES OF WESTERN NEW-YORK.

A COLLECTION OF MATTERS

DESIGNED TO ILLUSTRATE THE PROGRESS OF ROCHESTER DURING THE
FIRST QUARTER-CENTURY OF ITS EXISTENCE.

INCLUDING A MAP OF THE CITY AND SOME REPRESENTATIONS OF SCENERY,
EDIFICES, ETC.

ARRANGED BY HENRY O'REILLY.

" The names of the first settlers are interesting to us chiefly because they were the first settlers. There can be little new to offer; and what can there be interesting to the public in the lives of men whose chief and perhaps sole merit consisted in the due fulfilment of the duties of private life? We have no affecting tales to relate of them—no perils by flood or field—no privations induced by the crimes of others or their own imprudence. The most that can be said of them is, that they were moral, religious, prudent, quiet people, who, with admirable foresight, made the best advantage of their situation, and who lived in comfort, begat children, and died."

Gordon.

Title page of Henry O'Reilly's remarkable 468 page opus, produced when Rochester contained fewer than 20,000 persons and only the tiny library of the Athenaeum. Its numerous engravings were based on drawings by a young local artist, John T. Young. Courtesy of City Historian's Office

they joined Superintendent Mack in urging the establishment of a public high school, however, advocates of economy blocked action.

With several thriving seminaries and academies, what Rochester needed, many declared, was not a public high school but a college, and several denominational groups were eager to supply it. As the strongest local sect, the Presbyterians took the lead in a move to establish a University of Western New York at Rochester in 1845. Dr. Dewey, a Congregationalist, endorsed the project, as did a few Methodists, Baptists, and Unitarians, until they learned that the plan called for the naming of seventeen Presbyterians to the board of trustees. As local support for that project dwindled, both the Catholics and the advocates of education for women hastened to secure charters, but their projected colleges never opened.

Local Baptists, however, hearing of a move by some restless professors and trustees at Hamilton to relocate that Baptist college in Rochester, promised a warm welcome. Court action by loyal Hamiltonians blocked that action, but local Baptists rallied enough support from residents eager to secure a college for Rochester to establish both the University of Rochester and the Rochester Theological Seminary in 1850. Their joint opening in November, in the former United States Hotel building on Buffalo Street, was made possible, as Ralph Waldo Emerson would report the following February, by bringing "an Omnibus load of professors down from Madison, bag & baggage, Hebrew, Greek, Chaldee, Latin, Belles Lettres, Mathematics, & all Sciences" to staff both projects, and by placing "runners on the road to catch students."

Emerson was in Rochester on a speaking tour to address the Athenaeum, now the Athenaeum and Mechanics Association, in Corinthian Hall. When asked to name his price, he had responded, if the story can be trusted, that FAME was spelled "Fifty And My Expenses." Hosted by John N. Wilder, president of the trustees, in the Jonathan Child mansion he had recently acquired and where two of the new professors boarded, Emerson was clearly astonished by the sudden appearance of a university in a town not yet four decades old. His account was not quite accurate, however, for Dr. Dewey, who had arranged for his lecture, was now the science professor of the university, and with an enrollment of eighty-two students and six faculty members, it compared favorably with most colleges of the day.

If Emerson, after a dinner in the sumptuous Child mansion, was provoked at his own modest evaluation of fame and a bit churlish in his appraisal of the university, he nevertheless would return during the next few years for five more lectures in Corinthian Hall, including one on "Wealth" and another on "Culture."

Both of these topics were of interest to Rochesterians. The chartering of a second savings bank and a sixth commercial bank in the early fifties; the building of a chair factory that employed 250 workers, increasing the firms that employed upwards of fifty men to more than a score; the organization of five trade unions, two mutual benefit societies, and a building and loan association; and a renewed attempt to organize a board of trade—all attested to the appeal of wealth.

As for culture, a Daguerrian gallery and an Emporium of Art were opened in the Gaffney block, as was a new Metropolitan theater adjoining the Enos Stone block, while the enlargement of the Arcade provided improved facilities for the Athenaeum library. Corinthian Hall supplied a platform for many visiting lecturers—Wendell Phillips, urging the emancipation of slaves, and Louis Agassiz on science, among others—and for several local speakers who drew good crowds—including Frederick Douglass on the rights of Negroes and Lewis H. Morgan on Iroquois culture. Dr. William H. Channing, the Unitarian minister, delivered an address "In Defense of Popular Amusements."

It was a novel but not unwelcome clerical viewpoint. Visits by Barnum's Menagerie and other circus troupes had attracted crowds on numerous occasions into a canvas pavilion on Falls Field. Two cricket teams introduced the first organized games on Brown's Square, while a Union course provided a track for horse racing and grounds for an agricultural fair that drew thousands of visitors from up the valley. A stock company, shared in alternate weeks with Buffalo, presented Shakespearean drama and other classics, as well as *Uncle Tom's Cabin* and *The Honeymoon*, or *How to Rule a Wife*. No performer attracted larger crowds than Jenny Lind, the "Swedish Nightingale," who returned for a second concert to satisfy the overflow. A costume party in one of the large mansions numbered seventy-six guests and inspired the printing of an amusing account of *The Fancy Party*, in which the costumes and personalities were generously puffed up. But the "unsoaped" found a spokesman, too, in a second pamphlet on *The Great Uppercrust Party*, which burlesqued the show and put the town's "scrub nobility" in its place.

This section of the Robinson lithograph of Rochester (1868) shows Falls Field on the east bank of the Genesee River at the Main Falls. The field was for many years an informal park and location for circuses. Turned to commercial uses in the late nineteenth century, it was recently (1977) made a city park. Courtesy of Office of the City Historian and Genesee Country Village

Jenny Lind, the "Swedish Nightingale," was a favorite of local audiences and her concerts given here in July, 1851, were the major musical events of pre-Civil War Rochester. Courtesy of Local History Division, Rochester Public Library

Rochester viewed from Mt. Hope, 1854. The engraving by Felch follows an earlier (1849) picture by E. Whitefield. The original Clarissa Street Bridge is quite prominent in this view, as are the numerous church steeples that dominated the skyline of the young city. Courtesy of City Historian's Office

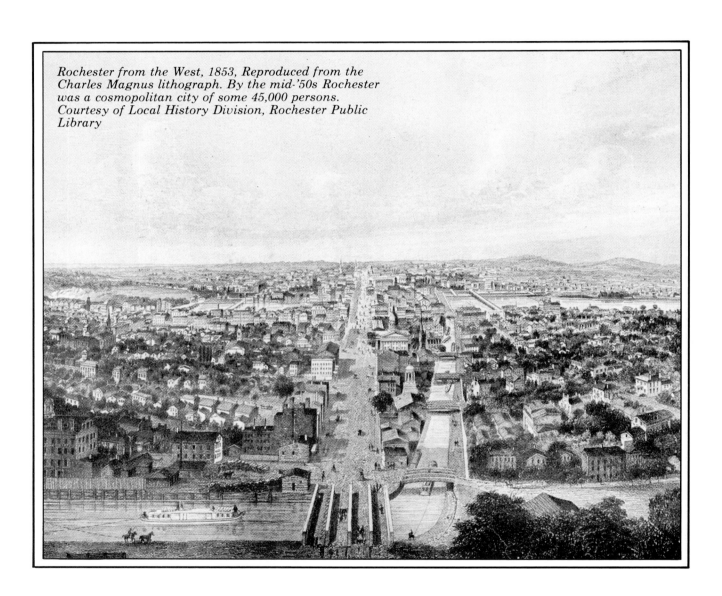

Rochester from the West, 1853, Reproduced from the Charles Magnus lithograph. By the mid-'50s Rochester was a cosmopolitan city of some 45,000 persons. Courtesy of Local History Division, Rochester Public Library

Chapter
5

The Cosmopolitan Flower City: 1855-1880

Two opposing views of Rochester in 1857 were jointly revealing. An aging miller, in a letter to a former neighbor describing the rebuilding of Main Street bridge, damaged by a flood in 1855, wrote disconsolately: "A number of workmen are hewing and hammering at it in an old fogy way, which, you know, is ever characteristic of Rochester." He concluded with a wish that he, too, had left when still young enough to move, for "the Flour City is dead." In contrast, Jeremiah O'Donovan, an Irish poet, in an account of his American travels published that year, pronounced Rochester, where he had spent a few weeks visiting his former countrymen, "the Promised Land."

Both views were in a sense correct. Flour milling was following the wheat farmers into the West, and while some millers remained, their days of leadership (when indeed their civic policies had had an "old fogy" character) were over. But newcomers were arriving from Ireland and other parts of the British

Isles, from Germany and Northern Europe, eager for new opportunities. First by filling the places of those who moved on, then by employing their skills in developing new industries, and finally by transplanting cherished aspects of their heritage, they were helping to build and shape the more cosmopolitan Flower City that emerged from the Flour City like a daffodil from a craggy bulb.

From Flour City to Flower City

The transformation was not instantaneous, nor was it unopposed. A friendly welcome had greeted most of the early migrants from abroad. Many of the Irish, who were at first the most numerous, had helped to build the canal and St. Patrick's Church, which they would soon replace with a cathedral. A stream of Norwegians, pausing for a few months in Rochester, manned the boat yard of Lars Larson, their most prominent (and most permanent) representative in Rochester. Migrants from England and Scotland had fitted unobtrusively into St. Luke's or the Presbyterian societies. The Germans, with language problems, had formed separate German Catholic as well as Lutheran and Jewish societies.

Many of the old Yankees regarded these newcomers with curiosity; the earlier attacks on "Popery" in the *Observer*, however, were now drowned out by the excitement over Rochester's booming growth. An English-born miller served as fourth mayor by appointment in 1837, and Irish-born John Allen, a popular leader of the local militia, which included many of his countrymen, won election to that office seven years later. O'Reilly, as we have seen, became a key figure in many aspects of the city's history.

But in 1845, when the state census tabulated 7,468 of the city's 25,265 residents as foreign-born, the unexpected strength of these newcomers stirred some concern. Almost 4,000 were listed as unnaturalized aliens without votes, but the Democrats who courted their support were encouraging many to seek full citizenship. Their success tipped the balance in local elections in six of the next eight years. Frustrated by successive defeats, a group of conservative Whigs organized a new American party, more popularly known as the Know-Nothings because of their reluctance to state their nativist principles. Backed by a new daily *American* published by the Jerome brothers, they successfully elected a mayor in 1854 and again in 1855. Neither man proved effective in the face of Democratic councils, however, and the nativist issue was soon submerged in the contest over slavery.

The Jerome brothers, Leonard and Lawrence, would later be remembered in Rochester chiefly because of the beautiful sisters they married and their distinguished offspring. Leonard left with his recent bride in 1856 and raised his family in Brooklyn and abroad. Jenny, his second and most beautiful daugh-

St. Patrick's Cathedral, as it appeared later in the 19th century. The church, which was torn down in 1939 to make way for Eastman Kodak's expansion, was located on Platt Street at the corner of Plymouth Avenue North. Courtesy of Local History Division, Rochester Public Library

The Rochester Novelty Works, one of many diversified manufacturing enterprises active in Rochester during the 1850s and 1860s, was located on Hill Street (later renamed Industrial Street), and was entirely dependent on steam rather than water power. Courtesy of City Historian's Office

*The Second County Court House/combined City Hall
was constructed at the beginning of the '50s and served
as Rochester's civic center until construction of a
separate City Hall in 1874. The gilded statue of Justice,
which now graces the front of the Third Court House
(County Office Building) is unblindfolded. Courtesy of
City Historian's Office*

ter, met and married Lord Randolph Churchill, and it was their son, Winston, whose spreading fame revived memories of the Jeromes in Rochester. A tradition, confusing Jenny with one of her cousins, that she had been born in Rochester and attended school here (though refuted in her autobiography) was widely enough held to persuade the University of Rochester to confer an LL.D. on Winston in 1942. The Prime Minister was valiantly defending Britain at the time, but cabled his thanks, adding, "as you tell me my mother was born in Rochester, and my grandfather published the Rochester *Plain Dealer*." Apparently Winston, or some assistant, did not at that delicate moment, when Britain was seeking American aid, wish to admit that his grandfather had published a Know-Nothing paper and substituted a more respectable title from Cleveland!

The cosmopolitan transformation had more than political overtones. The foreign-born, who numbered 19,389 by 1855, had brought new skills that soon enabled them to develop specialized shops that would free Rochester from its reliance on the now flagging mills. Patrick Cunningham's carriage factory, Henry Bartholomay's brewery, Myer Greentree's clothing shop, and John Jacob Bausch's spectacle shop were only a few of the many new enterprises destined to prosper in the years ahead.

But the industry that best represented the new cosmopolitan influence was the nursery trade. George Ellwanger from Germany, Patrick Barry from Ireland, and Joseph Harris and James Vick, both from England, took the lead. Trained abroad and alert to the advantages of applying European techniques and importing foreign seeds and plantings, they made Rochester—protected by the moderating temperatures of Lake Ontario, which never freezes over—the leading nursery center in America. It was fitting that Henry O'Reilly should be invited back in 1859 to write a brochure on "The Greatest Nursery in the World," in which he gave Rochester its new nickname—the Flower City. The fields of blooming daffodils and tulips, flowering ornamental and fruit trees, that virtually surrounded Rochester each spring by the late sixties, amply justified the cognomen. The stream of visitors from afar who journeyed to Rochester to see a blooming century plant at the Frost Nursery in 1869 further demonstrated its merits.

Rochester was becoming a part of a larger whole. The merging of the six short railroad lines east and west of the city into the New York Central in 1853 had rendered Rochester more accessible to distant influences. That consolidation, in which Joseph Field, an able former mayor, had participated, may have prompted Hiram Sibley and other Rochesterians to make a similar move in the telegraph field. The disjointed lines O'Reilly had built in the forties, several with Rochester backing, had connected many neighboring cities, but messages directed to more distant places had to be carried by boys from one office to another at each terminal, involving added time and expense and generally no profits for investors. Sibley and his colleagues, by securing the

George Ellwanger (1816-1906), from Germany, was co-equal in the partnership of Ellwanger & Barry. Ellwanger was also a promoter of the city's first horsecar line, a banker, and an Eastman Kodak trustee. He and Barry presented the city with 19 acres of nursery land in 1887, which became the nucleus for Highland Park. Courtesy of City Historian's Office

Patrick Barry (1816-1890), an Irish immigrant, established a national reputation as a writer, editor, and practical manager in the field of horticulture. With George Ellwanger he established the Mt. Hope Nurseries, and, like his partner, participated in a variety of local business affairs. Courtesy of City Historian's Office

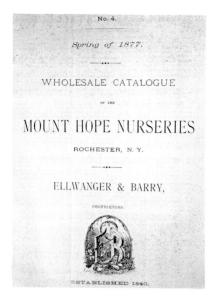

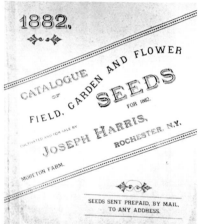

James Vick (1818-1882), an English immigrant, worked his way up from printer to editor of such publications as the Genesee Farmer *and the* Rural New Yorker. *Patrick Barry was his editor when he owned the* Horticulturalist. *After 1862 Vick devoted his energies to a career as seedsman. His estate and grounds on East Avenue became a subdivision with two streets that bear his name. Courtesy of Local History Division, Rochester Public Library*

Hiram Sibley (1807-1888), president of Western Union, which successfully consolidated the nation's telegraph lines during the '50s, was also a nurseryman, land investor, and patron of higher education. Cornell, the University of Rochester, and Mechanic's Institute all benefited to some degree from his considerable wealth. Courtesy of Local History Division, Rochester Public Library

Catalogs of the Flower City. Because the nursery and seed businesses were mail order, they placed many orders with job printers. Rochester's printing industry flourished accordingly. Courtesy of City Historian's Office

nationwide rights to a new, though much less efficient, telegraph sending machine, and by threatening to bypass the lines of companies that failed to cooperate, secured the lease or purchase of connecting lines throughout the interior. By 1857, they had established a virtually nationwide telegraph system under the name of Western Union, with its central office in the Reynolds Arcade.

The city's widening vista had cultural repercussions. No longer dependent on resident stock companies, the Metropolitan theater as well as Corinthian Hall featured programs by the Hutchinson family from England; the Italian operatic star, Adelina Patti; the Swiss bell ringers; and Sigsmond Thalberg, the German pianist. Thalberg made a second visit in 1858 with a concert orchestra that prompted his former countryman, John H. Kalbfleisch, to form a local orchestra. A Mannerchor was organized as well, and the two collaborated in celebrating the Schiller centennial at Rochester in 1859, thereby providing dramatic evidence of the new cosmopolitan influences. Henry Van Ingen from The Hague maintained a studio in Rochester, where he organized a local exhibit for some New York friends, and Edwin Scrantom, now Rochester's "Old Citizen," held an auction of a hundred paintings by contemporary European artists at his sales parlor in 1858.

The continued growth of the Athenaeum library, supported by the surplus from its annual lecture series, made an increasing number of books available to interested readers. Patrick O'Meara, a refugee from an abortive Young Ireland revolt now working as a butcher in Rochester, was a frequent user of the library. After two false starts, the successful launching of a German weekly, the *Beobachter*, in 1851, marked the beginning of foreign-language journals in Rochester.

But the most significant minority-group journal of the day was the *North Star*, established by Fredrick Douglass in 1847 and soon renamed *Fredrick Douglass' Paper*. Supported at the start by British friends (who had rallied to his aid, after his series of lectures as a fugitive slave in England, and had purchased his freedom), this weekly and his autobiography, first published in 1845, helped to make Douglass a national and international figure—the first Rochesterian to achieve that distinction. More important, by traveling and lecturing throughout the Northern states and by making his home on the city's southern border (near the site in Highland Park where his statue stands today) a station on the Underground Railroad, Douglass helped to focus local and national attention on the antislavery cause as the day of decision approached.

The Ordeal of Civil War

When William H. Seward delivered his famous "Irrepressible Conflict" speech at Corinthian Hall in

Corinthian Hall, built by William A. Reynolds in 1849 for the Athenaeum and Mechanic's Association, as it appeared in 1866. Corinthian Hall became the site of lectures, concerts, and historic speeches. The building is remembered today in the street name Corinthian Place. Courtesy of Local History Division, Rochester Public Library

Frederick Douglass (1817-1895) was not only Rochester's most famous black citizen, but the nation's outstanding black leader of his time. With his activities as lecturer and editor, he helped make Rochester a center of the antislavery movement. After the Civil War, when his career turned to public service, Douglass moved to Washington—but his burial place is Mt. Hope Cemetery. Courtesy of Local History Division, Rochester Public Library

The Striped Leaved American Aloe, or CENTURY PLANT,

NOW IN FLOWER

At FROST & CO.'S Genesee Valley Nurseries Rochester N. Y.

BENTON & ANDREWS, PRINTERS, ROCHESTER, N. Y.

The Century Plant, housed in a greenhouse at Frost & Co.'s Genesee Valley Nurseries, became a great curiosity and tourist attraction. In 1869 the plant protruded through a thirty-foot extension in the roof of the greenhouse and bore some 2,000 buds and flowers. Courtesy of City Historian's Office

October 1858, few in Rochester took the warning seriously. Two years later, the new Republicans mustered only a slim majority for Abraham Lincoln. Concerned over Lincoln's equivocal stand on slavery, local abolitionists, headed by Frederick Douglass and Susan B. Anthony, staged a meeting in Corinthian Hall demanding "No Compromise with Slaveholders," as a banner suspended in front of the Arcade proclaimed. Popular protests against the banner prompted its removal, and shouting opponents disrupted the meeting, which the police finally closed by dimming the gaslights. An adjourned session at the African Zion Church was poorly attended, revealing the essential weakness of local support for the cause.

News of the attack on Fort Sumter brought a different response to a totally different issue. Hamlet D. Scrantom, son of the first permanent settler and now mayor of Rochester, called a meeting in the council room in the city's portion of the new courthouse to pledge Rochester's support for Lincoln's call for volunteers to defend the Union. Martin B. Anderson, president of the university, addressing a vast throng outside, declared "the Rubicon is passed" and recommended resolute action. Two local militia companies, one of them Irish, enlisted en masse; Adolph Nolte, editor of the German weekly, recruited a company of his young countrymen who could follow orders in German. Isaac F. Quinby, a graduate of West Point and professor of mathematics at the university, was chosen colonel of the Thirteenth Regiment of New York State Volunteers as it entrained for Washington to defend the Capitol.

The "Bloody Thirteenth," as it was known after heavy losses in the first battle of Bull Run, was the first of several units recruited in the Rochester area as the war progressed. Relatives and friends gathered in the Arcade after successive battles to read the fateful bulletins and pore over the casualty lists. Private and public bounties helped to fill the new quotas, and residents who had formerly opposed the views of Douglass and other abolitionists rejoiced when, as the outstanding leader of his race, he journeyed to Washington to persuade Lincoln to recruit Negroes to battle for their own freedom.

The recruitment of the 140th, which became known as the Rochester Regiment, rallied support in 1862 from all segments of the population. The popular Patrick O'Rourke, who had grown up in Rochester and graduated at the head of his class, first at No. 9 School and then at West Point, was named colonel. A year later, when news arrived that the 140th had held Little Roundtop, a key position in the Battle of Gettysburg, all cheered until the casualty lists revealed that the colonel and twenty-five of his men had fallen in that crucial engagement. Protestants as well as Catholics followed the funeral bier of Colonel O'Rourke to St. Bridget's Church ten days later as Rochester learned a new sense of community.

The war to defend the Union called unexpected home-front energies into play. A Volunteer Relief Committee raised funds to assist the needy families of local recruits. A Hospital Relief Association rallied

Isaac F. Quinby (1821-1891) was a Professor of Mathematics at the University of Rochester when he was chosen colonel of the 13th Regiment of New York State Volunteers. He stayed with the 13th until after the Battle of Bull Run, subsequently assuming a number of arduous commands. Quinby not only was a West Point graduate, but had taught at the military academy as well, and had served in the Mexican War. Courtesy of City Historian's Office

Col. Patrick O'Rourke, Rochester's chief hero of the Civil War, fell while commanding the 104th New York State Volunteers at the Battle of Gettysburg. Courtesy of City Historian's Office

The University of Rochester's first permanent building, Anderson Hall, was built in 1861 with the aid of a state grant. The building still stands on the University's old campus. Courtesy of City Historian's Office

St. Mary's Hospital. This building, erected in 1863, housed many war-wounded; previously St. Mary's occupied temporary quarters. Courtesy of Local History Division, Rochester Public Library

support for St. Mary's and the City Hospital, both of which opened during the war and provided care for many wounded soldiers. Local bootmakers, clothing manufacturers, and gunsmiths filled rush orders, as did the flour millers and meatpackers.

While inflated prices and coal shortages brought hardships to many poor families, some men reaped large profits. When the federal government, in an attempt to meet its huge outlays, levied its first income tax and published the names and incomes of those reporting over $5,000, the Rochester list brought exclamations of surprise. A few millers were included, along with shoe, clothing, and wool merchants, and the publisher of the *Union*, among a dozen others, but Hiram Sibley of Western Union led all the rest, with a tax of $8,390 on $103,000. His telegraph lines were proving of crucial value to the North in the mustering of men and supplies, and the profits were handsome. Many in Rochester, after inspecting that list, acquired an enduring respect for inventions!

As the battles along the Potomac continued almost without letup, except when the armies went into winter quarters, Rochesterians felt an increasing need for distraction. Each winter brought an outburst of almost frantic gaiety—Christmas bazaars, boisterous ethnic rallies, welcome-home parties for returning units, a schedule of plays at the Metropolitan, and musicals as well as lectures at Corinthian Hall. Ice skaters crowded the large natural rink above the dam on frigid days, particularly in the hard winter of 1864-65.

Rochesterians got an unwelcome distraction that March when a sudden thaw up the valley sent a rushing torrent down the river, overflowing the aqueduct and Main Street bridge and inundating several downtown streets. As the city struggled to clean up after its worst flood, news of General Lee's surrender brought an outburst of joyous relief. Although 650 of the city's 5000 recruits (approximately one-tenth of its population) had made the supreme sacrifice, the Union had been preserved. Unfortunately, the prospect of renewed harmony was shattered a week later by the assassination of President Lincoln—a tragic ending that revived bitter wartime hostilities that were destined to plague local and national politics for years to come.

A New Leadership Emerges

During the next fifteen years, Rochester attracted 10,000 additional migrants from abroad, most of them from Germany, and, with the assistance of the postwar baby boom and some annexations, more than doubled its population. A new generation of leaders arose, among them several who gave a personal flavor to important phases of the city's growth. John Jacob Bausch, for example, stumbled on a chunk of hard rubber and, sensing its suitability for the manufacture of spectacle frames,

The Rochester Daily Democrat *and* American *for April 10, 1863 carried not only battlefront news but quartermaster's advertisements and market information keenly read by local provisioners. Courtesy of City Historian's Office*

The Great Flood, March 18, 1865. This view of Main Street looking northwest was taken from a building on Main Street Bridge. The Great Flood of 1865 was the most destructive in Rochester's history. There were considerable property losses, but no deaths. Courtesy of Douglas A. Fisher, Victor Historical Society

John J. Bausch (1830-1926), a German immigrant, opened an optical shop in Rochester in 1852 with the aid of his partner Henry Lomb. He achieved a breakthrough in the 1860s by successfully adapting hard rubber to the manufacture of spectacle frames and subsequently built one of the world's largest optical industries. Courtesy of City Historian's Office

Freeman Clarke (1809-1887), prominent banker, businessman, and University trustee, was elected to Congress twice and served as United States Comptroller in 1865, a critical year of that responsibility. Courtesy of Local History Division, Rochester Public Library

Iceskaters on the Genesee, 1862, photograph of a painting in the collection of the Rochester Historical Society. Courtesy of Local History Division, Rochester Public Library

secured the exclusive rights for such production. By recruiting technically trained artisans in Germany, he was able to include the grinding of lenses and the manufacture of microscopes in his new factory opened on St. Paul Street in 1874. In similar fashion, William S. Kimball, a tobacco merchant, developed a thriving factory around a tobacco-plug bailer and a cigarette-cutting machine developed by an inventor in his employ. George Ellwanger made annual trips abroad in search of choice bulbs and seedlings to enrich his nursery stock and brought works of art back with him. Kimball, too, became an art patron and ordered a giant-sized statue of Mercury to be mounted on the smokestack of his projected new factory.

None equaled Daniel W. Powers in the diversity of his influences. A private banker, Powers decided in the mid-sixties to construct a new, more elegant stone facade around his bank in the former Eagle Hotel at the Four Corners. Two fires in adjoining buildings enabled him to acquire their sites for expansion and prompted him to adopt the new cast-iron-front construction for these extensions, designed to match the stone-block section they flanked. The completion of the large Powers Block, with a sixth story under a mansard roof over the stone corner section, was celebrated by a grand illumination in 1871 that attracted a stream of visitors eager to ride on the first elevator in western New York.

As the owner of the largest building with the highest assessment, Powers was a staunch backer of the tax league, which was currently battling advocates of a water system. With a cast-iron sheath and marble floors in the corridors, Powers felt safe enough—until the great Chicago fire swept away several cast-iron structures there. Awaking to his own danger, Powers headed a committee that demanded the immediate construction of a water system, and the city built not one but two waterworks during the next two years.

With its safety assured, Powers ordered an extension of the mansard roof over the entire structure and proceeded to stock the top floor with paintings imported from Europe. Soon his gallery and a large adjoining room became the favorite center in Rochester for receptions, dances, and art exhibits. The block's success in attracting high-rental tenants spurred neighboring property owners to rebuild on a grander scale.

Civic and Cultural Leaders

Rochester's mounting civic needs intensified the political rivalries of former days. One of the few who managed to surmount the bitter hostilities left by the war was Henry L. Fish. A Democrat whose kindly manner and impeccable honesty won bipartisan support, he served two successive terms as mayor in the late sixties and initiated plans for a city hall and a

The nation-wide sales of the Kimball Tobacco Company depended in no small measure on Kimball's elaborate packaging, and the use of printed advertising of all kinds. Courtesy of Local History Division, Rochester Public Library

Gate House at Highland Reservoir, as it appeared in 1890. Rochester's "water works" comprised two separate systems. The "Holly" system, completed first, was a high-pressure downtown firefighting system, demonstrated in 1874. The domestic "Hemlock" system, which drew water from Hemlock Lake to Highland Reservoir thirty miles north, began serving subscribers in 1876. Courtesy of Local History Division, Rochester Public Library

Powers Banking House as it appeared shortly after the Civil War. Courtesy of City Historian's Office

In the decades after the Civil War, Daniel Powers made steady improvements and enlargements of his "fire-proof" block. This view is taken from an engraving published in 1871. Courtesy of City Historian's Office

During the mid-'70s, Powers built an observation tower and completed the first mansard roof. Note that the Elwood Building, completed in 1879, does not appear in this photograph; it would be built on the northeast corner of the Four Corners. Courtesy of Local History Division, Rochester Public Library

In this rare photograph, the Powers Block is seen in the left side of the picture undergoing one of its periodic enlargements and face-lifts. Main Street stretches eastward into the distance. The building's stage of completion places the photograph in 1880. Courtesy of Local History Division, Rochester Public Library

The Powers Block as it appeared "complete" with two mansard roofs and the observation tower as it was in 1883. Subsequent improvements would add an additional mansard roof and a larger tower. Courtesy of City Historian's Office

free academy. And when, after his retirement, rival factions within both parties secured the appointment by the state legislature of special commissions to undertake those projects as well as construction of the waterworks, thus removing them from local control, Fish stood for and won election to the assembly. There he backed Governor Tilden in his battle against the Tweed ring and, in the process, uncovered the corrupt activities of State Senator Jarvis Lord and his son George D. (who defeated Fredrick Douglass for assembly in 1871), the two local politicans who had engineered the creation of the commissions and had secretly acquired the coveted contracts they authorized. The Lords hastily left town, and Fish secured the substitution of an elective executive board to complete and manage the construction projects.

Despite incessant squabbles, the aldermen frequently reached agreement. They voted in 1871 to change the name of Buffalo Street to West Main Street (a slap at that booming rival), and three years later passed a revision of the city's boundaries that more than doubled its area. To improve service to the outer districts, they approved a lengthening of the lines of the horsecar company, launched in 1863, and a double-tracking of portions in the downtown area. They authorized an extension of the piers of Main Street bridge on the south side to permit the construction of brick buildings across the river, thus finally completing Rochester's unique "London Bridge."

Susan B. Anthony, battling for political rights for women, found little consolation in an engagement to deliver a series of speeches in support of President Grant, running for reelection in 1872 against Horace Greeley. Returning to Rochester in disillusionment, she read a call by a local editor for all citizens to register, and sprang into action. With Miss Anthony in the lead, fifty women registered, and fourteen cast ballots, despite official challenges, on election day in November 1872. Charged with illegal voting, Miss Anthony was tried before a federal court and, after a spirited defense, was convicted and fined $100, which she refused to pay.

The challenge posed by Miss Anthony in the 1870s was less political then intellectual, and it shared the limelight of public debate with another doctrinal issue, evolution, that aroused even more intense emotions. Lewis H. Morgan, who had backed the abortive attempt to launch a college for women, had also taken the lead in organizing a club in which a dozen of the city's leading "pundits" engaged in learned discussions of scientific and philosophical questions. The theories of Darwin, Huxley, and Spencer stirred heated arguments there and at public lectures before the Athenaeum, as well as in the Unitarian Church, where the Reverend Newton Mann emerged as the first Rochester clergyman to endorse evolution. Morgan, on a trip to Europe, hastened to visit these and other learned men, and on his return shared his experiences with the Pundit Club.

But it was young Henry A. Ward, grandson of Dr. Levi Ward, who brought the issue into dramatic focus. Ward returned after study and prospecting trips to Europe and the Near East with packing boxes

Henry L. Fish (1815-1895) owned a canal boating business and served in a variety of civic posts: alderman, supervisor, and school commissioner. A Democrat, he served as Mayor for two terms, 1867-1869—in fact, he was the first Rochester mayor ever to be re-elected. As Mayor, he promoted the construction of a City Hall but was incensed at the state's creation of a special commission to oversee construction. He accepted a Republican-Union nomination and won election to the Assembly against Jarvis Lord in 1872 and assisted Governor Tilden in uncovering scandals. Courtesy of Local History Division, Rochester Public Library

Henry A. Ward (1834-1906) was the grandson of Dr. Levi Ward, a Rochester pioneer. His study of natural science led to a brief professorship at the University of Rochester, but Ward's urge to travel and explore and his constant broadening of scientific interests eluded academic confinement. He became founder of the renowned Ward's Natural Science Establishment. Courtesy of Local History Division, Rochester Public Library

Susan B. Anthony (1820-1906), as she appeared in 1868. In that year she began publication of the women's rights journal The Revolutionist; the Fourteenth Amendment took effect, and four years later Anthony and her associates registered and voted in the national election. Courtesy of Local History Division, Rochester Public Library

Lewis Henry Morgan (1818-1881), lawyer, scholar, and leader among Rochester's intellectual circles, became recognized as the father of American anthropology. Courtesy of Local History Division, Rochester Public Library

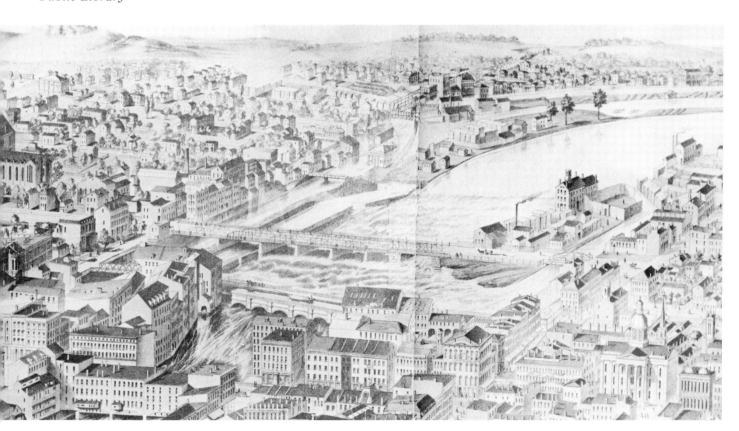

Rochester in 1868. Reproduced from the extremely rare William Henry Robinson lithograph. Courtesy of City Historian's Office, Genesee Country Village

loaded with geological and zoological specimens. He had raised a sum of $20,000 to buy this collection for the university where, with Dr. Dewey's backing, he had become the new professor of science. President Anderson could not refuse the generous gift, to which Hiram Sibley and others had contributed, but he was perturbed when his new professor appropriated the entire third floor of the newly opened Anderson Hall for the display of his collection. He was even more perturbed when a stuffed figure of a gorilla emerged as the prize exhibit!

Professor Ward, always busy collecting and classifying new specimens, generally shunned the public platform, but his artifacts spoke louder than words. President Anderson persuaded him to move part of the collection into a workshop near the college, which became known as Cosmos Hall and provided the nucleus for the independent Ward's Natural Science Establishment that stocked museums throughout the country. Ward included the gorilla in a collection he sold to Vassar College and resigned from the Rochester faculty, but a lengthy poem "To The Gorilla," written by a Pundit and published in the *Democrat,* explored in amusing fashion some philosophical aspects of the issue he had raised:

Are you the *key*, O Monkey, to unlock
    The sealed and scientific mystery?
Were Apes the parents of the human stock,
    Long ere the records of primeval history?
What countless ages did it take to span
    The ethnic chasm from baboon to man?

One verse is enough to suggest that Rochester's cosmopolitan era had nurtured a spirit of intellectual curiosity. Certainly the publication in 1877 of Morgan's seminal book, *Ancient Society,* was a scholarly contribution of the highest order.

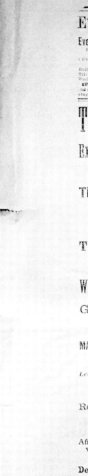

EVENING EXPRESS,
PUBLISHED BY THE
Evening Express Printing Company.
EVERY EVENING—SUNDAYS EXCEPTED.

VOLUME XVII.

THE GALLOWS.

Execution of John Clark, the Murderer.

The Final Scenes in the Terrible Tragedy.

The Prisoner "Dies Game."

Walks to the Platform Firmly

Greets His Friends Familiarly.

MAKES NO DYING SPEECH OR CONFESSION.

Leaves a Penitent Statement for Mrs. Trevor, and Asks Her Forgiveness.

Remarks that He Ought to Have Been Granted A New Trial.

Affectionate Parting with his Wife, Mother and Relatives.

Declares that he was Fully Prepared to Die, and thus Atone for his Crime.

A FULL HISTORY OF THE MURDER.

Interesting Sketch of Previous Executions and Murders.

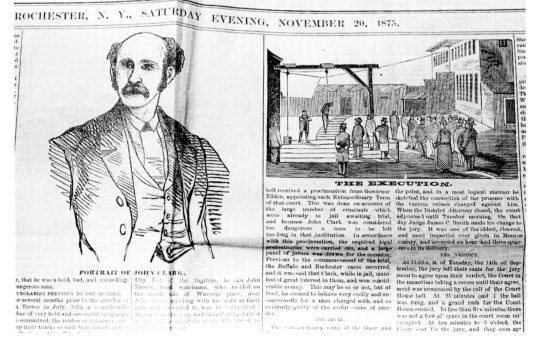

ROCHESTER, N. Y., SATURDAY EVENING, NOVEMBER 20, 1875.

PORTRAIT OF JOHN CLARK.

THE EXECUTION.

The local executions of murderers drew enormous public interest during the second half of the nineteenth century. Press and public alike seemed unanimous in their support of capital punishment. Courtesy of City Historian's Office

City Hall, late in the 19th century. Completed in 1875, the city hall designed by Andrew J. Warner has been the only separate city hall specifically built by Rochester for this purpose in a century and a half. "Old City Hall" was backed by the Erie Canal; in front was a pleasant lawn obliterated by expansion of the County Office Building in the 1920s. Courtesy of Local History Division, Rochester Public Library

"Genesee High Falls, Rochester, N.Y." from W.H. McIntosh, History of Monroe County, (1877). Courtesy of Local History Division, Rochester Public Library

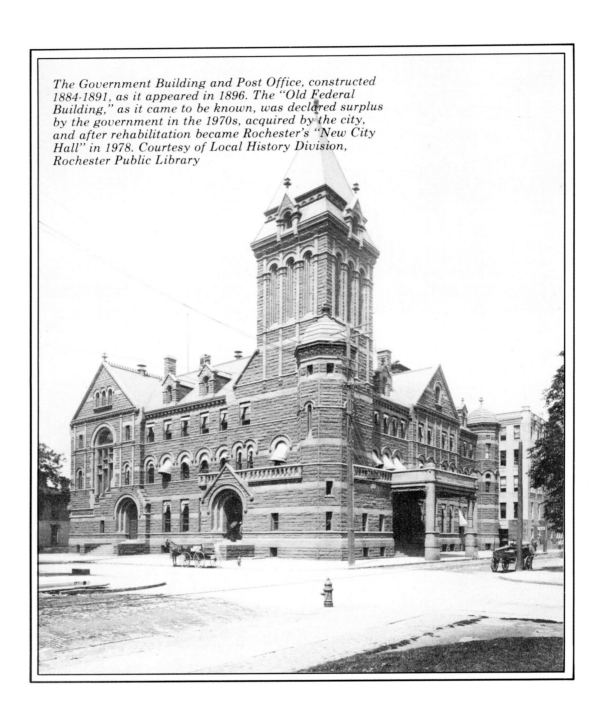

*The Government Building and Post Office, constructed
1884-1891, as it appeared in 1896. The "Old Federal
Building," as it came to be known, was declared surplus
by the government in the 1970s, acquired by the city,
and after rehabilitation became Rochester's "New City
Hall" in 1978. Courtesy of Local History Division,
Rochester Public Library*

Chapter

6

The City of Many Industries: 1880-1900

With the enclosing of Main Street bridge—Rochester's Ponte Vecchio or London Bridge—most residents lost sight of the Genesee River. Its raceways still served numerous mills and other establishments, and new users would appear (including a plant to generate electricity), but steam power, introduced at first as a supplement, was winning recognition as a substitute both for waterpower in production and for horsepower in transportation. It was manpower, however, that displaced waterpower as the wellspring of the Flower City's growth in the 1880s. The city's future lay, in fact, with the stream of residents surging back and forth across the bridge rather than with the silent river disappearing underneath.

The Lure of the City

If curious travelers from abroad now generally bypassed Rochester, their places were more than filled by the excursionists who arrived each spring and fall as regularly as the seasonal flight of birds. Memorial Day and the Fourth of July brought steamboat excursions from Canada as well as numerous visitors from nearby hamlets to see the parade on Main Street, join in the excitement at Falls Field or Charlotte, or watch the fireworks display in the dusk of evening.

The construction of new steam lines to the south and northeast greatly expanded Rochester's hinterland. The State Line Railroad reached Pittsburgh in 1883, and, with a spur to Buffalo, became the Buffalo, Rochester & Pittsburgh (B.R.&P.). The Genesee Valley Canal Railroad to Mt. Morris tapped a coal feeder from Pennsylvania. The Lake Shore Railroad pushed eastward to Oswego and beyond. Each extension of rail links was celebrated by excursions of excited townspeople into Rochester, and each, in turn, forged new commercial bonds. The erection of new railroad stations and hotels made Rochester a convention as well as a tourist center.

An unexpected display of regional interest in its semicentennial celebration awakened Rochester to its new role. Local historians had been working for many months on rival publications to mark the city's fiftieth birthday. William F. Peck, son of the pioneer editor Everard Peck, had a collaborative volume of 736 pages almost ready for distribution in May 1884, when the Common Council named a committee to plan a celebration. Mrs. Jane Marsh Parker, piqued at being excluded from that work, rushed to press a more sprightly account, titled *Rochester, A Story Historical*, and had copies on sale on June 4, when the official parade and other ceremonies attracted a host of sightseers into the city, filling the 300 rooms of the recently opened Powers Hotel and taxing all facilities elsewhere.

The first of a series of annual "Peapickers Excursions" on the B.R. & P. reached Rochester that October. Not all of these visitors were peapickers or farmhands, but their excitement over a trip to the city was evident as they crowded onto the horsecars (and after 1891 into the electric cars) for a ride to the lake resort at Charlotte, or to Driving Park to watch a horse race, or to Culver Field for a ball game. Most, of course, joined the downtown throngs, shopping in the large dry-goods stores on State Street or across the bridge at Main and St. Paul, and in the many specialty shops in between. Some hastened to take a ride on the elevator in the Powers Block to visit the art gallery, and a few among those who returned in succeeding years no doubt exclaimed over the second and third mansard roofs added by Daniel Powers as he struggled to maintain top place on the city's skyline.

Most of the excursionists—after a hearty dinner at the "Oyster Ocean" at the Four Corners, or per-

Cornelius R. Parsons, Rochester's popular mayor throughout the '80s, was known for his impeccable dress as well as his political acumen. Rarely seen without a white blossom in his lapel and a gold-headed cane, he served as mayor for an unprecedented seven terms and was subsequently elected to the State Senate. Courtesy of Local History Division, Rochester Public Library

Bartholomay Pavilion in 1890 was one of several pleasure spots at Charlotte. In the early '80s the development of the lake shore as a resort began with improvements in transportation and was vastly encouraged when the New York Central backed construction of a grand hotel by the Ontario Beach Improvement Company. Courtesy of Local History Division, Rochester Public Library

An 1888 view of City Hall Square with the Court House visible on the right and the front of City Hall on the left. The Free Academy is in the background. Courtesy of City Historian's Office

West Main Street near the Four Corners, 1885-1890; Rundel's "Art Gallery" (before 1885 he called it his "picture store") and the horsecar (streetcars were electrified after 1890) date this photograph. The columns of the second Court House are visible at the upper right. Courtesy of City Historian's Office

The Rochester Driving Park, on the city's northwest side, hosted the annual visit of the "Grand Circuit" as well as agricultural fairs and the like. It was built by a private association in the mid-'70s; the last visit of the Grand Circuit was in 1895. A section of Driving Park Avenue lies along the southern boundary of the old grounds. Courtesy of Local History Division, Rochester Public Library

The Powers Block at its full glory in 1896. The banner suspended above the Four Corners supports William McKinley's presidential campaign. The famed Powers Art Gallery, opened in 1875, would close after Daniel Powers' death in 1897. Courtesy of Local History Division, Rochester Public Library

haps, in the nineties, a visit to Rattlesnake Pete's saloon to marvel at his caged and mounted reptiles—would board their trains or boats for home, but some soon returned to follow up job leads they had found in the city.

Rochester's growth was, in fact, picking up momentum in the eighties. The stream of newcomers from abroad was swelling and now included Jewish as well as Catholic refugees from Poland and early migrants from Italy and the Balkans. Of the earlier ethnic groups, the Germans, with new arrivals, numbered 17,330 in 1890 and, with 20,000 American-born offspring, comprised one-fourth of the city's total population. The British, the Irish, and an increasing influx from Canada, constituted another, though less united one-fourth. In-migration from surrounding towns and states, amounting to some 10,000 persons in the eighties, replaced the out-migrants and gave residents of native parentage a full one-third of the population.

The cosmopolitan years had blurred many of the earlier ethnic differences, but a new division now developed. The long-awaited elevation of the New York Central tracks in the early eighties removed an old barrier to settlement in the city's northeast sector. As horsecars, and soon trolleys, advanced safely through underpasses, home construction followed, and since most of the newcomers in these years were of foreign birth, the district north of the tracks became an ethnic enclave. Many of the Polish immigrants clustered near the northern boundary, where they built St. Stanislaus Church in 1890. Polish Jews, settling along St. Joseph Street, renamed it Joseph Avenue and erected an Orthodox temple nearby on North Street. The Italians, predominantly transient laborers in the early eighties who crowded into lofts on Front Street, now included a number of Sicilian families that located north of the tracks near the old Irish quarter called "Dublin," renaming it "Mount Allegro"; by 1892 they had a sufficient number of males with first papers to form a marching club that staged a parade launching the city's preparation for the Columbian Exposition, scheduled to open in Chicago the following spring.

Manpower Industries

The Flower City's cosmopolitan growth, supported at the start by water-based industries and commerce, brought an infusion of new energies that transformed its economy. Numerous handicraft shops had appeared, and though some succumbed during the hard times, others consolidated and sent traveling agents out in search of distant markets. This pattern set by the nurserymen, took wider hold as the leading shoe, clothing, and wood workers formed partnerships that included enterprising salesmen in their top management. As the partners transformed their workrooms into factories and ex-

The Michaels, Stern & Co. factory building on Clinton Avenue North, completed in the mid-'90s, suggested the importance to which the clothing industry had grown. Courtesy of Local History Division, Rochester Public Library

An 1884 view of the Rochester Cotton Mill on Brown's Race. Courtesy of Local History Division, Rochester Public Library

86

The Second New York Central Station, built in 1882 in conjunction with the railroad's massive track elevation in the downtown section. This station was on the east side of the river, slightly west of the later Claude Bragdon station. Note the large train shed behind the station building. Courtesy of Local History Division, Rochester Public Library

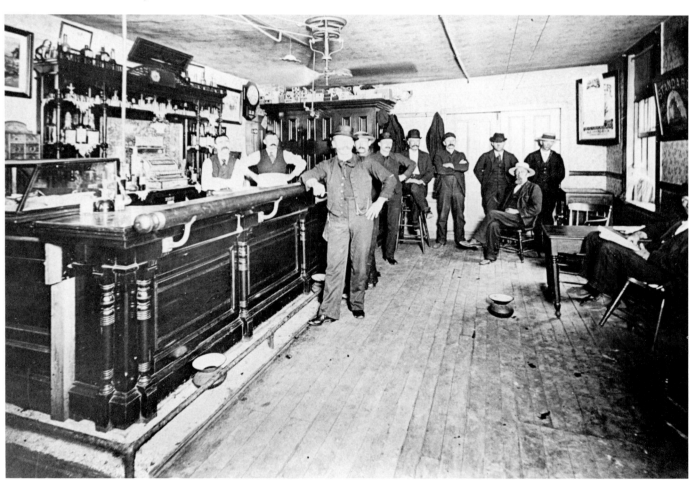

Interior of Francis Doud's saloon, 79 Front Street. In the mid '90s there were 560 saloons listed in Rochester's City Directory—one for every 250 men, women, and children. Courtesy of Local History Division, Rochester Public Library

panded their work forces, their increased reliance on manpower brought with it some troublesome labor-management problems.

The shoe manufacturers acquired industrial leadership in the late seventies and maintained it throughout the eighties. By specializing in women's shoes and employing girls to sew the cloth uppers, they developed a demand for skilled shoemakers to cut and welt the soles, thus absorbing the craftsmen and the markets of surrounding towns. The skilled shoemakers formed a Knights of St. Crispin local to safeguard their employment on the new welting and die-cutting machines; when their pleas for a restoration of wage cuts accepted in the depression were refused, many joined the new Knights of Labor to demand higher wages and shorter hours. To combat these demands, the shoe manufacturers, now more than a score in number, formed an Employers Protective Association and established contact with distant shoe centers.

The Flower City's central location made it a convenient site for conventions of the National Retail Shoe Dealers, as well as for the Shoemakers District Assembly of the Knights and, later, for the rival Boot and Shoe Workers International. A series of local strikes and lockouts brought the newly created State Board of Mediation, with William Purcell, editor of the Rochester *Union & Advertiser*, as chairman, into the picture. The shoe workers provided the largest contingent in the first Labor Day parade in 1887 and took an active part in the organization of the Central Trades Council a year later. Shoe manufacturers played a leading role in the establishment of the Chamber of Commerce in 1888 and supplied three of its first seven presidents. The depression of the mid-nineties would exact its toll, but the style setters and producers of quality shoes would emerge in a strong position.

Similar struggles marked the development of other manpower industries—in wood and metal working, brewing, and tobacco. But it was the clothing industry that became the largest employer locally in the nineties and experienced the sharpest controversies. Several of the clothing merchant-manufacturers had installed sewing machines in lofts adjoining their cutting rooms on Mill and Front streets, but the majority continued to distribute such work to individuals who took the bundles home to sew and finish at so much a piece. The influx of Jewish refugees from Poland, many unable to speak enough English to get factory jobs, provided a constant supply of such workers. As the industry expanded, a group of subcontractors appeared, relieving the manufacturers of the task of distributing and collecting the bundles, and some of these developed sewing shops of their own in lofts in the district north of the tracks, where the newcomers resided. This decentralized industrial pattern encouraged the development of sweatshops and made effective organization difficult.

When the elevation of the New York Central tracks prompted the erection of a new station on higher ground east of the river at St. Paul Street,

The Erie Canal Aqueduct over the Genesee River in Rochester. Illustration from H.R. Page & Company Rochester Illustrated *(1890). Courtesy of Local History Division, Rochester Public Library*

State Street in 1896, as seen from the Wilder Building. Photograph from W.H. Parish Publishing Company, Art Work of Rochester *(Chicago, 1896). Courtesy of Local History Division, Rochester Public Library*

West Main Street (looking east) from W.H. Parish Publishing Company, Art Work of Rochester *(Chicago, 1896). Courtesy of Local History Division, Rochester Public Library*

several of the clothing firms built new factories close by. The convenience of salesmen, who generally travelled with several trunks full of samples, was the chief consideration, but the location near the immigrant settlements north of the tracks proved an additional advantage. It enabled these firms to draw most of their operations into the new factories and to maintain production standards of brand-name quality. The larger factories also enabled the workers to develop firmer union ties, and the nineties saw the formation of rival Knights of Labor and United Garment Workers unions, bringing recurrent clashes between them, as well as with the Clothiers Exchange representing management. Most of the workers, recent immigrants from Eastern Europe, were Orthodox Jews, and religious differences accentuated economic differences with their more liberal German-Jewish employers.

The wages in the clothing industry, except among the skilled tailors and cutters, were meager enough to produce complaints, as Emma Goldman discovered. A 16-year-old recent arrival from Russia, Emma quit her job at the Garson factory after two months in 1886 when, as she later recalled, she was refused an advance from her $2.50 weekly wage to enable her to afford an occasional 25-cent ticket to the Yiddish theater. Having mastered enough English and mustered enough spunk to confront that boss, she tried several others in Rochester with similar frustrations. She soon left for New York City, where in time she became America's leading anarchist.

Most of her relatives and fellow countrymen in Rochester, however, persevered in the industry despite its hardships. A federal investigation of unsanitary conditions and child labor in the sweatshops cast a shadow over the industry, but when most of the subcontractors succumbed during the depression of the 1890s, the larger firms with model factories and brand-name products emerged stronger than ever.

New Industrial Accomplishments

The vitality of the cosmopolitan Flower City had varied manifestations. In addition to new products— such as the Cutler mail chutes, which found a market in the new skyscrapers of many cities, and the rival dental chairs of the Ritter and Archer companies— Rochester industrialists produced a number of civic and social innovations of value. Ellwanger & Barry, for example, donated twenty acres of their nursery grounds to form the nucleus of Highland Park, thus launching the park system in 1888. In the same year, Henry Lomb of Bausch & Lomb took the lead in the establishment of the Mechanics Institute to supply technical training for industrial workers. William S. Kimball was the first in 1889 to grant a half-holiday on Saturdays to his factory workers. Asa T. Soule, president of the Hop Bitters Manufacturing Com-

Emma Goldman (1869-1940), at the age of 17, from her autobiography Living My Life. *"Red Emma" lived in Rochester for only a few years, but harsh experiences and impressions she gained in the city's clothing industry helped shape her anarchist career.*

Driving Park Bridge, in a photograph taken February 8, 1896. Erected in 1890 by the Rochester Bridge and Iron Works, the bridge contains a single wrought-iron arch of 428-foot span—one of the longest in the world. It is the third high bridge built at the lower falls. Courtesy of Douglas A. Fisher, Victor Historical Society

Construction of Court Street Bridge, 1893. As in other times of depression, public works such as this helped relieve unemployment during the '90s. The stone arch design of the second Court Street Bridge deliberately imitated the successful aqueduct and Main Street Bridge. Courtesy of Douglas A. Fisher, Victor Historical Society

pany, backed the formation of Rochester's first professional baseball club, named the "Hop Bitters." It won admission to the newly formed National League in 1881 and, despite many losses, earned enough favor by defeating the Buffalo team on several occasions to assure support for new teams at Culver Field in the 1890s.

Perhaps the most spectacular Rochester industrialist of the eighties was Hulbert Harrington Warner, the patent-medicine king. In the promotion of his Safe Liver Cure pills, Warner introduced several advertising innovations, including what may have been the first widely circulated puzzle contest. His most noteworthy contribution was the building of an observatory for Professor Swift. Lewis Swift, a hardware merchant with a hobby in astronomy, had won four gold medals as the first discoverer of several new comets in the 1870s. On learning of these awards from the Imperial Academy of Science in Vienna, Austria, the local press had given Swift the title of Professor and launched a campaign to raise funds for a larger telescope. Swift's discovery of a fifth comet in 1881 and the arrival of another gold medal brought an offer from Warner to build an observatory on East Avenue to house the professor and his new telescope. The Warner observatory, opened the following October, was the first in America accessible to the public. Admission was gained by presenting a label from a Warner Safe Liver Cure package (did the product gain a scientific aura in the process?), or by purchasing a ticket for twenty-five cents at Warner's headquarters in his new building with a cast-iron front on St. Paul Street.

Swift's accomplishments in the discovery of comets and the charting of nebulae won widespread recognition. His public addresses in Corinthian Hall and elsewhere spurred the organization of an astronomical section in the newly formed Rochester Academy of Science. As the director of the country's sixth largest observatory, he was invited to attend the dedication in 1889 of the great Lick Observatory south of San Francisco. There, peering through its giant telescope, then the largest in the world, he exclaimed in delight. When asked what he saw, he replied, "Stars!" When asked what he had expected to see, he mumbled, "Clouds." The surprised bystander, a visitor from Southern California, grasping the situation, assured Swift that if he would bring his telescope to Pasadena, they would build an observatory for him on a nearby peak under a cloudless sky!

When Swift mentioned that offer back in Rochester, the clouds darkened. Indeed they soon became black for another reason, as the depression commenced. The first victim of the panic of 1893 was H.H. Warner. Buoyed by his election as the first president of the Chamber of Commerce, Warner had recently increased his firm's capital stock from $1.5 million to $3 million and, after negotiating a sale to British investors by guaranteeing them an 8-percent return, he had hastily invested the proceeds in a copper mine and was now unable to meet his commitments. With Warner's downfall, and no one to pay his bills, Swift shipped his telescope to Pasadena.

H. H. Warner (1842-1923), Rochester's "patent-medicine king" and first president of its Chamber of Commerce. His chief remaining monument is the Warner Building on St. Paul Street, embellished with a multistory cast-iron front and large "W's" set in medallions. Courtesy of Local History Division, Rochester Public Library

The color illustrations accompanying advertising literature for Warner's Safe Cures often depicted exotic tropical wharves and jungle scenes—the sources, presumably, of the rare botanicals in the medicines. Courtesy of City Historian's Office

The caption for these pictures on the inside cover of H.H. Warner's promotional pamphlet for 1882 immodestly described the Warner Observatory as "the most noteworthy building in Rochester." Courtesy of City Historian's Office

Professor Lewis Swift (1820-1913) posing with his telescope inside the Warner Observatory. Swift was born on a nearby Clarkson farm and did not come to Rochester until 1872. The self-taught comet discoverer once declared that "curve balls" in baseball were impossible. A demonstration next to a brick wall convinced him that they were possible, and his public retraction added luster to his local popularity. Courtesy of Local History Division, Rochester Public Library

Mounted on nearby Mt. Lowe, under the direction of the aging "professor," the Rochester telescope provided the stimulus for the development of the great Mt. Wilson and Palomar observatories.

Several other Rochesterians would catch a glimpse of the silver lining behind the dark clouds of that depression. In the early nineties, fifty-five Flower City firms had prepared exhibits for the Columbian Exposition—Bausch & Lomb, Cutler, Kimball, George Eastman with his camera, and Jacob H. Meyers with the first voting machine, among many others. But none sent as large a display as Professor Ward, who shipped thirty carloads of fossils, stuffed animals, meteorites, and skeletons. The Ward's Natural Science Establishment exhibit filled a gallery in the science building and won not only a gold medal but much popular attention; more important for Ward was a purchase offer of $100,000 from Marshall Field, who thus acquired the nucleus for the Chicago Natural History Museum.

That sale, announced as the depression was setting in, enabled Ward to repay his backers in Rochester and prompted new ventures at his establishment. But many local firms were less fortunate; most were forced to reduce their work forces, and some closed their doors.

As the crisis deepened, the number of families on the poor department's books mounted from 492 in November 1893 to 2,902 within fifteen months, despite the opening of a stone yard where able-bodied relief applicants had to break stone a half day each week to secure benefits. In spite of this check against the intrusion of "unworthy poor," the outlays soared from some $20,000 in normal years to $135,000 in the second hard winter. But this relief, supplemented by the soup kitchens maintained by several churches and the food and clothing distributed by several charitable societies, failed to supply the wants of unemployed workers estimated early in 1894 at over 4,000. The Common Council voted an extra $15,000 for park maintenance work and $61,000 for a new police headquarters; it funded new sewer and street construction projects—a boon to day laborers—but unemployed factory workers roamed the streets. Many were soon forced to seek jobs elsewhere, an out-migration that reduced the stability ratio of residents listed in the city directories from a high of 62.6 percent for 1889-94 to 58.4 percent over the next five years—the lowest ratio since the depression of the mid-seventies.

As the gloom deepened, the editor of the *Herald*, hearing that George Eastman was doubling his capital from $5 million to $10 million, hastened to warn his readers "to be wary of the novelty works on State Street," which, he surmised, was following the path of H.H. Warner toward bankruptcy. The *Herald's* startled owners, with a surer knowledge of Eastman's prospects, presented the editor with a one-way ticket out of town, but they never regained their canceled advertising!

George Eastman's accomplishments were not so widely known in the early nineties as they would become. Photography was still a specialty practiced

Portrait of George Eastman taken in 1884 with his American Film, the paper-backed predecessor of the true transparent flexible film he introduced later in the decade. Courtesy of Eastman Kodak Company

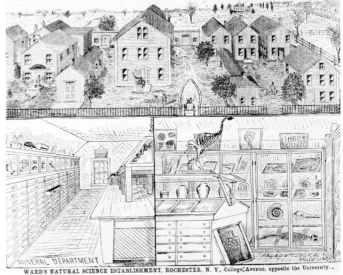

Ward's Natural Science Establishment, 1880s. Courtesy of City Historian's Office

This advertisement for the Eastman Dry-Plate and Film Company appeared in 1887, on the eve of the introduction of the Kodak. Courtesy of Eastman Kodak Company

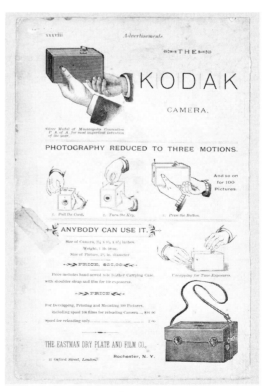

Early advertisements for the Eastman Kodak Camera. Courtesy of Eastman Kodak Company

by a few experts in elaborately decorated parlors. Eastman's Dry Plate & Film Company, organized in 1884 with a capital of $200,000, had made a promising advance, but even his magic box, called a Kodak and patented in 1888, still seemed a novelty to many. Priced at twenty-five dollars and advertised with the catchy slogan, "You press the button, we do the rest," it was attracting buyers, as visitors to the Chicago World's Fair, where Eastman himself snapped many pictures, could attest. Indeed, as the depression continued and even many well-to-do citizens had to cancel plans for expensive vacations, the opportunity to buy a Kodak and snap a hundred pictures, to be developed by the company for ten dollars with a new roll thrown in, seemed a real bargain. Mounting sales encouraged Eastman to expand his plant on State Street, renamed the Eastman Kodak Company, and to acquire a new site just north of the city line for development as Kodak Park.

Several other industrial specialists took advantage of the cheap labor available during the depression to build additions. Taylor Brothers, thermometer makers, responding to the increased demands of the U.S. weather stations and of the new chemical industries for temperature gauges, acquired the patent rights of two distant competitors and enlarged their plant on West Avenue. William Gleason seized the opportunity of slack orders in 1893 to perfect his gear-cutting machine and was soon flooded with orders from new bicycle firms and other industrial plants that required special gear-cutting machines.

Civic and Cultural Renewal

But if some firms prospered, many floundered, and unemployment mounted in 1894. Joseph T. Alling, president of the YMCA and teacher of a popular men's Bible class at Central Presbyterian, became concerned as many of the several hundred men in these groups lost their jobs. His own paper-manufacturing plant offered few opportunities; and his efforts to find jobs for them elsewhere proved disappointing—partly, he concluded, because of their poor training. Few, he discovered, had high school diplomas, and fewer still had received any technical instruction. Convinced that the public schools were at fault, Alling took the lead in organizing a Good Government movement to secure a reform of the school system. The task proved more difficult than he had imagined, but his determination persisted, and he expanded his campaign to include a revision of the city charter and a revitalization of all aspects of the city government.

The Good Government forces would not achieve effective control until the early 1900s, but a number of related reforms moved forward. The city's rapid growth in the eighties had brought the establishment of numerous charitable societies. With each staging an annual drive for support and engaging in sometimes overlapping functions, the need for coordina-

Joseph T. Alling (1855-1937) was Rochester born and educated, and became president of his father's paper company, Alling & Cory. Alling possessed a highly developed civic conscience. He was teacher of a men's bible class; president of the local YMCA; leader of the good government movement; and a trustee of the University of Rochester. Courtesy of Local History Division, Rochester Public Library

Mary T. Gannett and her husband, the Unitarian minister William C. Gannett, arrived in Rochester in 1889. Both were staunch advocates of social reform. Mary T. Gannett organized the Woman's Ethical Club, was active in the Political Equality Club, and presided at the founding of the Women's Educational and Industrial Union in 1893. Courtesy of Local History Division, Rochester Public Library

Kodak Park in 1895. Courtesy of Eastman Kodak Company

Faculty of the Rochester Free Academy on Fitzhugh Street. The Free Academy was well respected, and served as the city's only public high school from 1874 until construction of East High in 1902. Courtesy of City Historian's Office

Eastman Kodak employees, mid-'90s. Courtesy of Eastman Kodak Company

tion became apparent, prompting the formation in 1890 of a Society for the Organization of Charity. When the hardships of the depression forced that body to undertake relief activities, its resources proved sadly inadequate, and its function as an integrating agency lapsed to await the formation of United Charities a decade later.

Most of the ethnic groups had benevolent societies of their own; in 1893, women, too, discovered a special need. When a penniless woman, a stranger in the city, fainted in the street, the police picked her up and confined her overnight in jail for want of a better place. Susan B. Anthony, reading of the incident the next morning, again sprang into action. With Mary T. Gannett, wife of the Unitarian minister and president of the Women's Ethical Club, she organized a Woman's Educational and Industrial Union to provide facilities and services for the increasing number of women working in the city. Under the vigorous leadership of Helen Barrett Montgomery, it effectively promoted new community services.

The depression checked but could not halt the improvement of Rochester's cultural facilities. The Warner Observatory closed, but the Reynolds Library, organized in 1884 out of the book collections of the old Athenaeum library in the Arcade, found a new home and increased usefulness a decade later in the Reynolds mansion on Spring Street. The building of the Lyceum theater, which opened in October 1888 with a performance of Belasco's play *The Wife*, provided welcome competition with the burlesque performances that had invaded the Opera House.

The university under the presidency of David Jayne Hill was finally moderating its strong Baptist affiliation and acquiring a more ecumenical character. Bishop McQuaid successfully launched St. Bernard's Seminary in 1893 and five years later consecrated St. Patrick's Cathedral with impressive ceremonies attended by several respectful Protestant clergymen and public officials. Few but the Bishop could have recalled that Mayor Fish had been publicly criticized thirty years before for attending the Catholic Bishop's inaugural reception. Further proof that the Flower City had finally attained cosmopolitan maturity was provided by the dedication of a bronze statue of Frederick Douglass in June 1899 and by the success a year later of Miss Anthony's campaign to open the university to women.

After the death of Mortimer Reynolds in 1892 the library he established occupied the family home on Spring Street. The Reynolds Library maintained this headquarters until its formal association with the Public Library in the 1930s. Courtesy of Local History Division, Rochester Public Library

The Lyceum Theatre, located at 32 Clinton Avenue South, could seat nearly 2,000 persons. It opened in 1888 and for many years was the showplace for "serious" theater. Edwin Booth appeared here as Hamlet in his last Rochester performance in 1889. Courtesy of Local History Division, Rochester Public Library

The Frederick Douglass Monument, dedicated in impressive ceremonies attended by Governor Theodore Roosevelt, was originally located in a traffic island at the intersection of St. Paul Street and Central Avenue. Courtesy of City Historian's Office

St. Bernard's Seminary. Constructed (1891-1893) by the architect Andrew J. Warner on the city's northwest side, St. Bernard's Seminary was among the ambitious works undertaken by Rochester Catholics under the leadership of Bishop McQuaid. Courtesy of Joseph W. Barnes

ROCHESTER MADE

MEANS QUALITY

No. 1

Chapter
7

The Home of
Quality Products:
1900-1920

Two lessons of the 1890s supplied formulae for remarkable achievements at Rochester in subsequent years. Since most of the shoe and clothing firms that survived the depression had specialized in quality products, the merits of skilled manpower were highlighted and the need to promote it emphasized. That objective seemed even more essential in the technological field where firms based on useful patents required not only trained workers but also practical scientists to maintain their productive vitality. The early recognition of this need by Henry Lomb and Joseph T. Alling foreshadowed a broader grasp of the situation by George Eastman and many others in the early 1900s. Alling, meanwhile, had discovered an additional need for wide community support to assure effective programs.

Fortunately, an imaginative new executive secretary of the Chamber, Sidney R. Clarke, supplied two slogans that embodied these lessons. "Do It For Rochester," his slogan for 1907, injected new spirit into Chamber programs and into the city at large. A year later, his maxim "Rochester Made Means Quality" became the keynote of the first Rochester Industrial Exposition and a lasting motto for the Chamber.

"Do It For Rochester"

Only the slogan was new, for Alling and his Good Government colleagues had been promoting that formula for a decade before Clarke's arrival. But Alling's first victory, the election by the Democrats of Judge George E. Warner as mayor in 1895, had proved fruitless. Mayor Warner had resolutely blocked undesirable ordinances by vetoes, but the "veto mayor," as he was acclaimed, failed to rally support for needed programs. In his second term, when the city's resurgent prosperity called for new outlays for schools, parks, public health, and street improvements, the "Goo Goos"—as the Good Government people were called—became disillusioned with Warner's rigid economy and sought a new understanding with the Republicans.

George Aldridge, the Republican boss, had been induced by Governor Theodore Roosevelt in Albany to accept the new White Charter for cities, which abolished the executive board where Aldridge had built his power and made him eager to regain control of the mayor's office. He was ready to accept a small independent school board in trade for Good Government support in the city elections. When the Aldridge candidate for mayor, Judge George E. Carnahan, also proved acceptable, Alling switched sides and supported a Republican victory in 1899.

The new alliance brought numerous improvements but also opened new areas of controversy. Mayor Carnahan appointed able department heads and launched effective programs; however, when he attempted to block an Aldridge move for control of the Rochester Gas and Electric Company, the boss outmaneuvered him. Many applauded when, at the mayor's direction, the police made a vigorous attack on disorderly houses, the "Hard Cider" and "Goat Hill" gangs, and slot machine operators. But the Democratic editor of the *Herald* labeled the drive a sham, since it neglected serious crime. To prove his charge, he cited the activities of a "protected" gambling house and published sketches by John S. Clubb, the paper's cartoonist, showing men in fashionable garb gathered around a faro table. When the police finally raided the Manhattan Club at Main and St. Paul, they uncovered an array of gambling equipment said to have been installed many years before and used by its exclusive clientele unmolested during repeated antigambling drives. An investigation cleared the mayor of collusion, but the incident enabled Aldridge to drop Carnahan and nominate Judge A. J. Rodenbeck for mayor in 1901.

Rodenbeck proved to be an effective mayor. He added new park lands, pressed ahead with street

Rochester Day Parade, held during the Exposition of 1908. Courtesy of Local History Division, Rochester Public Library

Built as the Keeler and Kimball Building in the '90s, the Chamber of Commerce Building (so named because of the sumptuous twelfth-story Chamber headquarters) was one of Rochester's tallest skyscapers at the turn of the century. Courtesy of Local History Division, Rochester Public Library

Henry Lomb (1828-1908) became J.J. Bausch's partner before the Civil War; during the war he earned a captaincy and then returned to Rochester and the optical business. Not as active as Bausch in the affairs of the company, he devoted much time to community service. He was a founder of Mechanics Institute in 1885 and the school's principal leader for its first twenty years. Courtesy of City Historian's Office

George W. Aldridge (1856-1922) dominated Rochester politics from the mid-90s until his death. He was not only a local patronage "boss" but a powerful figure in state Republican circles. The highest government office he held was Collector of New York Port, awarded to him by President Harding in 1920. Courtesy of City Historian's Office

Horsecar Cherrelyn, 1903. Although the photograph is convincingly dated, the characters and meaning of the story have been lost. Courtesy of Local History Division, Rochester Public Library

improvements, and extended water services and garbage collection. He, too, crossed swords with Aldridge in a battle over utility rates and, while failing to achieve any rate reductions, he did push up their assessments and tax payments. He backed his able health officer, Dr. George Goler, in his efforts to check a severe smallpox epidemic, but failed to secure an appropriation for hospital facilities in time to render needed service. The resultant scandal, for which the council was chiefly at fault, marred the mayor's record and enabled Aldridge to replace him at the next election with James G. Cutler.

A successful manufacturer, who had visited many cities in America and abroad supervising the installation of his mail chutes, Cutler was a firm believer in municipal as well as business investments. A former president of the Chamber, he pressed for rapid improvements in the fire department, for recreational facilities in the parks, and for the repaving of several arterial streets with asphalt instead of macadam. That program won favor with the increasing numbers of bicyclists and motorists who were thronging the streets. Cutler also ordered an extension of street lights and of the underground conduits and moved for a reduction in utility rates. He was able to make the reduction without antagonizing Boss Aldridge since a Philadelphia-based trust had purchased control, thus eliminating local opposition to effective regulation. His able police chief, Joseph M. Quigley, who appointed the first Italians to the force, enlisted the cooperation of responsible members of that growing minority in a campaign to round up all knives and unlicensed firearms among them and to suppress the activities of a suspected Black Hand society. A drop in the number of violent crimes involving Italians from eighteen in the preceeding year to one over the next twelve months amply demonstrated the success of that drive and enhanced the reputations of Quigley and the mayor. But Mayor Cutler's battle in his second term for charter reforms that increased the mayor's authority prompted Aldridge to reassert his control and nominate a more complacent henchman, Hiram H. Edgerton, as mayor.

Much to the surprise of Alling, who had backed Edgerton's opponent, the new mayor soon demonstrated reformist tendencies. He was the first to propose the establishment of a public library, and he endorsed a move by the Chamber of Commerce for city planning. The Goo Goos had finally educated Aldridge to the merits of municipal improvements and had convinced him that the city was ready and able to pay for them.

Education and Social Reforms

The improvements achieved in municipal housekeeping were matched by new advances in education and in social welfare. Indeed, it was the accomplishments here that received the highest praise from Ray

James G. Cutler (1848-1927), architect, inventor, and businessman, served as Rochester's mayor from 1904 to 1908. Courtesy of Local History Division, Rochester Public Library

Hiram H. Edgerton (1847-1922) was a successful contractor who combined a modest life-style with a taste for politics. Beginning in 1871, he held a variety of minor posts until being elected president of the Common Council, in 1899, and finally mayor, in 1907. His mayoralty lasted until 1922. Mayor Edgerton was partly responsible for a long list of civic achievements, among them establishment of a public library and a museum, construction of a sewage-disposal plant, and major extensions of the municipal boundaries. Courtesy of City Historian's Office

The Elwood Building on the northeast corner of Main and State with its gargoyled tower was a familiar sight to Rochesterians until its demolition in the 1960s. The architect, James G. Cutler, designed the first successful mail chute for this building in 1879. He patented and manufactured the device and earned a substantial fortune. Courtesy of Local History Division, Rochester Public Library

Edward Boynton House, 16 East Boulevard, is Rochester's sole Frank Lloyd Wright house. It was constructed in 1907-1908. Courtesy of Joseph W. Barnes

Police helmets were discarded and billy clubs lightened in 1915, during Chief Joseph M. Quigley's administration. Courtesy of City Historian's Office

Stannard Baker in an ecstatic article, "Do It For Rochester," published in the *American Magazine* in September 1910. Baker, a crusading progressive, was most excited by the defeat of Aldridge in his campaign for Congress that year, but he also lauded the Rochester reformers for the positive measures they had adopted.

The chief civic gains were in education. Under the leadership of Professor George M. Forbes of the university and Helen B. Montgomery, the first woman commissioner in Rochester, the small school board rapidly upgraded the teaching staff by making appointments and advancements on the basis of training and experience rather than political pull. It included electives in manual and mechanical training and, in 1908, opened an experimental Factory School that quickly won popular favor. The school board also engaged a supervisor of physical training to organize programs in each school and equipped the new East High with the first gymnasium. It reorganized the program of evening classes to accommodate pupils who had to work during the day as well as adult immigrants who wished to learn English or civics, and it promoted the organization of parent-teacher groups in all schools.

The new board's most remarkable innovation, however, was the opening of three schools for evening use as social centers in congested neighborhoods. The adult civic clubs formed at these centers soon spread to other districts, and a League of Civic Clubs, organized in 1909, held annual assemblies that attracted national speakers—among them, Lincoln Steffens, outstanding critic of civic corruption, and reform governor of New York, Charles Evans Hughes. Inevitably, the free discussions at the public forums gave expression not only to sharply opposing religious views but also to radical socialist harangues and harsh attacks on Boss Aldridge. Aldridge bided his time until a teenage group in a Jewish neighborhood staged a dance at the social center in No. 9 School on Sunday evening rather than on Saturday, their Sabbath. The announcement brought an outburst of indignation from several clergymen horrified at dancing, especially on Sunday and at a public school. Amidst the furor, Aldridge pressed for a cut in the school budget to eliminate the social centers, and Mayor Edgerton diverted the money thus saved to the playground movement as a more fitting use of public funds.

Few could protest such expenditures, least of all Walter Rauschenbusch. Born and educated in Rochester, with graduate study abroad, Rauschenbusch had been called back to join the faculty of the Theolgical Seminary in 1897 and had quickly become a spokesman for humanitarian reform. Engaged by the YMCA to make a survey of the city's social conditions, he had uncovered many challenging needs. Six of the twelve recommendations he submitted in May 1904 were quickly taken up, including the provision of educational and other facilities for new immigrants, the enforcement of child-labor laws, the promotion of an enjoyment of nature and of recreation in the parks, and the strengthening of cultural facilities.

Helen B. Montgomery (1861-1934) was a leader of the Women's Educational and Industrial Union and a social reformer. In 1899 she was elected to the Rochester school board and served for ten years as its first female member, accomplishing a great deal in helping the city school system's growth and modernization. Courtesy of Local History Division, Rochester Public Library

Dr. Max Landsberg (1845-1927), Rabbi of B'rith Kodesh for forty-four years, was active in the intellectual life of the city in association with such contemporaries as the Rev. Newton Mann and Walter Rauschenbusch. Founder of the United Jewish Charities of Rochester, he headed the New York Association of Charities and Corrections. Courtesy of Local History Division, Rochester Public Library

Walter Rauschenbusch (1861-1918), a Rochester native and University of Rochester graduate, became a professor of church history at the Rochester Theological Seminary. His book Christianity and the Social Crisis *(1907) was important to the social-gospel movement. Courtesy of Local History Division, Rochester Public Library*

Playing at Number Fourteen School playground—a photograph originally published August 31, 1907 in The Playground, *the journal of the Children's Playground League. Rochester was a leader in the playground movement. Courtesy of City Historian's Office*

East High School, on Alexander Street, opened its doors in 1903. Courtesy of Local History Division, Rochester Public Library

Number Nine School, on Joseph Avenue, was in the heart of the city's immigrant neighborhood on the near northeast. The social-center movement was dealt a severe blow when Jewish teenagers held a dance here on a Sunday; Protestant and Catholic clergy loudly objected. Boss Aldridge seized the opportunity to weaken "socialistic center" support and provoked a sharp confrontation with reformers and "goo-goos." Courtesy of Local History Division, Rochester Public Library

107

Two of his recommendations, however, proved controversial. Rauschenbusch had discovered that over one-fourth of the city's men and women between the ages of 25 and 40 were unmarried, and he proposed an increase in wages to encourage early marriages as a means of reducing vice and crime. He opposed gambling and the saloon, but in place of a negative attack he recommended band concerts and other recreational opportunities for poor working people, especially on Sunday, their one free day. His account of hundreds of immigrant workmen housed several to a room in downtown lofts, with no escape other than the streets or cheap saloons, highlighted their plight. Soon the People's Sunday Evening and two similar programs in downtown theaters endeavored to supply an alternative. But the real substitute for the saloon as "the poor man's club" was to be the new Bijou Dream, Fairyland, and a dozen other five-cent motion-picture houses that appeared on downtown streets before 1910.

The reports of Dr. George Goler, the city's chief health officer, had supplied some of the data assembled by Rauschenbusch. In public addresses on "The Submerged Tenth" and "Slums in Our Town," Dr. Goler had warned of deterioration in the city's domestic accommodations. Its housing facilities, which in 1890 supplied 27,000 families with 24,000 dwellings, 44 percent of them owner-occupied—a higher standard than that of any other major city—had suffered a decline because of stagnation in home building during the depression and the rapid inmigration at the turn of the century. The crush of newcomers had pushed rents up 20 percent in two years, forcing many poor families to double up. Homeowners, especially on the narrow lots in the poor northeast district, were erecting second dwellings on the rear portion of their lots, crowding the land and overtaxing the water and drainage facilities. Dr. Goler was able, with the assistance of the fire marshall, to halt conversion of some outmoded warehouses downtown into unsanitary tenement firetraps. A new building ordinance in 1911 gave him wider authority but failed to remove all the hazards, as a new survey sponsored by the Women's Educational and Industrial Union that year revealed.

Rochester's Civic Awakening

The Rochester City Club, organized in 1909, provided an open forum for the discussion of these and other civic problems. Professor Forbes and Edward J. Ward, director of the social centers, invited Alling, Rauschenbusch, and other friends of the centers to a luncheon to discuss their threatened demise. Successive Saturday luncheons at the Powers Hotel attracted an increasing attendance that prompted the chartering of the club and the election of the Reverend Paul Moore Strayer, head of the People's Sunday Evening, as toastmaster. Among the active participants were Dr. George Goler, the health officer;

Labor Day Parade, 1910. Courtesy of Local History Division, Rochester Public Library

East Main Street in 1910. Rochester's first motion-picture house, the Bijou Dream, is visible at the extreme left. Sibley, Lindsay, and Curr's new department store at Main and Clinton (completed 1905) is visible at the extreme right. Courtesy of Douglas A. Fisher, Victor Historical Society

Dr. George W. Goler (1864-1940), Rochester's outstanding Chief Health Officer, was an early exponent of milk inspection—a measure which reduced childhood mortality significantly. He vigorously combated deplorable housing conditions as well as epidemic diseases. Mayor Edgerton considered him "the biggest crank and the best health officer in the United States." Courtesy of Local History Divisioin, Rochester Public Library

The Main Falls of the Genesee and the New York Central Railroad Bridge, about 1910. Courtesy of Local History Division, Rochester Public Library

The east side of State Street near the Four Corners, 1902. The sign on the pole, advertising "BURLESQUE" and "SMOKING CONCERTS," indicates how far down the Corinthian Theatre had come. Courtesy of New York Museum of Transporation

Charles Mulford Robinson, an advocate of city planning; and George Van Schaick, organizer of a Legal Aid program for Rochester. With a membership of 310, the club ended its first year on the Fourth of July with a banquet at which 200 newly naturalized citizens, each accompanied by his club sponsor, were formally welcomed to the community.

Although the City Club limited itself to an open discussion of current issues, the Chamber of Commerce, responding to a similar civic awakening, was taking more positive action. Secretary Clarke's slogans had supplied the formulae, and Edward G. Miner, who became president in 1909, provided the leadership. He had taken the initiative the year before in organizing the first Industrial Exposition in Convention Hall, and he now made it an annual affair of broader community significance. He named a housing committee to spur home construction and raised funds for a Civic Improvement Committee, with Charles M. Robinson as chairman, charged with the preparation of a city plan for Rochester. Largely self-educated, Miner was a lover of books and endorsed Mayor Edgerton's proposal for a public library. He named a public safety committee to help the city formulate new traffic regulations to control the flood of automobiles that was increasingly jamming Main Street.

The Chamber's approach to civic improvements enlisted both public and private support. The 1911 Brunner-Olmsted plan for Rochester's development proved premature, but Mayor Edgerton finally launched both a public library and a public museum in 1912. An art exhibit included in the third and fourth Industrial Expositions stimulated the gift by Mrs. James Sibley Watson of the Memorial Art Gallery. And as the Chamber's membership and activities expanded, overtaxing the facilities on the top floors of the Commerce Building, George Eastman announced a gift of $500,000 for a new Chamber of Commerce headquarters on St. Paul Street.

Eastman had become increasingly involved in community affairs in the early 1900s. With the development of motion pictures, the rapid expansion of the market for his cameras and film required constant expansion and produced fabulous returns. A gift of $200,000 to the Mechanics Institute in 1900 had been made in recognition of his own need for trained workmen. When Rush Rhees, the new president of the university and a trustee of the institute, approached him for funds for a new physics building, Eastman gave the $67,000 required for its construction, but he warned Rhees not to expect any more, explaining that he was not interested in general education. President Rhees, however, would soon spend a half year in Europe, visiting the leading scientific institutes and colleges of the day, in preparation for a new scientific emphasis at the university.

Eastman, meanwhile, was discovering new interests. His decision to build a new mansion on East Avenue included plans for the installation of a pipe organ, because of his mother's love of music; her poor health alerted him to the city's need for improved

The Brunner, Olmsted, and Arnold city plan for Rochester envisioned a grand city hall at the intersection of Main Street and the not-yet-constructed Broad Street. Courtesy of Local History Division, Rochester Public Library

Mayor Edgerton and his cabinet on New Year's morning, 1914. Hiram Edgerton had won his fourth consecutive mayoralty contest, and, along with his chief department heads, posed with floral tributes. Seen to the left of the mayor is City Engineer Edwin A. Fisher. Third from the extreme right is Assessor Joseph C. Wilson. Courtesy of Local History Division, Rochester Public Library

Streetcar workers pause for a portrait: the intersection of Court and James Streets on the east side of downtown, September 21, 1911. Courtesy of New York Museum of Transportation

George Eastman's house on East Avenue, completed in 1905. Courtesy of Local History Division, Rochester Public Library

Kodak office workers, 1906. Courtesy of Eastman Kodak Company

hospital care, prompting a gift of $400,000 in 1909 to hasten the reconstruction of the City (General) Hospital. He had welcomed the establishment of United Charities during a local recession the year before and regularly referred all requests for aid to its secretary, to whom he periodically sent a check to cover such outlays. And in 1912, when the General Education Board offered $200,000 to the university if it would raise $1 million for an endowment, Eastman pledged half that sum to assure its success. He had set aside an equal sum the year before as a benefit fund for his employees, and he now declared the first of a series of annual wage dividends, paying 2 percent on all wages received over the previous five years to each of his 6,609 workers.

No other Rochesterian could match Eastman's gifts, though several were contributing more generously in time and in proportion to their resources. Most citizens, however, were still preoccupied in the early 1900s with their private affairs. Many, like Henry D. Silver, a modest grocer who moonlighted as a huckster, and in fair weather as a housebuilder, were saving to pay off a mortgage or for a vacation trip in a slack period. It was on such a trip to Virginia Beach that Silver, who fortunately kept a diary, learned from another vacationer that he could double the value of his nest egg by investing it in Swift's stock, which paid 7 percent, as against 3 percent at the bank. That discovery and his continued labors progressively raised his goals. After paying off his mortgage and accumulating $10,000 in stock, Silver acquired a "fat head," as he later put it, and bought an automobile for $1,100. When he tried to start it up after the first cold spell in December he found "the D— thing froze up" and had to pay fifteen dollars to get it fixed. He paid another fifteen dollars for admission to a "gas engine" class at the Mechanics Institute, but in three months learned only that "a million things could happen and every one would stall you."

Silver's experience on the road when warm weather returned was equally discouraging, and after struggling for two years to keep it in working order, he concluded that "only a dam fool or a millionaire would own a car." He finally sold it for $150, only to discover a few months later that his oldest son, a carpenter at 18, had bought a motorcycle and was striking out to seek his fortune in Florida. Henry was now pursuing his fortune at Bonbright's, the stock broker in the Powers Block, where he had invested an extra $10,000 borrowed from the bank, but he still spent most of his time tending his store. He found his greatest enjoyment in reading the successive works of Dickens, borrowed from the Reynolds Library, and in writing his diary in his attic retreat safely above "the fierce bunch of quarreling children" in the rooms below. After seven years in the market, trying to keep his income in line with his annual outlays of $1,200, Silver advised his children to "borrow books, not cash" and "don't speculate!"

George B. Selden (1846-1922), a local attorney who filed for the first American patent for a gasoline-driven "road engine" in 1879, is seen here posing with the prototype automobile constructed to prove its practicality in the course of a lawsuit against Henry Ford which dragged on from 1903 to 1911. Courtesy of Local History Division, Rochester Public Library

A test of the George B. Selden automobile in New York City proved the workability of the 1877 design, but at the end of a protracted lawsuit Henry Ford "broke" the Selden patent in 1911. The Rochester patent attorney had already collected generous fees from the Association of Licensed Automobile Manufacturers. Courtesy of City Historian's Office

Main and Water Streets, c. 1919. From the collection of the Rochester Museum and Science Center, Rochester, New York

The Erie Canal, Court Street Bridge, and the Lehigh Valley Railroad Station, c. 1910-1915. This view looks south from the Second Erie Canal Aqueduct (Broad Street Bridge). Three water courses, all at different levels, stood side-by-side here. From left to right, the canal, the Johnson & Seymour Mill Race, and the Genesee River. Courtesy of Douglas A. Fisher, Victor Historical Society

Party of Rochesterians sightseeing in Washington, 1906. Courtesy of Local History Division, Rochester Public Library

Rochester In World War I

The First World War greatly expanded Rochester's horizons. Its outbreak in Europe in 1914 revived submerged loyalties in several of the city's ethnic neighborhoods and stirred a new interest in community affairs even among many who, like Henry Silver, had lived in secluded or private worlds. The appearance of large black headlines in successive daily issues early in August created a new demand for local papers. Local Austrians and Hungarians, some 2,000 in number, rallied at the Ruthenian Church in support of the fatherland. French and Belgian residents gathered at Our Lady of Victory Church where, aided by their more numerous Dutch sympathizers, they recruited twenty-seven young men who hastened to the defense of Belgium. Young men from Britain and Canada rushed across the border to enlist. Most of the German-born were now advanced in years and fully naturalized, and few were eager to fight for the kaiser, nor were many Russians anxious to rally to the czar. But among the Italians, now the largest ethnic minority in Rochester, were several hundred still listed as Italian reservists and, as the war progressed, more than a thousand returned to help defend their homeland.

The invasion of Belgium had brought a local drive for Belgian relief, headed by Hiram W. Sibley, and soon a number of similar agencies joined the Red Cross in appeals for funds and supplies for war victims. The City Club provided a forum for the discussion of the issues involved, for debates over rationing and other measures, and for pleas for national defense. A mass meeting at Convention Hall in support of neutrality was followed a month later by a more tumultuous meeting there endorsing universal military training and conscription. A succession of military parades early in 1916 set the stage for a great Liberty Day parade in October in support of the Liberty Loan drive, which promptly surged "over the top."

These efforts were dwarfed by the response that quickly built up after the declaration of war. To coordinate the multitude of relief efforts, their leaders formed a Patriotic and Community Fund, which, with George Eastman (who had previously shunned such assignments) serving for the first time as chairman, conducted a united drive that rallied support from 117,064 citizens and gathered pledges totalling $4,838,335. Volunteers working in these drives, and in the stations and canteens of the Red Cross, the YMCA, and the YWCA, brought unprecedented numbers of citizens into active community service.

Alerted in 1915 by a deluge of U.S. defense orders and of military orders from abroad, Rochester industrialists quickly retooled for production. Of the eighty-one firms that filled orders from the newly established Rochester Ordnance District, Bausch & Lomb earned the greatest praise. Its success in the production of optical glass, formerly imported from

Scenes from military parades early in 1916. Courtesy of Douglas A. Fisher, Victor Historical Society

Parade of mothers of servicemen at the Rochester Exposition, Edgerton Park, September 4, 1918. About 6,000 mothers participated in this emotional event on "Defenders of Liberty Day." The women walked quietly in procession to receive their medals—some with gold stars. Army aviators flew overhead sprinkling flowers. Courtesy of City Historian's Office.

Wartime industry: "bloomer girls" in the Kodak camera works, 1918. Courtesy of Eastman Kodak Company

Germany, and in the manufacture of gunsights, range finders, and other optical implements, was judged a "paramount achievement." Eastman's contributions to military and aerial photography, and the devices developed and produced by a dozen other technical firms, demonstrated the quality as well as the versatility of Rochester products. A Community Labor Board, with union as well as industrial members, managed, despite rapidly rising living costs and fluctuating wage rates, to keep work stoppages at a minimum.

Concern over the number and welfare of the city's servicemen was the driving force behind many community efforts. By the close of 1917, Rochester had recruited 6,695 men and women into the war services. Most were still in training camps, but a few had already seen action at sea or abroad. The first fatality occurred on January 2, 1918, when William S. Ely, grandson of a noted Rochester physician, died in a plane accident in France. Continuing enlistments, and the second and third draft calls, raised the city's total to 18,119, approximately one recruit from every third family (including the Silvers, whose second son enlisted), plus several hundred in civilian service at the front. As the casualties mounted, exceeding 500 before the armistice was signed, Rochesterians learned a new sense of community involvement.

The false announcement of an armistice on November 7 brought out a tumultuous throng, exceeded only by the prolonged demonstration on the 11th marking the true end of the war. More orderly ceremonies greeted the returning units, including two military parades in April and May, when over 100,000 citizens lined Main Street to cheer the battle-scarred heroes of the 108th and the 309th regiments, with many Rochester men in line. Rochester was one of two cities in the nation to publish a full record of its participation in the war—the *Rochester and Monroe County World War Service Record*, published in three volumes from 1925 to 1929.

Rochester was a more self-conscious community in the wake of war. The city launched new public works and expended nearly $3 million to supply jobs while industry was retooling. The City Club provided a convenient forum for the discussion of these problems, as well as the peace terms and the League of Nations. The four Rochester dailies took strong editorial stands on the League, with all but the *Democrat* in favor; yet in November the voters gave their support to Warren G. Harding, who called for reservations. Most citizens were more directly concerned at that point over the health hazards revealed by the ravages of influenza, which had taken a toll of 1,100 lives in 1918, overburdening all available health facilities. The success of the war-chest drive earlier that year made it a model for a new Community Chest drive. With Eastman again serving as chairman, the Chest enlisted widespread popular support and assured resources for expanded hospitals and other welfare agencies in the years ahead. The slogan "Do It For Rochester" had finally caught on.

Mayor Clarence Van Zandt examining a volume of the World War Service Record *prepared by City Historian Edward R. Foreman. Behind them stand two officers of the American Legion. May 1, 1926. Courtesy of Local History Division, Rochester Public Library*

Main Street on Armistice Day. Courtesy of Local History Division, Rochester Public Library

ROCHESTER TIMES-UNION
AND ADVERTISER

VOL. 1. NO. 296.

ROCHESTER, N. Y., MONDAY, NOVEMBER 11, 1918.

8 PAGES. TWO CENTS.

WAR ENDS
Huns Surrender To Foch;
Germans Sign Armistice

Washington, Nov. 11.—The State Dept. announced today at 2.46 o'clock that Germany had signed the armistice terms of the Allies. Hostilities will cease at 11:00 a. m. French time This makes peace secure. The terms will be dictated by the Allies. The acceptance of the armistice is equivalent to unconditional surrender and strips Germany of all military power. The armistice was signed at 5 a. m. French time. Terms made public during the day.

Kaiser, Having Lost His Throne, Flees To Holland; May Be Interned; Crown Prince Also Is Fugitive

Old Man Who Accompanied the Defeated Monarch May Be Hindenburg—Train Carefully Guarded— Emperor Karl Also Seeks Refuge— Will Kaiser Be Punished?

Rochester To Celebrate; Ask Morse For Details

The Times-Union *front page for November 11, 1918. Courtesy of Local History Division, Rochester Public Library*

George Eastman in
1922. Courtesy of
Eastman Kodak
Company

Chapter
8

In Prosperity and Depression: 1920-1940

By 1920, Rochester had discovered that quality production could offset its poor access to the minerals and fuel generally considered essential for industrial success. The city's future lay in light industry. For this it would need skilled workers and ingenious technicians, and to attract and hold them it would require quality services. The quest for quality was vigorously pressed in the twenties under the active leadership of George Eastman, with the backing of the Chamber of Commerce and a battery of civic and educational institutions. The goal was well defined and widely accepted: to make Rochester, as Eastman put it, "the best city in which to live and raise a family." The leaders, however, were not in full agreement as to tactics, and their conflicting programs would be sorely tested in the Great Depression.

Managerial Reforms in Government

Eastman's increasing participation in community affairs now paced Rochester's development. In spite of an aversion to party politics, he experienced a mounting concern over civic problems and found the Bureau of Municipal Research, which he had launched in 1915, an effective agent for testing and improving governmental programs. Under the leadership of Leroy Snyder, its first director, the bureau had promoted tighter budgetary procedures, recommended reforms in street paving, cleaning, and snow removal, and achieved advances in other phases of municipal housekeeping. When Snyder's successor, James W. Routh, provoked by opposition to some proposed reforms in garbage collection in 1921, exclaimed publicly that "many officials in city hall are solid ivory from the neck up," Eastman promptly accepted his resignation and replaced him with Stephen B. Story, who proved a more diplomatic director.

The political situation changed drastically a year later, when the death of Boss Aldridge precipitated a battle for control of the party and the city. Advocates of a city-manager charter suddenly won a hearing. With Eastman's backing, the bureau made an extensive survey of the experience of a score of cities that had adopted or rejected city-manager government. The City Club, with Snyder as president, staged a debate on the merits of the manager plan, and the newly formed Women's City Club, whose members voted strongly in support of the plan, took the lead in forming a City Manager League to promote its adoption. George Eastman, in a rare public statement of his views, expressed favor, and Frank Gannett, with Snyder now serving as his chief counselor on civic affairs, devoted many columns in the *Times-Union* to exposition and support of city-manager government.

Faced with such widespread agitation, Mayor Clarence D. Van Zandt named a committee to draft the proposed revisions. To expedite matters, the committee decided to submit an amendment, replacing the board of aldermen and elective mayor with a small council empowered to choose a mayor and a manager. Van Zandt, chosen by Aldridge shortly before his death as Edgerton's successor, took a neutral stand and won reelection with a promise to abide by the popular will. After considerable arm-twisting, the aldermen, confident that their many supporters would defeat the plan, agreed to place the amendment on the ballot.

Public interest mounted as the campaign progressed. The league's district canvassers boosted the number of registered voters to an unprecedented total of 104,000—almost 90 percent of those eligible. Only some 65,000 actually turned out on election day, but nearly two-thirds voted in favor of the amendment. In their haste to press the issue, however, the reformers had left its implementation in the hands of

Frank E. Gannett (1876-1957) was an Elmira newspaper publisher who came to Rochester in 1918 and merged the old Union and Advertiser *with the* Evening Times *to form a new afternoon paper: the* Times-Union. *During the '20s as his newspaper empire grew, Gannett's editorial policies (expressed in the "flagship"* Times-Union*) were reformist, but in the '30s he became a virulent anti-New Dealer and even, in 1940, tried to win the Republican presidential nomination himself. Courtesy of Local History Division, Rochester Public Library*

Magnolia Trees on Oxford Street. Residential embellishments like this were sometimes a direct inheritance from Rochester's "Flower City" heyday. Courtesy of New York Museum of Transportation

*Packet boat "Palmyra" on the Erie Canal. Courtesy of
City Historian's Office*

*Construction of the Rochester Harbor of the Barge
Canal, 1919. Site south of Court Street dam. Courtesy of
Canal Society of New York State*

the aldermen. Despite the mayor's efforts, the hostile aldermen, by awaiting a judicial decision affirming its validity and by other tactics, managed to delay the election of a small council and the selection of a manager until January 1928.

Despite its widespread support and final triumph, the city-manager government continued to face partisan obstructions. When Story, the civil engineer who had directed the bureau's survey, was named manager, he promptly chose able department heads on a nonpartisan basis. But his appointment of a talented park director imported from California antagonized supporters of a local candidate who had come up through the ranks. When a lad drowned at Ontario beach on a hot day before the beach was officially opened, the director was held negligent for failing to provide supervision and forced to resign.

That controversy widened the split already dividing the nine-member council. The traditional parties had defeated a nonpartisan election provision, and although both had endorsed two or three council candidates firmly committed to efficiency in government, most of their nominees felt stronger bonds to their constituents. A major objection to the manager plan had been the fear, particularly in the ethnic-dominated wards, of a loss of representation. The Republicans, whose slate proved victorious, had stressed that issue; only two of their councilmen had ethnic affiliations, but two others had strong district ties. When Joseph C. Wilson, the one councilman able to achieve a measure of harmony, died shortly after his selection as mayor, the eight remaining councilmen proved unable to agree on a replacement or on several other controversial issues.

Industrial Management

While the bureau took the lead in promoting efficiency in government, the Chamber, also benefitting from Eastman support, tackled other pressing problems. The city's continued growth and the arrival of some 12,000 new immigrants during the twenties, mainly from Italy and Eastern Europe, prompted the organization of new ethnic societies, such as the Italian and the Ukrainian civic leagues. To forestall the development of subversive groups, a Chamber committee took over the New Citizen banquets of the City Club and in some years scheduled as many as six banquets in order to provide a proper greeting for all new citizens. In 1920, and again eight years later, the Chamber collaborated with the Art Gallery in staging a Homelands Exhibit and Music Festival at Exposition Park in which the various ethnic groups displayed native artifacts and presented programs on their designated days.

The Chamber also faced the sober problem of assuring jobs and housing for the city's mounting population. A committee on housing discovered a widening gap between the supply of houses and the

Joseph C. Wilson (1851-1930) became first mayor under the new Council-Manager form of government in 1928. Wilson had served as an alderman, city assessor, treasurer, and comptroller. He was a successful jeweler, an officer of Acme Sales, and a director of the Haloid Company, which his grandson of the same name would head during its transformation into the Xerox Corporation. Courtesy of Local History Division, Rochester Public Library

Intersection of Main Street and South Avenue, facing south, early 1920s. From the Collection of the Rochester Museum and Science Center, Rochester, New York

New Citizens Banquet at the Chamber of Commerce.
Courtesy of City Historian's Office

Repairing track in State Street, August, 1921. The
streetcar company (now owned by New York State
Railways), like other Rochester employers, drew on the
growing Italian population for heavy labor of all kinds.
Courtesy of New York Museum of Transportation

demand of an increasing number of families. An earlier move backed by Eastman to build model tenements had been blocked by Dr. Goler for its failure to meet residential standards, and the committee turned to the home builders and mortgage lenders for a solution. It prodded the trolley company to extend its lines to encourage tract developments on the outskirts of the city, which were sponsored in some cases by building and loan societies and in others by local industries, including Eastman Kodak, chiefly for their skilled employees. The Chamber lent its support to the development of an industrial suburb named East Rochester; it also backed a move by the bureau for the creation of a Civic Plan Committee to provide expert guidance in this field.

Unfortunately, rival interests blocked major advances in some areas, particularly in planning. The mounting congestion on Main Street had demonstrated the need for parallel streets to relieve the east-west traffic; advocates of a north-side and a south-side parallel, however, were unable to agree on priorities. That impasse was partially broken when the completion of the New York State Barge Canal, which skirted Rochester's southern border, replaced the old Erie Canal, and released its trough through the city for a subway, prompting the construction of Broad Street over its course in the central district.

Major decisions remained. Debate over the extension of Broad Street east to Park Avenue, over the opening of a north-side parallel, and over the location of new public buildings prompted Story to engage the Bartholomew Associates of St. Louis as consultants to prepare a master plan. George Eastman had settled an earlier debate over the proposed location of a new city hall at the canal crossing on West Main Street by buying the old Kimball tobacco factory and making it available for use as a city hall annex; he further promised a free title to the site if the city found it suitable for that use. The Bartholomew plan approved that site for a civic center and recommended the eastward extension of Broad Street, among other major improvements, but the onset of the depression had already made discussion of such plans seem academic.

The city's economic health was, of course, the basic requirement, and expanding production during the twenties had provided an increasing number of jobs. Eastman was able and ready to pay good wages, even wage dividends, and his example raised standards in other local firms. Except in the shoe, clothing, and brewery industries, most Rochester firms also discouraged efforts by their workers to form unions. The Industrial Management Council, now an independent subsidiary of the Chamber, supported that policy, but the strength of AFL unions in the building trades made indirect negotiations through the construction contractors necessary in order to facilitate expansion.

Eastman again took the lead. Responding to the argument that construction workers, because of the seasonal nature of their jobs, needed higher hourly rates, he formed a Community Conference Board

The Bartholomew master plan (1930) envisioned this grandiose civic center flanking the Genesee River below Court Street Bridge. The river water would be used to supply a series of reflecting pools, fountains, etc. Only bits and pieces of the civic center concept were ever carried out. Courtesy of City Historian's Office

Erie Canal Aqueduct, drained of water, c. 1919-1920. Well before construction of the Barge Canal, which skirted Rochester to the south, the presence of the Erie Canal in the heart of the city had become a nuisance. Many considered the canal "dirty," "evil-smelling," and a safety hazard. Courtesy of Douglas A. Fisher, Victor Historical Society

The old Kimball Tobacco Factory became not only a city hall annex, but also a temporary home for the Central Library until construction of the Rundel Building across the river. Courtesy of Local History Division, Rochester Public Library

with labor as well as management representatives to promote harmony by mediating disputes and by spreading construction activities into the winter months. In the clothing industry, the Clothiers Exchange, representing most of the leading firms, had signed a contract in 1919 with the Amalgamated Clothing Workers providing for a permanent arbitrator of disputes, thereby achieving a basis for even greater harmony.

Social and Cultural Advances

The trend toward expert management found expression in social and cultural developments as well. Here, too, Eastman's influence was important, though not always decisive; his most dramatic contributions were in the areas of music, medicine, and higher education. Both the Community Chest and the Council of Social Agencies attracted broad participation, by subscribers in the first instance and by cooperating agencies in the second; able managers, however, organized the annual drives and named the numerous committees that promoted new programs. In public education, recreation, and religion, other able citizens took the lead. Even the city's centennial celebration represented an organizational triumph.

A drive for quality services marked most of these efforts. In the field of public education, the fruits of the good government movement were finally apparent. A move by the Board of Education for fiscal independence was defeated, but the schools, under the able leadership of Superintendent Herbert S. Weet, added new services for handicapped children, greatly expanded the high school program, and won authorization for a $10 million bond issue to finance the construction of fourteen new schools. The athletic program in the high schools was enlarged to include interscholastic contests, particularly in basketball, spurring the development of school loyalties.

The parks and playgrounds attracted an increasing flow of active and passive visitors. Sports events ranging from tennis, golf, skating, and bathing to soccer and baseball drew spectators as well as participants. The now annual Lilac Weeks at Highland Park, the fruit blossom displays at Durand-Eastman, and the rose festivals at Maplewood Park brought streams of tourists from afar. Concerts by the park band and innumerable picnics attracted other thousands to the parks throughout the summer months. The Rochester Baseball Club, now affiliated with the St. Louis Cardinals, outgrew its park on Bay Street, where in 1928 it captured the International League pennant. Rechristened the Red Wings, it opened a new park on Norton Street the next year with a second pennant victory and retained the pennant for two more seasons.

By 1929, automobile registrations in the county had increased to 110,000—more than one to a family —thus marking a transformation in the recreational

Herbert S. Weet (1871-1953) was Rochester's Superintendent of Schools between 1911 and 1933, a period of great expansion for the school system; nineteen new schools were added during that period. Weet was a pioneer in the use of junior-high schools, school psychologists, and special programs for the handicapped. Courtesy of Local History Division, Rochester Public Library

Near the mouth of Red Creek in Genesee Valley Park. Courtesy of Local History Division, Rochester Public Library

Promenade of Sea Breeze amusement park, c. 1925. Courtesy of New York Museum of Transportation

The art deco Genesee Valley Trust Building, built in 1929-30, added a distinctive note to the Rochester skyline with its "Wings of Progress" sculpture. Courtesy of Local History Division, Rochester Public Library

The Lincoln-Alliance Bank Building was the largest of several new office towers constructed during the real-estate boom of the 1920s. Courtesy of Local History Division, Rochester Public Library

May 19, 1923. The cover of the following day's gravure section shows the Bay Street Ball Park filled with an attentive home crowd. The Rochester Tribesmen defeated the Buffalo Bisons 4 to 1. Rochester was leading the International League with 20 wins and 5 losses. Baltimore, with 17 and 10, was the closest rival. Courtesy of City Historian's Office

as well as the daily life-style of most residents. The annual auto shows now eclipsed the horse shows in popularity. Five country clubs and a half dozen other well-equipped social clubs shared the leisure time of many affluent families. Summer cottages on the lake or bay, or to the southeast on the Finger Lakes, easily accessible by family car, vied with more distant resorts for vacation time, which now became a cherished right for most citizens.

Rochester's most striking advances occurred in higher education and the arts. Rush Rhees had finally won Eastman's full backing for the transformation of the struggling college into a major university with a strong emphasis on science. They rallied enthusiastic community support for the construction of a men's college on the new River Campus and for the creation of a separate women's college on the Prince Street Campus. Eastman agreed to match an ambitious offer by the General Education Fund to establish a first-class medical school at Rochester and secured a pledge from the daughters of his first backer, Henry A. Strong, to build the Strong Memorial Hospital in his honor as an adjunct to the medical school. Eastman's most dramatic philanthrophy, however, came in his support of music. He almost single-handedly funded the new Rochester Philharmonic Orchestra, established the Eastman School of Music as part of the university, and built the Eastman Theater to assure adequate facilities for their performances.

These developments, coming in rapid succession in the early twenties, attracted a host of talented professionals to Rochester and added to its excitement. New support was generated for the Memorial Art Gallery on the Prince Street Campus, and for the public library and the museum, which still occupied temporary quarters at Exposition Park. One objective of the Eastman Theater—to provide a suitable hall for the presentation of distinguished motion pictures—proved impractical, as the competing production companies developed rival theater chains and resisted Eastman's attempt to make selective bookings. Instead, the theater collaborated with Frank Gannett in promoting radio programs featuring performances by the Rochester Philharmonic Orchestra as pioneer offerings of WHAM.

Both Gannett and Eastman soon sold their interests in WHAM to the Stromberg-Carlson Company, a Rochester producer of telephonic instruments, which now added radios to its line. Gannett then joined Lawrence G. Hickson, the city's radio pioneer, in establishing a second broadcasting station, WHEC. Thus, by 1927, Rochester had two stations broadcasting news and weather bulletins, music, and lectures. Speakers in the City Manager League campaign made good use, a year later, of these new outlets reaching into some 30,000 homes. Franklin D. Roosevelt, nominated for governor at the Democratic state convention at Rochester in October, hastened to take advantage of the new medium, which rapidly expanded its coverage as the local stations affiliated with NBC and CBS, respectively, thereby greatly enriching their programming.

Interior of the Eastman Theatre. Courtesy of Eastman Kodak Company

Colgate-Rochester Divinity School, completed in 1931, was the product of a merger between the old Rochester Theological Seminary and a Baptist seminary at Colgate. Its stately campus was another symbol of the extraordinary expansion of Rochester's institutions of higher education in the late '20s. Courtesy of Joseph W. Barnes

Traffic back-up on Main Street, c. 1928. Courtesy of New York Museum of Transportation

The University of Rochester's School of Medicine and the associated Strong Memorial and Municipal Hospitals (in one building complex) were completed in 1925-26. The nearby River Campus, designated for use as a Men's College, was constructed next, in 1927-1930. Courtesy of Eastman Kodak Company

With these varied accomplishments, it was not surprising that Rochester made early and ambitious plans for the celebration of its approaching centennial. City Historian Edward R. Foreman launched preparations in 1929, a few months before the stock market crash, and no depression could quell the community's high spirits. A mayor's committee headed by Carl S. Hallauer directed the program, which included the construction of a large stage at Exposition Park, now renamed Edgerton Park, the collection there of historical displays for a six-month exhibit in the summer of 1934, and the nightly performance for two full weeks of an historical pageant, *Pathways of Progress*, depicting the dramatic phases of Rochester's growth. Only a proposed reenactment of Sam Patch's leap over the falls was canceled by order of the commissioner of safety. Special ethnic programs helped to boost paid attendance over 300,000 and assure financial solvency.

Aerial view of downtown Rochester, c. 1930. The new Broad Street Bridge is lined with parked cars; Main Street Bridge, lined with buildings that were already old in 1930, presents a curious Venetian appearance. Courtesy of New York Museum of Transportation

Rochester's Response to the Depression

Rochester met the onset of the depression with a remarkable display of community effort. Reports of mounting unemployment late in 1929 prompted the Council of Social Agencies to take the lead in forming a Civic Committee on Unemployment. Representatives of the Chamber, the Community Chest, the Bureau of Municipal Research, the Federation of Churches, the Central Trades and Labor Council, and the city government joined to back an expanded welfare drive early in 1930 and created a battery of subcommittees to promote new industrial employment, introduce a share-the-work plan in hard-pressed firms, and encourage the city to expand public relief. One subcommittee, under Earl Weller of the bureau, endeavored to determine the number actually unemployed and to persuade the state to collect such data. When its findings revealed a total of some 17,000 unemployed by November 1930, the serious nature of the depression became all too apparent.

Rochester's confidence remained strong during 1931. References to foreclosures as "Bow-wows" disappeared from *Rochester Commerce*, as did the annual statistical surveys of economic progress, but the Civic Committee backed a second Community Chest drive in one year to meet rising welfare needs and launched a separate drive that collected pledges from citizens to spend over $6 million during the next two years on new projects designed to create jobs. The city commenced construction of the Veterans Memorial Bridge and other public works and increased its welfare outlays 44 percent. When these efforts failed to meet the needs of the unemployed, the council voted a fund for work-relief projects, anticipating the adoption of that program by Governor

Highlight of the prolonged and very successful centennial celebration in 1934 was the "dramatic spectacle" Pathways of Progress, a costumed extravaganza with enough thematic optimism to balance the gloom of the Depression. Courtesy of Local History Division, Rochester Public Library

Clinton Avenue, looking north toward Main Street, early 1930s. Courtesy of New York Museum of Transportation

Roosevelt, and Rochester was the first city to apply for such state funds when they became available. In response to protests that the city's outlays were excessive and wasteful, Weller released a bureau study showing that the value of the completed projects greatly exceeded the outlays and thus represented prudent investments.

The city's self-reliance faltered, however, in 1932. An address in January by Daniel W. Hoan, socialist mayor of Milwaukee, describing the advantages enjoyed by a city without debt, prompted executives of the bureau to send Weller on a junket to study the fiscal and welfare situation in Dayton and two other civic-minded cities. His report that, although their unemployment problems and welfare needs were comparable, their relief provisions and their debt charges were considerably less, strengthened the advocates of retrenchment in Rochester. The Republicans, who now held eight of the nine council seats, chose a new mayor and a new manager and promptly slashed nearly $4 million from the city budget. The library, the museum, and the parks suffered the most drastic cuts. When a citizens' protest brought restoration of some of these cuts, the city's effort to borrow $3.6 million to maintain its services attracted no bids, and the mayor and the manager resigned to be replaced by a team more acceptable to the bankers.

Hard-pressed Rochesterians were able to smile sorrowfully over a mistaken assumption made by some New York papers in their reports of the death of George Eastman in March 1932. He had shot himself, not over financial reverses as the reports surmised and as some others were doing, but because of a fear of debilitating infirmities. He left munificent bequests to the university and other institutions, but his leadership and the confidence it engendered were gone.

These developments contributed to a shift in Rochester's political allegiance that November, when the city voted Democratic for president, governor, and senator. The strong stand taken by the Democrats against the Volstead Act and Prohibition was a major factor in their victory, for Rochester—despite the long agitation of the "Little Giant," Clinton Howard—had never favored Prohibition. Bartholomay, the largest brewer, had become a milk company, yet numerous bootleggers enjoyed a thriving trade even after some dramatic efforts by the federal agents to halt rum-running across the lake had reduced their supplies. But the severity of the depression was the chief cause for the political overturn.

The debilitating effects of widespread unemployment had reached a peak in 1932. Apple vendors, who had first appeared on Main Street two years before, were now increasing in number. Applicants for public assistance had become too numerous for proper investigation by the department's staff, prompting a resort again to a rock pile to help screen out shiftless vagabonds. Diversified charitable societies, most of them backed by the Community Chest, were supplying unprecedented aid to the most

Kodak offices and camera works in 1925 and 1933. Courtesy of Eastman Kodak Company

destitute, and the projects of the Civic Committee on Unemployment were providing many jobs, but they were at best temporary and failed to fill the demand. Many still unemployed and unwilling to accept charity were again seeking jobs and shelter elsewhere—a back-to-the-land movement, as J. Franklin Bonner, a county planner, euphemistically described it. The city's stability ratio, which, based on the *Directory* listings, had hovered between 62 percent and 66 percent for each five-year span during the two previous decades, dropped to 57.6 percent in the dark years 1930-34, the lowest ratio since the troubled Civil War period. This outward migration relieved the pressure for jobs somewhat and reduced the danger of violence, but many who remained were clamoring for more positive action.

As a result, Rochester welcomed the new federal leadership and the new resources made available in the mid-thirties. Weller accompanied City Manager Theodore C. Briggs to Washington in search of funds to speed the completion of the new public library, among other projects. Although they failed to win backing for the parallel streets and other ambitious plans, Rochester secured over $2.5 million from the Public Works Administration (PWA) for construction projects and double that sum for work relief from the Works Progress Administration (WPA) in the first year of the New Deal. Rochesterians rallied to the support of the National Recovery Administration (NRA). So many local firms adopted the prescribed codes and earned their Blue Eagle banners—reading "Member NRA We Do Our Part"—that the city staged a mammoth parade in September. An estimated 175,000 onlookers cheered the slowly advancing procession of two hundred industrial floats and seventy-five bands, supplying patriotic music for some 65,000 marchers.

Dissenting voices soon appeared, however, particularly among industrialists incensed by the encouragement given by Section 7-A of the Industrial Recovery Act to union organizers. WPA workers, too, were dissatisfied with the modest wages they received and became disgruntled when many projects proved temporary. The great majority, however, were grateful for the 16,000 jobs the New Deal supplied in 1934. Rochester gave the Democrats control of the council in 1935—the first time in thirty-six years—and boosted President Roosevelt's plurality the next year to 32,900, enabling him to carry the county as well. Frank Gannett, who had added the *Democrat & Chronicle* to his chain of newspapers, moderated his early enthusiasm for the New Deal and took a neutral stand in 1936; he finally joined the opposition in protest against Roosevelt's court-packing move and backed the successful drive of the Republicans to retake control of the city a year later.

Official cooperation with the New Deal was waning. Many WPA projects were now nearing completion—new schools, highways, airport runways, and the like—and resistance to the provision of matching funds for new projects was mounting. The experimental grants available from the newly

Victor station of the Rochester & Eastern Railway c. 1925, one relic of the interurban era which still stands. The Rochester & Eastern, which provided fast service to Canandaigua and Geneva, was abandoned in 1930. Courtesy of New York Museum of Transportation

The monumental Veteran's Memorial Bridge, completed in 1931. Courtesy of Local History Division, Rochester Public Library

created U.S. Housing Authority did not interest Rochester. Economy was the watchword of the Republicans who, now under the leadership of Thomas E. Broderick of Irondequoit, again won control of the council in 1939. Harold W. Baker, the former bureau executive chosen city manager by the Democrats and retained for two years by the Republicans, had cooperated too readily with New Deal agencies and was now replaced by Louis B. Cartwright, the city comptroller. Cartwright shortly announced the party's intention not only to balance the budget but to pay off all city debts within the next decade.

Rochester was only mildly stirred that year by a report that a national survey had rated it near the top among central cities of its size. Only Minneapolis excelled it in the combined categories of health, education, recreation, and economic and social well-being. The survey, however, had overlooked the negative category of public debt, which was now Rochester's most deplored "Bow-wow."

A wintertime view of Andrews Street Bridge and North Water Street, which was once densely filled with small manufacturers. Courtesy of New York Museum of Transportation

Thoughtful reserve marked the faces of spectators during the nighttime parade of Blue Eagle banners in September 1933. Courtesy of Local History Division, Rochester Public Library

136

*Construction of John Marshall High School began in
1933, with the help of WPA funds. Courtesy of Joseph
W. Barnes*

*Mercury and the Wings of Progress, 1951. Courtesy of
Local History Division, Rochester Public Library*

Chapter
9

Metropolitan and International Horizons: 1940-1960

Rochester's civic lethargy in the late thirties was due in part to an increasing concern over troubles abroad. Its 50,000 residents of Italian origin, stirred by Mussolini's dramatic rise, had become divided and defensive over his invasion of Ethiopia. Its 20,000 Jews, alarmed by Hitler's pogroms in Germany, were organizing to aid and find homes for a new flood of refugees. The City Club, turning from civic to international issues, drew packed audiences to hear nationally prominent speakers successively defend the Loyalists and the Nationalists in the Spanish civil war, support and oppose the Zionist claim to Palestine; it listened in stunned silence as Maurice Hindus, a distinguished author and lecturer just back from Eastern Europe, predicted in February 1939 the outbreak within a year of the most disastrous war in history.

Rochester in World War II

When the war erupted on September 1, many agreed with Frank Gannett that America should stand apart. Many more rallied to support a drive hastily organized by the city's 10,000 residents of Polish extraction to raise relief funds for their invaded homeland. When Hitler launched his three-pronged attack on Norway, Belgium, and Holland, leading citizens formed a branch of the Committee to Defend America by Aiding the Allies. An opposing group, supporters of the America First Committee, urged strict neutrality. But as France collapsed and the air attack on Britain intensified, indignation and alarm mounted. Helen Rochester Rogers headed a committee that collected fifteen hundred overcoats for Britain; other citizens' committees raised $50,000 for British war relief and lesser sums for six other war-ravaged countries.

Rochester's lethargy disappeared as the challenge of war became more imminent. Defense orders stimulated local firms early in 1940. Bausch & Lomb began again to manufacture telescopic sights and fire-control instruments; Stromberg-Carlson constructed a telephonic switchboard for the Signal Corps. The board of education scheduled several evening technical courses that enrolled two thousand workers eager to prepare for skilled jobs on orders still to come. As local defense contracts mushroomed from $10 million to $75 million within a year, local defense bond sales multiplied. Rochester mustered in and dispatched one thousand National Guardsmen to camp before the passage of the Selective Service Act, cosponsored by the Rochester area's congressman James W. Wadsworth; thirty-three of the initial 30,842 registrants volunteered for the first unit to leave for training camp in 1940.

Debate continued to rage over lend-lease and other policies until the attack on Pearl Harbor on December 7, 1941, forged a new unity of purpose and effort. Of approximately sixteen hundred aliens registered late that year in Rochester, only one violated the restrictions on possession of radios and firearms; most were eager to attain full citizenship in the country for which many of their sons were serving.

Residents of all ranks and stations were eager to contribute their talents. Firm executives, such as Marion Folsom of Kodak, hastened to Washington to serve on emergency boards; three university scientists left on a secret research mission to Los Alamos. Over two hundred physicians from the county and thirty clergymen volunteered for service in the field; as the war progressed, five hundred Rochester nurses left for battle areas, and two hundred other local women joined the military auxiliaries.

As the number of inductees increased, reaching 18,000 by the end of the first year of war, the demand for trained workers to replace them mounted. The Rochester Office of Civilian Protection prepared a

Japanese-American Harry Yazuda of San Francisco chose relocation in Rochester over continued internment in Utah; photographed in December 1944, Yazuda had become a member of the typographical union and, according to the War Relocation Authority, was planning to stay in Rochester. Courtesy of Local History Division, Rochester Public Library

Marion B. Folsom (1893-1976). As George Eastman's personal assistant, he was responsible for drawing up Eastman Kodak's pension plan; later he made valuable contributions to the planning for national Social Security. His increasing involvement in governmental affairs during and after the war led to posts as Undersecretary of the Treasury and Secretary of Health, Education, and Welfare in Eisenhower's administration. Courtesy of Local History Division, Rochester Public Library

master file of the skills of 24,000 citizens employed in technical fields. Mechanics Institute as well as the university and the public high schools conducted training courses that upgraded the skills of some 22,000 men and women. Unemployment disappeared, except for brief periods of industrial retooling, and Rochester's work force increased by 80 percent, reaching 120,000—more than one-third of them women—by the summer of 1943. As a result, local firms were able to accept and fill new government contracts, which reached a total value of $1.2 billion by November 1945, and thirty-eight companies won Army-Navy E awards.

Rochester's patriotic response took many forms. Its penchant for organized drives was again demonstrated as the Community Chest campaigns surged above $2 million annually, while two separate Red Cross drives topped $1 million. Successive tire, scrap metal, and other salvage drives generally exceeded local quotas, and one week-long collection totaled 27,300 tons. The city, shifting to buses, ripped up its old trolley tracks to add to the pile. Some grumbling was heard over various rationing programs, but the home front could not falter as reports of casualties came back from Rochester units on the battle lines in Italy, France, and the Far East. Local recruits from Monroe County soared past 42,000 by the summer of 1945; the number of service fatalities climbed to 1,139 by August, with another 2,000 severely wounded and 100 still listed as missing.

As the war effort surged toward a triumphant conclusion, local determination mounted that peace this time should be assured. America would have large and costly responsibilities, Gannett as well as Congressman Wadsworth and Professor Dexter Perkins repeatedly declared. All mourned the sudden death of President Roosevelt, whose third- and fourth-term campaigns had been bitterly opposed by Rochester's official leaders but supported by its voting majorities. Many applauded when Harper Sibley, representative of the U.S. Chamber of Commerce, and Professor Perkins, conference historian, returned from the international conference at San Francisco to report on the successful negotiation of a world charter for the United Nations. Professor John R. Slater expressed the yearnings of many in his prayer at the university's V-E Day ceremony: "Lord have mercy on us....Give wisdom and patience to all who try to build over the ruins of a thousand years a new temple of freedom and justice."

Postwar Planning and Practice

The Rochester Chamber had made an early start on postwar planning. A lingering aversion to that term had prompted L. Dudley Field, its president in 1942, to call its effort a Council on Postwar Problems, but the twenty-five civic, social, and governmental groups that participated in the numerous general

German POWs cleared snow from Broad Street Bridge under armed guard, February 1945. A contingent of POWs was housed for much of the war in Cobbs Hill Park. Courtesy of Local History Division, Rochester Public Library

Liberty Bridge over Main Street was designed to stimulate patriotic effort during the drive for the Fifth War Loan, June 12-July 8, 1944. A bond purchaser was entitled to ring the bell. Courtesy of Local History Division, Rochester Public Library

On the home front, February 1943. Courtesy of Local History Division, Rochester Public Library

and committee sessions of the council during the next four years were endeavoring to reach agreement on their future plans. The industrial subcommittee reported active planning for expansion by 52 of the 121 firms with more than fifty employees. The civic subcommittee listed a number of desirable postwar projects, with an estimated total cost of $27 million—a figure that seemed excessive to the editor of the *Democrat*, a supporter of the official hold-the-line policy.

The Council on Postwar Problems would soon pass from the scene, but it opened debate on several emerging issues. The education subcommittee launched a Voluntary Educational Council to promote cooperation between public and private educational institutions and develop training programs for returning servicemen. Its proposals for guidance counseling and for the creation of a metropolitan school district, however, proved too visionary. The subcommittee on social welfare, headed by Mrs. Harper Sibley, recommended advances in recreation, character-building, housing, and family services that would in some cases take years to accomplish, but the Council of Social Agencies and the newly reorganized Better Housing Association prepared to battle for their adoption.

The urgent needs of returning servicemen were already highlighting some of these issues. Over 6,000 were on hand to march in the parade on V-J Day in August 1945, cheered by 100,000 onlookers, but their major concern was to find suitable jobs. As the number of returnees increased to 30,000 by the next April, the search for jobs and housing intensified. Some found their old jobs waiting for them; many seized the opportunity to acquire academic and technical training; others found jobs through the employment offices of expanding local firms—the Bond Clothing Company's mammoth new plant, Stromberg-Carlson's Radio City station, and Kodak's new color-film plant, among many others.

It proved easier to find a job than a house or apartment in Rochester. Goaded by Helen Jones of the Better Housing Association, the city created a Service Housing Bureau which converted an old school building into apartments and refurbished several abandoned lofts; veteran applicants, however, persistently outnumbered units more than ten to one. A mass meeting at Convention Hall petitioned for public action, but Mayor Samuel B. Dicker and the majority of the council, committed to economy and opposed to public housing, refused to act. Less constrained by tradition, a group of bankers headed by Elmer B. Milliman joined in the construction of a nonprofit project named Fernwood Park, which provided 152 apartments to veterans at moderate rentals. The wide praise it received stimulated other business leaders to undertake two similar projects, while the city converted several additional structures to residential use. Many veterans with secure jobs and growing families moved to the suburbs to build new houses with VHA loans.

The migration to the suburbs was broadening

Mrs. Harper Sibley during her years as a civic leader in Rochester promoted improved housing and social services, fostered the creation of R.A.U.N., and fought urban decay. Courtesy of Local History Division, Rochester Public Library

Dexter Perkins, professor of history and long-term chairman of the department at the University of Rochester, won national recognition in his field of diplomatic history. Regarded as an authority on international events in his home community, he was also repeatedly honored as a teacher of first rank. Courtesy of Local History Division, Rochester Public Library

F. Harper Sibley (1885-1959), grandson of Hiram Sibley, was a director of Western Union and numerous banks and other corporations. He was President of the U.S. Chamber of Commerce in the late '30s and took an active interest in foreign-mission work and the relief of refugees. Courtesy of Local History Division, Rochester Public Library

Mrs. Alan Valentine, wife of the president of the University who served from 1935 until 1950, was trained in architecture. During her Rochester years she rendered valuable service as a leader of the Citizen Planning and Housing Council and as a member of the City Planning Commission.

V-J Day. Courtesy of Local History Division, Rochester Public Library

The Bond Clothing factory on North Goodman Street under construction in 1947. In subsequent years the giant building would house the telecommunications division of General Dynamics Corporation. Most recently it has become headquarters for the optical division of Bausch and Lomb. Courtesy of Local History Division, Rochester Public Library

Rochester's horizons. A proposed metropolitan school district failed to win support, but the Chest became the Community Chest of Greater Rochester, as it extended its services and solicitations into the surrounding towns. City Planning Commission staff members began to work more closely with the Regional Planning Board. Their collaboration was especially urgent in highway planning, as the construction of the New York State Thruway raised the problem of opening proper links to the city. The final decision, to come in from the east in the old Erie Canal bed, solved two troublesome questions—the abandonment of the subway and the location of the expressway; it also accelerated migration into the eastern suburbs lining that route. Industrial expansion, too, was occurring on the outskirts, especially in Henrietta along the rail and highway routes skirting south of the city. The first large suburban shopping plazas, five of them with parking facilities for over two thousand cars each, made their appearance at strategic traffic junctions on the periphery of Rochester.

But suburban migration had the dual effect of draining talents and taxpayers from the city while burdening it with increased responsibilities. The eagerness of returning servicemen to establish families created a baby boom that gave the city an annual surplus of thirty-five hundred births over deaths in the early forties. With these babies and a continued influx of newcomers offsetting the out-migration, Rochester experienced a slight increase in population, to a record high of 332,488 in 1950. But as the out-migrants, attracted by new homes in the suburbs, swelled to 100,000 in the fifties, the city's population decreased by 16,000. Most of the newcomers—refugees from trouble spots abroad and migrants in increasing number from the South—were handicapped by poverty and welcomed the opportunity to move into the aging quarters abandoned by the suburban migrants.

The resettlement of deteriorating sections of the inner city posed other problems as yet only faintly perceived. An influx of black people had commenced during the war, when some of the migrants from the South who were bused north to work in the fruit orchards along the lake moved into the city each fall to await the next harvest. Some found shelter with families in the traditional Negro district on the southwest edge of the old Third Ward, but most of these newcomers lodged in the now partially vacated dwellings of former immigrants northeast of the tracks. Baden Street Settlement, founded in 1901 to serve the needs of the poor Jews from Eastern Europe who were then crowding that area, saw its former clientele dwindle as a result of out-migration and hastened to draw its new neighbors into recreational and counseling programs. Montgomery Neighborhood Center, newly established on the west side to serve the small residue of old Negro families there, opened its facilities to the newcomers as well. With the return of peace, the influx mounted rapidly, as news of Rochester's thriving industries and low unemployment spread, attracting migrants from

The first section of Route 490 East (or Eastern Thruway Connection) was opened between Fairport Road and Victor in 1955. Courtesy of Local History Division, Rochester Public Library

Fernwood Park, Rochester's first major postwar housing project, was financed at the initiative of local banks as a nonprofit venture. It was ready for occupancy in 1947. Courtesy of Local History Division, Rochester Public Library

Governor Thomas E. Dewey broke ground for the New York State Thruway in ceremonies at nearby Fishers, October 1946. Courtesy of Local History Division, Rochester Public Library

other Northern cities as well as from the South. No one foresaw the magnitude of the movement, which brought a twofold increase in the city's nonwhite population during the fifties.

Some of the implications of these trends had surfaced in the election of 1948. Harry Truman's unexpected victory in the city had convinced its Republican leaders that the migration of many party members to the suburbs was to blame and prompted a reappraisal of their programs. Reluctantly, party chairman Thomas E. Broderick approved the construction under state auspices of Hanover Houses, the city's first public housing project. A move to locate it on an undeveloped subdivision near the city's northern border, reclaimed for taxes during the depression, was loudly protested by neighboring house-holders, and a site was chosen in the Baden-Ormond district north of the tracks, where slum properties could be demolished without protest.

Other troubling problems pressed for solution in the late forties. Prodded by the Chamber's Civic Development Council, City Manager Louis B. Cartwright relaxed the hold-the-line policy in order to undertake long-deferred street improvements and to grant modest salary increases to city employees. The frustration many felt was revealed when the superintendent of parks, finally given a $200 raise, resigned in indignation. In an attempt to reduce its burdens, the city turned the airport over to the county for needed improvements. The schools avoided a teachers' walkout when a last-minute grant by the state enabled the board to add $600 to their salaries. It was not until three years later that the council finally abandoned its hold-the-line policy with the decision to go ahead with construction of the War Memorial—the first move toward the development of a Civic Center.

Brighter Horizons in the Fifties

Important industrial advances renewed Rochester's self-confidence. The launching of its first television station, WHAM-TV, by Stromberg-Carlson in 1949 highlighted other developments by that firm. Pfaudler, Taylor Instruments, General Motors, and Bausch & Lomb, as well as Eastman Kodak and a dozen other local companies, each added new products, built new additions to their factories, and in several cases developed new branches abroad. None, however, expanded as dramatically as Haloid which, under the leadership of Joseph C. Wilson (grandson of a former mayor), developed a new electrophotographic process and placed its first Xerox machines on the market in 1950. As its copying machines opened a fabulous new market, the company, renamed Haloid-Xerox, built a spacious new factory in suburban Webster, increased its local employment tenfold in as many years, and helped to boost total industrial employment in the county to 106,000 in 1959, when the total output of

Construction for the Community War Memorial. The site had been occupied by the Kimball Tobacco Factory with its chimney-top statue of Mercury. Courtesy of Local History Division, Rochester Public Library

The Rochester Community War Memorial, in a photograph taken not long after the building's dedication on May 30, 1956. The photographer was in an upper story, or in the tower, of the Powers Building. In the extreme left side of the photograph two buildings may be discerned facing the Rundel Building: the Milner Hotel and the Genesee Amusement Company. They would soon be demolished for the extension of Broad Street and construction of the Downtowner Motor Inn. Courtesy of City Historian's Office

The new Rochester-Monroe County Airport terminal building, nearly completed in 1953. The old Municipal Airport operated from the south end of the field, on Scottsville Road, where general aviation operations are now located. The enlargement of the airport and the transfer of its operations from Rochester to Monroe County involved a series of complex legal steps. Financing, for example, came from the county while the city expanded the territory of the municipal airport through purchase and annexation. Courtesy of Local History Division, Rochester Public Library

The Baden-Ormond district in Rochester's near-northeast had become badly run down by the mid-'50s. Courtesy of Local History Division, Rochester Public Library

149

local manufacturers for the first time exceeded $1 billion in value.

Invigorated by these industrial achievements, the city tackled several long-deferred tasks. It built new incinerators to dispose of its garbage, opened water-intake lines from Lake Ontario, and constructed a filtering plant, launched an urban-renewal project to clear the slums around Hanover Houses, and authorized the Board of Education to construct the spacious new East High School. These projects, planned and launched by Cartwright, were vigorously carried forward by Robert P. Aex, his successor, and by Peter Barry, who replaced Dicker as mayor in 1955. Together they pressed the state for progress on the Eastern Expressway, partially opened in 1960, and launched construction of downtown parking ramps and of the long-debated Broad Street extension. That improvement tied in with and assured the construction of the new Midtown Plaza, the nation's pioneer enclosed downtown shopping mall.

Renewed prosperity brightened Rochester's social horizons as well. An increasing number of the homes on the more spacious lots in the suburbs supplied new luxuries to affluent families, including a thousand private swimming pools by 1960. Sportsmen in the city rallied to purchase the Red Wing baseball franchise (and stadium) when plans for its removal by the St. Louis club were revealed. Rochester Community Baseball, Inc., headed by Morris E. Silver, secured a new association with the Baltimore Orioles and maintained a place for the Red Wings in the International League. The Rochester Royals, after several victorious basketball seasons at Edgerton Park, moved to the new War Memorial but, unable to fill its larger galleries, soon gave place to the Rochester Americans, whose flashing skates and skilled playing developed an enthusiastic following in 1956 and assured their hold in succeeding years. Amateur teams crowded the park facilities each summer, affording abundant opportunities for youths. Senior citizens acquired a headquarters for numerous programs with the opening of the Danforth House in 1950. Entire families enjoyed the annual series of Opera Under the Stars launched at Highland Park in 1953.

Rochester's metropolitan expansion presented new problems in some fields. Jazz and other dance bands multiplied, affording entertainment in the city and the suburbs, but the Philharmonic Orchestra, with many of its patrons removed to the suburbs, had difficulty filling the Eastman Theater. Vigorous drives by the Civic Music Association managed to sustain the orchestra, but Will Corris, whose annual seasons of drama at the Auditorium suffered a similar suburban palsy, had to suspend his efforts in 1956. The City Club, benefiting from the increased interest in international affairs, held lively sessions during the early fifties when the Korean War commanded attention, but as that engagement became protracted and the five-day week acquired wider acceptance in Rochester, the club's attendance, too, suffered attrition.

The increased flow of cars in and out of the city,

Future site of the Rochester-Monroe County Civic Center, as it appeared around 1892 (photographer F.W. Swift). The view is from the top of the Wilder Building. Courtesy of Douglas A. Fisher, Victor Historical Society

Peter Barry (1912-1973) was Rochester's mayor from 1955 to 1961. Among the city's accomplishments during his term in office was the construction of Midtown Plaza, its associated underground parking garage, and the extension of Broad Street, all the product of cooperative effort between private enterprise and municipal initiative. Peter Barry was the great-grandson of Patrick Barry, the nineteenth-century nurseryman. Courtesy of Local History Division, Rochester Public Library

The Joseph C. Wilson Center in suburban Webster is the Xerox Corporation's chief manufacturing and research center. Courtesy of City Historian's Office

East High School, completed in 1959. Courtesy of Local History Division, Rochester Public Library

the transmission of radio and television programs over a broad receiving area, and the distribution of daily papers carrying suburban as well as city news into homes throughout a six-county metropolitan district were all obliterating Rochester's boundaries. Branch factories, branch banks, branch stores, and delivery services operated by the city's leading industrial and commercial concerns, along with the wide services of its gas and electric and telephone companies, were helping to integrate the area's economy. County government was increasing its functions, as demonstrated by the successful merging of the city and county health bureaus into the county health department in 1958. But the only municipal function that managed to assume a metropolitan stance was the public library, which merged its services with the county system and developed in 1956 a tri-county federation, the Pioneer Library System, that became a model for the nation.

Rochester's horizons, broadened by World War II experiences and by the increased number of foreign branches and outlets of its industrial firms, were extended anew by the Korean involvement. Prominent among the new institutional responses was the Rochester Association for the United Nations (RAUN). Founded in Mrs. Sibley's spacious parlor in 1945 to rally citizen support for that body, the RAUN saw America's intervention in Korea as a demonstration of its commitment to the United Nations and held several annual convocations at Eastman Theater to promote international cooperation. The Korean War was more than an academic question in Rochester, however, for, with 20,000 men and women from the county involved directly or in support capacities for various periods in that protracted engagement, even the city's absorption with postwar recovery assumed a broader outlook. At a critical moment in December 1950, when 450 Rochester men were known to be on the battlefront, the local Red Cross assembled and dispatched the first shipment of whole blood, a service that continued as the number of fatalities among Rochester's recruits mounted to 176 over the next five years.

New military orders helped to boost Rochester's industrial production to new highs, enabling the city to sustain new ventures, several of them international in character. One such effort was the Teen Age Diplomat program, organized in 1952 to promote an exchange of local high school and college students with similar students from foreign cities. Another was the Seminar in American Studies in Salzburg, Austria, of which Professor Perkins became board chairman in 1949 and principal fund raiser for two decades, dispatching selected professors from American universities to conduct intensive four-week seminars for graduate students recruited from cities throughout Western Europe. The Jews of Rochester, who had contributed $1.2 million annually to assist in the resettlement of refugees from Hitler's purges—some of them in the Rochester area—redoubled their efforts after 1947 in behalf of newly independent Israel and raised $8 million over the next decade for its support. A series of Confer-

ences on High Energy Physics, launched at the university by Dr. Robert E. Marshak with the support of local firms in 1950, and subsequently held there and abroad in alternate years, was another significant attempt to bridge international boundaries.

Rochester's expanding horizons, however, could not obviate a number of internal trends that were troubling many citizens. The leaders of neighborhood settlement houses in the old and decaying ring surrounding the central business district were concerned over mounting hostilities between the older ethnic residents and landlords who had held on there and the newcomers, many of them poor blacks from the South. Friction in the neighborhoods and complaints of discrimination had prompted the opening of a local office of the State Commission Against Discrimination, but difficulties continued as the influx of newcomers mounted. The protests of Mrs. Sibley and leaders of the Federation of Churches, among others, deploring the neglect of these internal sores, went largely unheeded, however, amidst Rochester's excitement over its more dramatic accomplishments.

A 1949 view of Eastman Theatre and its surroundings. Courtesy of Eastman Kodak Company

Rundel Memorial Building. Headquarters of the Rochester Public Library and the Monroe County Library System, the Rundel Building was constructed in the 1930s with funds largely supplied by the bequest of Morton Rundel. Its front entrance has been extensively modernized (1977-78). Courtesy of Joseph W. Barnes

*Clock of the Nations in Midtown Plaza. This shopping
complex was among the first modern downtown
shopping malls in the nation in 1961; subsequent
expansion and improvements have maintained its high
caliber. Courtesy of City Historian's Office*

The Genesee River Gorge and the Lower Falls. The wild beauty of the Genesee River Canyon has been preserved within the City of Rochester to a remarkable degree. Courtesy of Joseph W. Barnes

Chapter 10

Rochester — A Grass-Roots Metropolis: 1960-1978

Several old and new challenges, sorely testing Rochester's self-confidence and high spirits, helped to unveil new horizons in the sixties and seventies. Rapid demographic, economic, and political shifts brought new leaders and new programs to the fore. Vigorous grass-roots movements—sparked by the inner-city riots of 1964, the accelerated migration to the suburbs, and the upsurge of citizen participation —produced significant changes. Yet, in the 1970s, residents who had survived the turmoil of Rochester's transformation could take delight in the new splendor of the city's downtown, the renewed amenity of many city and suburban neighborhoods, the continued productivity of its technology, and the broader scope and vitality of its cultural institutions. They could also find comfort and reassurance in the spreading patches of green grass—both the seeded variety and the symbolic—appearing on all sides.

Demographic Shifts
and Repercussions

Demography is perhaps too learned a term to use in describing the population changes that have transformed the Rochester metropolis during the last two decades. Yet a city that has long found its chief source of power in its inhabitants should not be surprised when the people speak up, move, and vote in unconventional ways. And in a population as heterogeneous and changing as that of Rochester, the orchestration is not always harmonious—although civic leaders as well as historians must try to interpret the cacophony.

The flight to the suburbs, already pronounced in the fifties, accelerated in the sixties and continued with only slight abatement in the seventies. Though offset in part by new in-migration and new births, this outward movement reduced the city's population from a high of 332,488 in 1950 to 296,230 in 1970, and to an estimated 270,000 at mid-decade. The county's nineteen towns for the first time surged ahead of the city and finally doubled its total in the late 1970s.

In essence, this migration marked the outward expansion of metropolitan Rochester, which was also spilling over into neighboring Livingston, Wayne, and Orleans counties and into nearby Ontario and Genesee towns. But the movement was more than a shift in numbers. In their quest for newer homes on larger lots, city residents were selling or renting older dwellings to less affluent newcomers and investing the returns in outlying properties. Suburban shopping plazas now attracted their patronage and by the early seventies would threaten the commercial vitality of the downtown district. The increased civic needs of the mushrooming suburbs prompted the county to appropriate a larger share of the sales tax and to expand its services chiefly in the towns.

These shifts posed a serious challenge to the central city, already confronted by another perplexing demographic situation. Many newcomers to the city were blacks, and though the rate of their influx had dropped off from the twofold growth of the fifties, they more than doubled Rochester's nonwhite population in the sixties, reaching a total of 52,105 in 1970. Blocked by poverty and discriminatory practices from the more salubrious outer wards, most of them settled in the aging quarters surrounding the central business district. Arriving, like most migrants before them, as young adults, they soon produced numerous children, and with a new stream of migrants from Puerto Rico that numbered some five thousand in the sixties, they imposed severe burdens on the aged dwellings, schools, and other facilities of the inner-city wards.

Though few of Rochester's leaders in the early sixties foresaw the hazards these trends portended, a succession of incidents progressively alerted them to action. Mounting signs of juvenile disorder brought increased Community Chest support for youth

programs at three settlement houses in the blighted districts, and the creation of a Human Relations Commission and a City-County Youth Board with access to state funds promised more effective action. But the protracted discussions that led up to these measures, as well as the delayed opening of long-awaited new schools in the congested wards, had aroused the indignation of many blacks and contributed to a political turnover in 1961, when the Democrats unexpectedly captured control of the City Council and elected two blacks to the Board of Supervisors.

A series of probing articles in the *Times-Union* in June 1960 had contributed to the awakening. The "New Negro," columnist Desmond Stone had discovered, did not want "help" or "better treatment" but equality and independence. Outspoken blacks in the NAACP, supported by an influx of new members, had relegated the earlier white leaders to the back

Aerial view of Eastway Plaza. Courtesy of Local History Division, Rochester Public Library

benches. The public schools, settlement houses, and other agencies recruited able Negroes for their staffs, and friends helped them find desirable homes, but the improved status of some middle-class Negroes failed to satisfy the desire of the mass of blacks for equality.

The incident that best revealed the depth of resentment was the arrest in 1962 of Rufus Fairwell as he closed the service station at which he was employed. Offended by the assumption that, as a black, he was an obvious suspect, he refused to identify himself and suffered injuries in resisting arrest. In the civil rights atmosphere of the sixties, popular indignation mounted as the case progressed, and a United Action Committee of black leaders, who now took pride in their distinctive color, joined with white sympathizers in raising a fund to press for justice. Several other incidents involving blacks and the police prompted the formation of an Integrated Non-Violence Committee that spurred the new Democratic administration to create a Police Advisory Board to enlist citizen assistance in reducing tension. The charges against Fairwell were dropped, and a suit he brought against the city for damages was settled out of court for $12,000.

Several other community agencies took remedial action. The Housing Authority finally opened its new Chatham Gardens project and collaborated with the Human Relations Commission in making it an integrated community. The Youth Board enlisted the aid of industrial and union leaders in promoting an on-the-job training program supported by federal funds with assurance of apprenticeships and jobs for the blacks enrolled. The Board of Education prepared a plan for the reduction of de facto segregation by the transfer of some nonwhite pupils from inner-city districts to adjoining, predominantly white, schools. Despite protests from some of the affected neighborhoods, most Rochesterians felt confident that the city's long experience in absorbing newcomers of varied origins and heritage would again assure success.

The Inner-City Riots and FIGHT

All Rochesterians were shocked when rioting broke out north of the tracks on July 24, 1964. The police, summoned by the Mothers Improvement Association of the Eighth Ward to remove a drunk from a street dance they were conducting on that hot Friday evening, met resistance from several black youths who sprang to his defense. A call for reinforcements brought several police cars to the scene, including one with a K-9 Corps dog, which incited indignation that erupted in rioting and spread rapidly throughout the area. All efforts by Police Chief William Lombard and several black leaders to restrain the violence proved futile, and rioting and looting continued throughout the night. In the ominous quiet that settled over the area the next morning, property owners attempting to board up the shattered windows of their looted stores and refuse workers sweeping up the debris provoked threatening shouts from sullen bystanders. While most Rochesterians listened with astonishment to news broadcasts at home that day, city officials and other leaders conferred on plans to cope with a possible renewal that evening.

It was the vicious character of the rioting on Saturday night that demonstrated the depth of hostility smoldering in the black community. Despite a citywide curfew and the constant patrol of some 550 city, county, and state police officers, racing gangs of disgruntled blacks, accompanied by a few Puerto Rican and white youths, pillaged many stores and set scattered fires throughout the blighted northeast and southwest districts. Efforts to quell the rioting produced numerous arrests and many injuries, including four accidental deaths (all of them whites).

As Sunday dawned, the arrival of a detachment of fifteen hundred National Guardsmen restored a sense of security. Respected black and white leaders issued pleas for reconciliation. The Reverend Arthur Whitaker of Mt. Olivet Baptist Church spoke for many when he declared that "violence cannot be

William Warfield, the great baritone, in a Rochester dressing room December 1956. Warfield grew up in the Hudson Avenue neighborhood. Courtesy of Local History Division, Rochester Public Library

Commissioner of Public Safety Harper Sibley, Jr. confers with Chief of Police William Lombard, July 1965. Courtesy of Local History Division, Rochester Public Library

Chatham Gardens, the Rochester Housing Authority's project opened in 1965, was conceived in part as an alternative to the mistakes of Hanover Houses. Courtesy of Local History Division, Rochester Public Library

condoned but it must be understood." Most Rochesterians spent the day quietly at home pondering the implications of the riots. Whether because the message had been delivered or because of the new show of force, Sunday night passed without serious disturbances. Monday brought a welcome sense of relief, as cleanup operations commenced and activity in the business district returned to normal. The courts hastily granted suspended sentences to two-thirds of the 976 persons arrested for looting and curfew violation; a closer scrutiny of the remainder revealed that the majority had been residents of the city for more than five years and that less than one-fifth were newcomers within the year.

It was clearly a local problem calling for local solutions, and many agencies already involved redoubled their efforts. Several firms expanded their job-training programs; youth agencies intensified their recruiting and counseling programs; church groups created a revolving fund to finance the purchase and improvement of homes in all parts of the city by nonwhites. A voter registration committee launched a campaign to register an additional 10,000 blacks. Convinced that a still more concerted effort was necessary, several business leaders backed the formation of a Rochester branch of the Urban League to promote on-the-job programs. The city's antipoverty task force organized Action for a Better Community (ABC) and secured federal grants for several educational and welfare projects geared to the nationwide war on poverty.

To some blacks, these efforts appeared tardy and tinged with paternalism. When the Board of Urban Ministry invited Saul Alinsky, a Chicago organizer of minority groups, to help develop a more indigenous black movement in Rochester, approximately one hundred black groups joined in the formation of FIGHT to work for Freedom, Integration, God, and Honor, Today. Scorning rival efforts as "welfare colonialism," the new organization, under the leadership of Minister Franklin Florence, rallied support from many blacks who had never before participated in community programs. It aggressively challenged the white leadership of agencies serving the inner city, including the housing authority with its long-awaited plan for urban renewal in the now blighted Third Ward. FIGHT's most dramatic assault, however, was on the job-training program of Eastman Kodak. Demanding the exclusive right to recruit some six hundred hard-core unemployed blacks for the program and to represent them during and after training, FIGHT gained wide publicity but failed to breach the company's traditional refusal to accept outside representation of its work force by unions or other independent agencies.

While FIGHT's abrasive strategy, which won the support of militant blacks, created deep fissures in the white community, it also spurred new efforts to cope with the city's basic problems. Perhaps the most significant of these was the establishment in 1967 of Rochester Jobs, Inc. (RJI). An outgrowth of discussions at the Colgate-Rochester Divinity School among several industrial and community leaders RJI engaged Edward Croft of the state employment bureau as director and won the cooperation of ABC, the Urban League, and FIGHT in a program to train fifteen hundred unemployed for industrial jobs. The experience of working together healed some of the earlier wounds, and FIGHT, on observing some of the Urban League's trainees receive jobs at Kodak, hastened to reach a more conciliatory agreement with that firm and abandoned its plan to stage a national pilgrimage to Rochester on the third anniversary of the riots. It was Detroit, not Rochester, that suffered the brunt of black rage in July 1967.

Rev. Franklin Florence at the Kodak stockholder's meeting in Flemington, New Jersey, May 1967. Courtesy of Local History Division, Rochester Public Library

Bernard R. Gifford at the construction site of FIGHT Square, November 1969. Courtesy of Local History Division, Rochester Public Library

Civic and Economic Resurgence

The black upsurge had a lesser impact on other phases of Rochester's civic and economic life, already beset by urban-suburban rivalries and fiscal dilemmas. Despite shifts in political leadership, the city's successive administrations launched, with state and federal assistance, unprecedented housing and other construction projects. These, together with private reconstruction, transformed the face of metropolitan Rochester. Although its vibrant prosperity during the mid-sixties was tempered somewhat by fluctuations in the national economy, Rochester's technological energies proved sufficiently resilient to maintain a dynamic metropolis.

The Democrats, who, with some black support, had captured the city council in 1961, faced a stringent fiscal situation throughout the booming sixties. The efforts of Mayor Henry Gillette to launch municipal improvements were hampered by a loss of sales tax revenues to the county. Although the city's thriving retailers collected ever-increasing tax payments, partially relieving this constraint, Mayor Frank Lamb in his turn suffered an additional tax diversion in 1965 that delayed urgent inner-city projects. As a result, the city was forced to accept the county's offer to take over maintenance costs of the parks, the central library, and the museum, but it retained responsibility for its playgrounds, branch libraries, and other municipal services.

Mayor Gillette had secured the creation of a Department of Urban Renewal and Economic Development to press ahead with the Genesee Crossroads project straddling the river north of Main Street bridge and to expedite redevelopment in other parts of the inner city. Mayor Lamb backed these efforts, but the inevitable delays stirred complaints of inaction. Before the Third Ward plan was approved, the leaders of FIGHT, having shifted from their advocacy of "integration" to a demand for "independence," insisted on black participation in planning and development, which further postponed that project. The city, however, hastened to incorporate the principle of neighborhood participation in its successful application for a Model City redevelopment project north of the tracks.

Rochester's low-cost housing needs were not exclusively a minority group concern. Business leaders, alert to the demand for new workers in the city's thriving industries, formed the Metropolitan Rochester Foundation to promote the construction of moderate-income housing in the suburbs as well as the city. Several of its projects were for senior citizens and served to release their former dwellings for the families of new workers. When opposition developed to the location of such projects in the towns, the foundation joined the city in inviting the state's newly chartered Urban Development Corporation (UDC), with authority to cut local red tape, to make a

The Genesee Crossroads Urban Renewal Project, 1965-1977. One of the most dramatic and sweeping downtown renewal projects in the nation, Rochester's Genesee Crossroads Project accomplished the removal of deteriorated buildings on both sides of the Genesee River north of Main Street Bridge as well as the buildings on the bridge itself which had blocked sight of the river. Private and public capital was invested in several new office buildings, two new hotels, a new federal building, and the Plaza Apartments. Carroll Park on the west side of the river, linked to the east side by the distinctive Y-shaped Sisters Cities pedestrian bridge, has proved to be a popular gathering place at noontime and during musical events, festivals, and firework displays. Courtesy of Floyd J. Evershed

study of greater Rochester's needs and to launch effective action under local leadership.

Such action would require broad cooperation between the city and the towns, now politically divided. The city Democrats, hoping to strengthen their black support, had elected Laplois Ashford to the school board and nominated him for the city council. But Ashford's leadership of the Urban League, which had not pleased the leaders of FIGHT, dampened the ardor of many blacks. His defeat at the polls, together with the prospect that a Republican council might achieve better cooperation with the county, turned the city back to the Republicans in 1969.

Stephen May, chosen mayor by the Republicans, pressed forward with the redevelopment program. The city and county signed a contract with UDC-Greater Rochester, Inc., giving it authority to construct housing and promote industrial development throughout the county. Under the management of Richard Pine, it not only completed the Gleason Estates in Pittsford but undertook six other projects in the towns and launched ten residential projects in the city during the early seventies. The demolition of deteriorated structures on these sites and the early progress of construction, together with the progressive completion of the Crossroads and Civic Center developments, drastically altered the city's appearance.

Private construction more than kept pace with these developments. New bank and office towers—Marine Midland and Lincoln First—arose in the vicinity of the soaring Xerox office building near Midtown Plaza, introducing spacious open plazas in the process. New hotels and office buildings, including a new Federal Building and the striking high-rise Plaza Apartments, occupied open-spaced Crossroads sites. The city demolished the aged structures lining Main Street bridge to restore a full view of the Genesee and built a handsome new Y-bridge, christened the Sister City Bridge in recognition of that program promoted by former Mayor Lamb; it provided a colorful pedestrian link between the river plazas.

Despite the modern appearance of the city's downtown and of the new housing projects arising on scattered sites, opposition mounted against the demolition of cherished parts of old Rochester. The Landmark Society took the lead in the creation of a Preservation Board to safeguard designated landmarks; together they secured the establishment of the East Avenue Preservation District and of similar districts in three other areas where neighborhood associations made determined moves for such safeguards. Their success prompted other neighborhood associations to undertake the restoration of residential and business properties in their areas, thus reviving old amenities and, in the case of Park Avenue, developing a thriving new center of urban life.

Grass-roots neighborhood associations sprang to action in old inner-city districts, as well as in the outer wards. After protracted delays, Fight Square

was finally completed in the Third Ward, along with St. Simon's Terrace and Los Flamboyanes, black and Puerto Rican projects in the Model City area; and these served as focal centers for resident and neighborhood associations. Together these movements represented a resurgence of confidence in the city.

When the Republican administration failed to improve relations with the towns, the voters again turned to the Democrats, who promptly named Thomas P. Ryan, Jr. mayor. Yet in 1977, when the Democrats won control of the county legislature, as its board had been renamed, rivalries between the city and the towns persisted. The report of a protracted Urban Policy Conference of leading citizens in 1972, which had recommended, among other reforms, a two-tier system of governmental responsibility, remained on the shelf.

In the economic sphere, however, greater Rochester was developing as a unified metropolis. Its leading merchants were operating the major stores in the proliferating suburban plazas, as branches of their downtown establishments. Several of the leading industries had opened or were now opening branch factories in the towns. Thus the booming Xerox Corporation, as it was now called, concentrated production at its factory complex in Webster, and management in its Xerox Square tower downtown. The Sybron Corporation, a newly formed conglomerate of several prestigious Rochester firms, managed its scattered plants from headquarters in Midtown Tower, while the Gannett Company, with an expanding network of newspapers and broadcasting stations throughout the country, was one of several firms to locate its headquarters in the new Lincoln First tower. The UDC-Greater Rochester not only helped the city develop an Outer Loop Industrial Park on an old landfill on the west side, but redeveloped the abandoned car shops in East Rochester as an industrial park; it also assisted Bausch & Lomb in relocating its production facilities in the former Bond Clothes factory, thus saving that optical firm from migration elsewhere.

Like other aging cities in the Northeast, Rochester was losing some factories to the sunny South, but the vitality of its technology was spawning new firms. A prize example was R F Communications Associates, organized in the early sixties to provide design consultation in the field of electrical communications. Its proficiency prompted the Harris Corporation of Cleveland to absorb it and build a modern office and plant on University Avenue for the production of its quality control and communication products. Among the numerous other new firms springing from the city's technology was EDMAC Associates, launched by several highly skilled former employees of the Electronics Division of General Dynamics who had decided to remain in Rochester when that corporation moved out in 1970. The successful development of its manufacturing, assembling, and testing plant in East Rochester again demonstrated the entrepreneurial vigor that characterized the metropolitan labor market, al-

Among Rochester's urban renewal projects of the mid-60s was one of the nation's smallest; clearing the triangle of Main, North, and Franklin Streets to create Liberty Pole Green. Courtesy of City Historian's Office

South Avenue, looking north, a view which reveals two of Rochester's most up-to-date structures. The Guggenheim Museum-like ramp garage is the city's newest and is one of the nation's most advanced. The soaring white skyscraper in the right side of the illustration is the tower of Lincoln First Square. Courtesy of City Historian's Office

Turning Basin, located within Turning Point Park, the City of Rochester's newest park. Courtesy of Joseph W. Barnes

Rochester Philharmonic Orchestra Headquarters, located in the Grove Place Preservation District, a small residential area adjacent to downtown Rochester which has experienced an "urban renaissance." Courtesy of Joseph W. Barnes

ready first in the nation in its proportion of technical-professional workers. These and other firms created a continuing demand for highly skilled workers and helped to account for the industrial backing given RJI's recruiting and training programs, which comprised a major portion of its activities and consumed half the $19 million expended in its first decade in upgrading the skills of the unemployed and fitting them into the Rochester economy.

Social and Cultural Trends

Rochester's social and cultural developments were also interlinked and displayed a similar grass-roots quality. New racial and ethnic tensions, coupled with the uprooting and resettlement of old neighborhoods and the growth of new, widely different communities, had a disrupting effect. To counter the fragmentation that sometimes appeared to threaten the entire metropolis, individuals with similar special interests joined to form innovative associations, often of a sophisticated character. Others banded together to preserve and restore traditional values. The diversity of activity, though seemingly chaotic, offered a rich variety of open choices in self-expression and added to the quality of life in greater Rochester.

The public schools encountered all the city's demographic, metropolitan, and fiscal problems in their most acute form. Since the suburban migration removed more children than adults, the enrollments in the outer-ward schools declined, while the large but poor families settling in the inner city over-crowded its more aged schools. Attempts to rectify this situation by a linking of school districts brought loud protests from parents defending the integrity of their neighborhoods and blocked more forthright efforts to reduce the imbalance. The number of schools with predominantly nonwhite pupils increased from six to nine, but the development of a voluntary busing program opened opportunities for integrated education, as some twelve hundred black children traveled daily to outer-ward schools and, in time, several hundred more were bused to receptive suburban schools.

While promoting voluntary integration, the school board provided several new schools and developed programs to upgrade the quality of the educational experience. The integrated and innovative programs of the special World of Inquiry School and the School Without Walls—promoting a voluntary individual and team approach to the world at large and the city, respectively, as an incentive to the mastery of basic learning skills—and the collaboration with the Urban League's Project Uplift, all won national support and recognition. Efforts to meet the needs of Spanish-speaking pupils, and in the mid-seventies those of the children of Vietnamese refugees, evidenced the flexibility of the program. Despite serious outbreaks of disorder in several

Concept for a high-rise City-County Office Building straddling Exchange Street, which was to have "finished" the civic center. The building never advanced beyond the model stage, in part because of political differences between the two municipalities. Courtesy of City Historian's Office

168

Peace demonstrations at the University of Rochester and downtown, 1971-72. Courtesy of Local History Division, Rochester Public Library

schools, the increased number of nonwhites attending high school represented a real accomplishment.

The school board had early learned to respect neighborhood movements. It had long valued the contributions of strong PTAs, and when the inner-city schools failed to maintain active groups, the board made a deliberate attempt to organize parent advisory committees in each elementary school there. The board recognized the Rochester Teachers Association as a legitimate representative of its teachers and began to engage in collective bargaining shortly after the city took that step in 1961. Since several of the leading Rochester firms remained nonunion, the organized public workers and teachers quickly gained influence in local labor councils, with the teachers bringing a professional status to the movement.

The crucial importance of technical and professional training had spurred the rapid development of institutions of higher learning. The newly opened Community College and the relocated Rochester Institute of Technology, in Brighton and Henrietta, together with the increased facilities at St. John Fisher and Nazareth colleges in Pittsford, met some of greater Rochester's expanding educational needs. Five other colleges on the area's outer fringe also experienced new growth. None, however, rivaled the University of Rochester in its diversified facilities for scientific and professional study and research. Its eminence made the university a center for animated debate over civil rights in the mid-sixties and for antiwar demonstrations a few years later. The latter activity stirred some resentment among the friends of the several thousand Rochesterians serving on the battlefields of Indochina, where 225 lost their lives.

But the university's ties with the city were secure and the benefits mutual. These were especially evident in medicine, as graduates of the School of Medicine filled many posts in the seven area hospitals and numerous local health centers and comprised a major portion of the city's practicing physicians. The school's research facilities helped to maintain the high standard of medical care enjoyed by Rochesterians. The interlocking relationships between the courses in advanced science and technology at the university and the city's industrial specialties were also close.

It was, however, Colgate-Rochester Divinity School that now made the most dramatic response to local community challenges. Alerted by the widespread civil rights agitation of the fifties, the seminary had endeavored to recruit able black students. More than a score were enrolled in 1967, when several staged a sit-in demanding the appointment of black professors and black trustees. As a result, the school developed a black studies program in the field of religion that won wide commendation. The school maintained close ties with the liberal and civil rights movements in Rochester's Protestant churches, and in a bold extension of its new ecumenical policy, Colgate-Rochester reached an agreement with St. Bernard's Seminary for a joint program on Protestant-Catholic issues and views.

Holy Redeemer Church. Courtesy of Joseph W. Barnes

St. Stanislaus Church. Courtesy of Joseph W. Barnes

The Spiritualist Monument on the site of Plymouth Church, near Plymouth Avenue and Troup Street.

Some area churches had suffered an internal trauma when asked to back the Board of Urban Ministry's pledge of support for FIGHT. All survived that challenge, but several in the inner city succumbed as the suburban migration scattered their members to the towns where new churches welcomed them. In adjusting to these shifts, the Council of Churches, revising its charter, gave birth to the Genesee Ecumenical Ministries (GEM), a more inclusive organization that drew into active colloboration the Catholic Diocese as well as most Protestant denominational bodies and the newly formed United Church Ministry of black minority churches. The Jewish Community Federation, absorbed by concerns over Israel and other international issues, deferred affiliation.

GEM included the Board of Urban Ministry as a participating agency and formed a Judicial Process Commission to promote a concern for the welfare and rights of prisoners. Three inner-city churches merged as the Downtown United Presbyterians to serve their old neighborhood at Brick Church. Others sold or leased their edifices to new black congregations, and Minister Florence found a new home for his Central Church of Christ in the old First Presbyterian. Perhaps the most striking example of the grass roots resurgence in the religious field was the occupation and restoration of the century-old Leopold Street shule by the Church of God and Saints of Christ, a congregation of black Jews with ecumenical views.

Other cultural trends were similarly eclectic. The museum built the spectacular Strasenburgh Planetarium on its expanded campus, added new educational features, and changed its name to the Rochester Museum and Science Center. The International Museum of Photography increased its collections of photographs and films and made the George Eastman House a focus for specialists in its field the world over. A variety of specialized museums sprang up in the towns, among them the Genesee Country Museum in Mumford, with its cluster of historic houses and shops grouped around a spacious green simulating many aspects of early American village life. The new Margaret Strong Museum, still in the formative stage, cooperated with the Memorial Art Gallery in the preparation of special exhibits of Victorian folk art. The gallery added a new wing and expanded its exhibit and lecture programs. A half dozen private art galleries and three institutional art centers—the Wilson Art Center at the University, the Nazareth Art Center, and RIT's Bevier Gallery—provided additional exhibit areas. Annual Clothesline Shows on the gallery grounds and curbside shows on downtown streets attracted artists and craftsmen from near and far and created a festival atmosphere on long holiday weekends. The facilities of Midtown Plaza, Lincoln First, and the Xerox Auditorium and Square mounted varied exhibits, including the Rochester Peoples Exhibition, while the numerous displays and events commemorating the nation's Bicentennial spilled over into many stores.

In music, in addition to the scheduled perform-

Chapel of the State Industrial School, later known as "Assembly Hall" during Exposition Park days, as the "Stardust Ballroom" to a later generation, and finally as the "Edgerton Park Recreation Center." This remnant is all that remains of the old Industrial School complex. Courtesy of Joseph W. Barnes

A modern landmark: Temple Beth El on the city's southeast side, by architect Percival Goodman.

*Leopold Street Shul.
Located in Rochester's
near northeast, a section
which has traditionally
sheltered the city's most
recent immigrants, this
synagogue was erected by
Beth Israel Congregation
in 1886. Orthodox Jews,
chiefly from Poland,
arrived in Rochester later
than German Jews, but
there were enough to form
a minyan in 1867. The
near northeast has become
a heavily black-populated
section in the years since
World War II. Leopold
Street Shul has been
purchased and renovated
by a congregation of black
Jews, the Church of God &
Saints of Christ, Inc.
Courtesy of Joseph W.
Barnes*

ances of the Rochester Philharmonic Orchestra—at Eastman Theatre, at various suburban halls, and at the Highland Park Bowl—a chamber orchestra, the Oratorio Society, the Opera Theatre, and a number of popular bands provided a wide choice for varied tastes. In drama, in addition to occasional visits by Broadway shows and the periodic revival of summer theater, the Ge Va Theatre and Mime Workshop presented frequent performances of quality. Successive ethnic cultural festivals staged at the museum or at the new Manhattan Square supplied outlets for dramatic expression of a grass-roots character. Interested residents, choosing from the wide variety of programs listed in weekly cultural calendars, enjoyed such rich opportunities that comparative appraisals of the quality of life in large American cities have repeatedly rated Rochester near the top.

Such ratings have also judged the city's recreational opportunities for both spectators and participants as exceptional. In addition to the traditional seasons of baseball at Silver Stadium, soccer at Holleder Stadium, hockey in the War Memorial, and varied amateur sports in the parks, Rochester has witnessed an upsurge of private recreation in cycling and jogging, bowling and golf at numerous halls and courses, and skiing at thirty-five resorts in its snowbelt region. While motoring for pleasure—because of traffic and energy considerations—has become largely an accessory to other recreational objectives, motorboating and sailing on nearby lakes and bays has increased in popularity.

Though greater Rochester is still best characterized as a community of free-standing homes with its recreational and other domestic activities centering in the family and neighborhood, new trends are apparent here as well. The proliferation of radio and television sets, served by three commercial networks and a local public station, has reinforced the home setting but reduced the need for private yards—except, of course, among the ever-numerous garden lovers. The steadily increasing proportion of senior citizens has prompted the construction of many new highrise and condominium apartments to accommodate them, and both have contributed to the development of a new, more flexible life-style. The most striking manifestation of the new style has been increased popularity, among young and old alike, of dining out. A profusion of restaurants in the restoration areas of Park Avenue and Alexander Street, as well as downtown and on the outskirts, has provided new options for residents as well as visitors.

The most spectacular dining setting is that afforded by the Changing Scene restaurant atop the new First Federal building downtown. There, residents and visitors alike can enjoy a panoramic view of the entire metropolis. And while their eyes slowly circle the city, identifying office towers, massive industrial, commercial, and institutional blocks, and the highways fanning to the outskirts, they cannot help noting some interesting revivals of old Rochester: the statue of Mecury again on a lofty pedestal downtown, the Campbell-Whittlesey house and other Third Ward restorations, the three-tiered

roofs of the Powers Block, the new city hall in the dignified old Federal Building, the Upper Falls Park on old Falls Field overlooking the Main Falls. They cannot actually see the falls without a visit to that new park, but they will have a clear view of the Genesee stretching north and south and, in most seasons, of a surprising number and extent of patches of green grass and foliage bordering the river and cropping up at unexpected sites—a reminder of the city's rich agricultural and horticultural past, and a symbol of the ongoing, creative vitality of its inhabitants.

St. Luke's Church, where Nathaniel Rochester served as vestryman.

*St. Mary's Church on
Washington Square,
consecrated 1858.*

Images Of Rochester

Nineteenth century settler Edwin Scrantom placed a letter into the time capsule of the old City Hall and asked that it be opened at the end of the 20th century. He expressed his best wishes to the residents of the city, wrote of early Rochester and wondered what the future would bring. Rochester's founding pioneers would be proud to see the city as it enters its third century. Many of the infant industries of the nineteenth century have not only changed to meet the times, but have become leaders in their fields. The skyline that struck Nathaniel Hawthorne on his visit in the 1830s has become even more striking as new office headquarters and hotels are built. The city's museums attract thousands of visitors every year. The Genesee, once the workhorse that powered our early industries, is now opened to residents by a hike/bike trail. The old Genesee Valley Canal is a Trail as well. The mouth of the river empties into Lake Ontario offering peaceful boating and walking along the beach. The Erie Canal has become a major tourist attraction with new boat docks and facilities as well as a new generation of "canawlers." Scrantom's letters were replaced with messages from today's Rochesterians and placed in a new time capsule in the same cornerstone. Our grandchildren will inherit the city we preserve for them. Here is a pictorial glimpse of our historic Rochester.

The World Canals Conference met in Rochester in 2000, marking the 175th anniversary of the Erie Canal. People from all over the world came to ride on the canal and to learn of its impact on the history of New York state as well as America. Courtesy of City of Rochester

The Ontario Beach Carousel at Ontario Beach, originally carved by Gustav Dentzel, was restored during the Parks Centennial in 1988. Courtesy of City of Rochester

Rochester from the west looking across the Genesee River from behind the buildings facing West Main Street. First Federal Plaza stands on the left with the circular top that offers a panoramic view of the city. Across the river stands the Hyatt Hotel and Lincoln Tower to its right. The Main Street Bridge today, without the buildings that stood on it until the early 1960s, has remained central to Rochester's downtown. Courtesy of City of Rochester.

A colorful hot air balloon offers tethered rides during the city's Sesquicentennial in July 1984. Courtesy of City of Rochester

The atrium of City Hall. Photograph by Robert V. Fuschetto

The Powers Building reflected in the glass curtain of its newest neighbor, the Crossroads Building. Photograph by Robert V. Fuschetto

New lights, paving stone sidewalks, bus shelters and bus lanes, new trees and historical markers beautified Main Street in the late 1980s. Courtesy of City of Rochester

Gatehouse of Mount Hope Cemetery (1874-1875).
Photograph by Robert V. Fuschetto

Gravesite of Susan B. Anthony and her sister Mary, champions of women's rights. Photograph by Robert V. Fuschetto

Gravesite of Frederick Douglass, black abolitionist. Photograph by Robert V. Fuschetto

Eastman Quadrangle of the University of Rochester.
Photograph by Robert V. Fuschetto

Interior of the Memorial Art Gallery. Photograph by Robert V. Fuschetto

The Anthony home on Madison Street, maintained as a house museum by the Susan B. Anthony Memorial. Photograph by Robert V. Fuschetto

The International Museum of Photography at George Eastman House. Photograph by Robert V. Fuschetto

Above: Near the home of Susan B. Anthony at 17 Madison Street, a larger than life sculpture of Anthony and her friend, Frederick Douglass, was unveiled and dedicated on August 26, 2001, during the annual 19th Amendment Celebration co-sponsored by the Susan B. Anthony House and the Susan B. Anthony Neighborhood Association. The Celebration is held at Susan B. Anthony Square. Let's Have Tea, *sculpted by Pepsy M. Kettavong, portrays the friends discussing the many causes they supported most forcefully—the abolition of slavery and the right to vote. Courtesy of Studio America*

Left: Among the popular "Horses on Parade" project is Help Down Here On Earth, *created by Randy R. Rossow and dedicated to all the angels on earth. This horse is sponsored by Randy R. Rossow Enterprises, Inc. and Donna Borgus. The High Falls Brewing Company and Dixon Schwabl Advertising sponsored the project and auctioned more than 150 horses to raise over half a million dollars for local not-for-profit agencies. The horses were to be auctioned in 2001. Courtesy of Studio America*

The Laser Light Show has become a popular attraction as beams are projected onto the Genesee River gorge wall at High Falls in the Browns Race Entertainment District. Courtesy of City of Rochester

Douglas Road, one of many fine residential side-streets in the East Avenue Preservation District. Photograph by Robert V. Fuschetto

Headquarters of the Schlegel Corporation at 400 East Avenue, formerly the Sibley residence. Photograph by Robert V. Fuschetto

Home in the Third Ward Preservation District. Photograph by Robert V. Fuschetto

Canoeists paddle on the peaceful river near Veterans'
Memorial Bridge. Courtesy of City of Rochester

Leisure boats near the pivoting railroad bridge at the mouth
of the Genesee River. Courtesy of City of Rochester

*Rochester Red Wings' new Frontier Field in August
1997. Courtesy of City of Rochester*

*The Middle Falls gently cascades over rocks in one of the city's
remote peaceful areas. Courtesy of City of Rochester*

Crowds look forward to the colorful pansy bed displayed during the annual Lilac Festival at Highland Park. Courtesy of City of Rochester

Chapter

12

The Dawning of a New Century

In 1988 Rochester and Monroe County jointly celebrated the centennial of the Parks System. Before the Civil War, pioneers spent decades cutting down trees to clear land for homes and businesses as well as roads to other villages and shipping points along the river and lake. Their children and grandchildren, alarmed at the rapid disappearance of the wilderness where they had grown up, called for preservation of forests and setting aside of open spaces. The pioneers, too, had mourned the loss of particular trees, but they did not express the need for preservation until after the Civil War when the desire for open land was made a more pressing need by returning soldiers who played the new game baseball among the flower beds in neighborhood squares. The militia, too, marched in the squares and disturbed the tranquility. Though it was realized that land was important for both active and passive activities and that the city had grown to need more recreational space, the offer of twenty acres from Ellwanger and Barry Nursery was first turned down as being too expensive for the city to maintain. The gift was finally accepted in 1888 and became Highland Park, the nucleus of today's parks system.

The following year noted landscape architect Frederick Law Olmsted was hired. He identified the Genesee River as the central focus of the parks system. His working maps identified North Park (today's Maplewood and Seneca Parks) and South Park (today's Genesee Valley Park). Recognizing the need for both passive and active recreation, Olmsted planned trails that offered spectacular views of the river and forests. To add to the pastoral setting at Genesee Valley Park, Olmsted added a flock of sheep tended by a dog and shepherd. Canoeing, fishing and nature observing were within walking distance of the city.

Over the years the County's parks have expanded to more than 11,000 acres offering skiing, kayaking, canoeing, hiking, camping, fishing, bird watching, horseback riding, picnicking and outdoor concerts. At Highland Park, the city's Lilac Festival began as an occasional event in the first decade of the twentieth century. It was later called Lilac Sunday and has now become nationally acclaimed among flower lovers, attracting thousands of people for more than a week-long festival. Historically narrated wagon rides, craftsmen, tethered balloon rides, ponies, entertainers and food vendors add to the Lilac Festival's joyous atmosphere. Lamberton Conservatory shows its best plants and arrangements at this event.

Seneca Park Zoo has been redesigned to better accommodate the animals that include elephants, polar bears, large cats, seals, monkeys and more. Modern practices encourage having animals native to the zoo's climate, but visitors especially clamor for the elephants. Rochester has bred several animals in captivity, helping to preserve endangered species.

When Nickel and Penny, two popular polar bears purchased partly with the nickels and pennies of school children, died, their popularity prompted the replacement with two new, young polar bears.

The Sesquicentennial

By the time Nathaniel Rochester died, the One Hundred Acre Tract had grown to become a village. Though he didn't see it become a city in 1834, many of his fellow pioneers did. They celebrated the fruition of their vision of community, kept strong by dedicated pioneer families. Despite the nervousness experienced by pioneers as immigrants arrived with their own visions, each group brought its skills and leaders and contributed to the strength of the community.

When the city celebrated its centennial in 1934, it had not yet experienced some of its greatest challenges, though it was in the midst of the world's worst depression. The year presented an opportunity to review its past, its strengths and to plan its future. George Eastman passed on two years earlier, leaving his company, Kodak, in good hands and the community as beneficiary of much of his wealth. The city population was near its highest ever. "Rochester Made Means Quality" had overtaken the "Flower City" as a logo. Clothing manufacturing was a major industry

Crowds wander among the fragrant lilacs in May 1999 during the last Lilac Festival of the twentieth century. Since the first decade of the 20th century the festival has grown from Lilac Sunday to more than a week-long festival that attracts thousands from great distances. Courtesy of City of Rochester

being overtaken by photography and its support businesses. Italians were the largest immigrant group.

The apprehension some pioneers expressed for the future of Rochester during the Pioneer Festival in 1847, would have been alleviated if they had been present at the city's Sesquicentennial. Sesqui chairman and pioneer descendant Edward Peck Curtis, Jr., with Mayor Thomas P. Ryan, Jr., celebrated the "new blood" brought to the city since its founding by New Englanders and Pennsylvanians. The vision of Rochester had been recast numerous times to meet the changing needs of the residents. New populations including Blacks, Southeast Asians, Puerto Ricans and others have arrived since its centennial. While the population of the county has increased, the city's has decreased. Precision instruments and high-tech businesses grew while tourism, education and medical research took on new emphasis. The Genesee River powered its last waterwheel decades earlier and the Erie Canal gave up its freight to tractor trailers and railroads, carrying instead tourists and travelers seeking the leisure offered by boats forbidden to travel more than ten miles per hour.

What to celebrate of its 150 years? Certainly the canal's part in making Rochester the "Young Lion of the West" and assuring its role in Rochester's growing tourism market. People who traced their lineage to pioneer roots were presented a Pioneer Certificate

Lauren McCracken of McCracken Farms shares a seat with Andrew Wolfe of Wolfe Newspapers during the Lilac Festival parade in 1993. Courtesy of City of Rochester

The tugboat DeWitt Clinton *pushes the float in the Great Canal Caper in July 1984, the city's Sesquicentennial. Courtesy of City of Rochester*

by the Rochester Historical Society. Newer arrivals were celebrated in a number of ethnic festivals, plays and performances. The *Sketches of Rochester* by Henry O'Reilly, recognized as the city's first history, was reprinted from the 1838 edition along with the 1834 map of the city and an index. The arrival of the Tall Ships at Charlotte attracted thousands of visitors. Floral arrangements and gardens were exhibited all over the city. Historical markers were placed and Sesqui minutes were broadcast on radio and television.

The Ice Storm of 1991

It took Northeastern settlers years to get used to what came to be known as "lake effect" weather. Over the summer Lake Ontario, as a large body of water, gathers heat and holds it well into December, before cooling so much over the next few months that the warmth of spring is delayed—enough that the chance of frost lingers until May 26. What would have been spring rain turns to snow crossing Lake Ontario. It drops as snow near the lake before warmer air turns it back to rain.

Friendly rivalry between Buffalo and Rochester encouraged comparison of annual snowfall, but cities in the Northeast were unprepared for the great ice storm of March 1991. It became the storm of the century. Certainly modern weather predicting abilities and heavy equipment made Rochester better prepared than the city would have been seventy years earlier, however snow removal equipment was of little help in rescuing a city literally encased in ice. More disturbing was the damage to telephone and electric lines. Out-of-date utility maps were of little help to out-of-state utility repairmen brought in to speed the recovery of the Northeast. It was more than a week before utilities and communications were fully restored to the region. Schools were closed for a week in some areas. Many of the county's oldest trees were

damaged or destroyed by the weight of the ice. People willingly donated to restore the plantings. Predicted deep snows did little to unsettle the nerves of veteran Rochesterians. It is the unpredictable March weather that brought apprehension to all who remember the ice storm of 1991—the same weather that makes this area one of the greatest agricultural and fruit growing regions in the country.

A City of Culture and Education

Not far from Main Street the East End Cultural District showcases the Eastman Theatre built by Kodak founder George Eastman in 1922. Today, the Eastman School Library, dormitories and small retail shops are located there as well. Condominiums are tucked among some of the beautiful old homes now occupied by people returning to the city to live in the heart of culture and a vibrant urban lifestyle. A new YMCA anchors the site across Main Street from the Eastman Theatre. Not far away is the successful Geva Theatre where live performances attract large audiences.

The Margaret Woodbury Strong Museum has earned world-wide attention as a museum of popular culture. Built by the estate of Margaret Woodbury Strong to house her personal collection of dolls and toys, it greatly broadened her vision. It is visited annually by tens of thousands of people and attendees of conferences and lectures on history and popular culture.

Rochester Museum and Science Center expanded, reorienting the entrance to its complex of educational buildings, gardens and the planetarium. With an emphasis on science and technology, Rochester Museum & Science Center attracts thousands of visitors and students annually to its interactive exhibits, interprets regional history and offers classes. The Planetarium presents programs as well as educating the public about our universe.

Lamberton Conservatory in Highland Park is famous for its beautiful flowers and displays. It's a wonderful way to preview spring in the Flower City. Courtesy of City of Rochester

Piers calm the water at the mouth of the Genesee River. The railroad bridge is in the distance. The piers reduce the accumulation of sediment that once caused boats to run aground in the nineteenth century. Courtesy of City of Rochester

William Warfield grew up in Rochester and became a world famous baritone. He performed for the city's Sesquicentennial in 1984. Courtesy of City of Rochester

The Memorial Art Gallery joined its buildings through a beautiful addition between its main gallery and Cutler Union and includes the works of Pierre August Renoir and John James Audubon. Associated with the University of Rochester, the gallery also offers art education to the public.

The Rochester Historical Society, founded by the city's early pioneers, occupies the Silas O. Smith home on historic East Avenue. Its collection is one of the best in the region and includes letters, diaries, photographs, books, furniture and clothing arranged in the rooms of the home.

The Landmark Society of Western New York in historic Corn Hill offers tours of its buildings as well as of the Stone Tolan House, an eighteenth century inn built by Orringh Stone as a home and inn on East Avenue, once the road between the Falls settlement and Pittsford. The Society offers classes and guided and self-guided walking tours, and publishes books about the city's architecture, gardens, historic Mt. Hope Cemetery and the grand Erie Canal.

The International Museum of Photography at the George Eastman House has a vast collection of rare photographs and a research library.

The Susan B. Anthony House Museum has grown to include Anthony's sister's home as an educational center.

The local History Division of the Rochester Public Library has one of the most extensive collections of letters, diaries, manuscripts, maps, photographs and postcards in Western New York. Recently expanded, the library attracts many genealogists and researchers to study this collection.

Rochester's Strength—Its People

Rochester has always been a city that attracted new immigrants, whose skills and culture strengthened its place in New York state's economy. In the next few decades Hispanics will likely become one of the largest minority populations in the city. The Hispanic population grew by 48 percent in the 2000 census in Rochester and by 60 percent in the six county region including Monroe, Genesee, Livingston, Ontario, Orleans and Wayne counties. In Monroe County Hispanics comprise 5.3 percent of the population. Growth of the Hispanic community rose to 28,032 in the city and is attributed to an above-average birth rate as well as to newcomers from Puerto Rico and the New York City area.

The African American population remained the largest minority in the city comprising 39 percent of the population and 13.8 percent in the county. In 1990 the percentage of African Americans stood at 11.8 percent. The largest suburban African American population was in Henrietta at 6.9 percent followed by Gates at 6.4 percent.

The Asian population rose to 2.4 percent in the county, up 32 percent in the city alone, where the population stood at 4,943 in 2000. Their largest suburban population was in Brighton where Asians comprise 8 percent of the population. The total popu-

A bronze statue to fallen deputies of the Monroe County Sheriffs Department stands in front of the remodeled Hall of Justice on Exchange Street. Courtesy of Studio America

lation of the six-county region grew by twice the estimates to 3.4 percent of the 1990 figures or 1,098,201. Monroe County grew by 3 percent though no growth was predicted. The county attributed the unexpected six-county population increase to job growth that not only offset lay-offs and downsizing by major companies like Bausch & Lomb, Eastman Kodak and Xerox, but created new jobs as well.

The 2000 census revealed a continued downward trend in the city that began following World War II and the popular desire to have a house in the suburbs. In the past decade the population dropped by 5.1 percent to 219,773. The automobile made it possible

The University of Rochester Interfaith Chapel across the Genesee from the river trail. The riverside was the first site suggested as the location of the University in the nineteenth century. It was first situated near downtown before moving in the early twentieth century to the riverside. Courtesy of City of Rochester

Several new homes are ready to be occupied during the Home Expo 1997. Courtesy of City of Rochester

for people to move out of the city in search of larger home lots and the quiet of rural life after World War II. The expressways made commuting to city jobs from the suburbs manageable. In 2000 it was estimated that Rochester area workers spend eight hours of their work-week in cars commuting to and from their jobs, a small amount of time compared to most cities.

The growth of suburbs also brought a movement of retail shopping centers outside of the city.

Manufacturing, in search of growth space, sometimes located in the suburbs, attracting housing developments and retail, thus contributing to the city's declining population. While the inner ring of suburbs grew slightly or maintained population—Brighton and Greece grew by 3 and 4 percent respectively—a few outer ring suburbs experienced tremendous growth. Victor outpaced other suburbs with a 39 percent increase climbing to 9,977 while Webster climbed to 37,926—up about 6,300.

Suburbanites say they moved to more distant suburbs where less developed land is affordable even though the commute is greater. In some places, suburban growth has required reconstruction of sections of the expressway. The city government has worked to replace aged housing and invigorate communities and to reintroduce retail centers and grocery stores to neighborhoods. Neighborhood associations have flourished in numerous parts of Rochester.

Many people have moved into new and remodeled homes near downtown to be close to the cultural and entertainment center. City residents can enjoy movies, restaurants, nightclubs, bowling, baseball and hockey games and visiting entertainers, all within walking distance. Riverfront activities and hike/bike trails attract suburban residents who now find the city a vibrant center with numerous opportunities.

Vision 2010

In 1993 Rochester Urban League President William A. Johnson Jr. was elected mayor, succeeding Mayor Thomas P. Ryan Jr. Ryan was the first mayor elected under the restored strong mayor form of government after having served under the city manager system that was favored by George Eastman in the early part of the century.

Mayor William A. Johnson became the city's first African American mayor. As he entered his third term, Johnson listed among his accomplishments the city's first new comprehensive plan since 1964. "Rochester 2010: The Renaissance Plan" is a blueprint for the city's redevelopment. It includes 11 campaigns that include "center city" as the core of regional growth and planning. Citizen involvement is key to the mayor's plan for revitalizing aging neighborhoods and addressing the problems of education, employment, housing and poverty. With the five percent drop in the city's year 2000 population count and resultant reduced tax base, recognizing the "center city" as the heart of the region is critical to the economic health of the greater multi-county area.

In Mayor Johnson's tenure, many dilapidated

About 1990, then Mayor Thomas P. Ryan, Jr. opened the Home Expo in front of one of its showcase residences. The city's aggresive program of revitalizing neighborhoods has been very successful. Courtesy of City of Rochester

Mayor William A. Johnson, Jr. reads to children during Rochester's Day of Caring. Courtesy City of Rochester

houses have been removed, nearly 350 new homes have been constructed and more than 1,300 rehabilitated. Streets and parks have been rebuilt and residents have united in the successful Neighbors Building Neighborhoods Program. Several housing developments have been built such as First Place, Brown Street, West Square Manor and Susan B. Anthony Square. Many people have chosen to live downtown in refurbished older homes or newly-constructed condominiums, as in the East End. These residences are bought up as soon as they become available. People are attracted by the Rochester Philharmonic Orchestra, Little Theatre, Geva Theatre, Eastman Theatre, Frontier Stadium, museums, restaurants and nightlife.

The new Convention Center in July 1989. Courtesy of
City of Rochester

The Monument to Soldiers and Sailors in Washington
Square Park entered its third century as a memorial
to those who died during the Civil War in the country's
bitter battle to end slavery and preserve the Union.
Abraham Lincoln stands atop of the statue. Courtesy
of Studio America

Main Street before the mid-1980s reconstruction.
Courtesy of City of Rochester

Emphasis has been placed on attracting new jobs while retaining established businesses. Rochester's colleges play a major role in attracting companies seeking well-trained employees and facilities that offer additional training. Rochester Institute of Technology, University of Rochester, Monroe Community College, St. John Fisher College, Nazareth College, Roberts Wesleyan College, Empire State College and business schools like Rochester Business Institute offer a broad range of career training and continuing education courses.

A growing number of tourists come to Rochester attracted by music and theatre, fine museums, the laser light show at the Browns Race Entertainment District and the Erie Canal.

Rochester's Neighborhoods

George Eastman's quip that Rochester is a good place to live and raise a family is as true today as when he said it nearly a century ago. Almost 220,000 people make Rochester their home. The city offers many different lifestyles from condos on the lake to downtown loft apartments to sprawling 4,000 square-foot-homes.

Rochester's growth follows the Genesee River, revealing that Rochester's infancy depended upon waterpower. Many of the city's neighborhoods were once early riverside settlements that grew into one another and became absorbed by the growing city.

Mayor Johnson's Vision 2010 Plan initiated in 1994, created Neighbors Building Neighborhoods, through which more than 2,000 citizens from across the city joined in planning their own neighborhoods divided into ten Sectors. Many Sectors encompassed what had been several smaller neighborhoods in the city's early history. Citizen planning enabled each neighborhood to maintain the unique character for which the city is known.

Moving counter clockwise from Rochester's earliest settlement, *Sector One* began at the Charlotte neighborhood. Though it was annexed in 1916, the residents identify themselves as from Charlotte. First settled by the Hinchers in 1792, the mouth of the Genesee River at Charlotte was designated by New York State as an official harbor in 1805. In 1822 the first lighthouse was built, with a keeper's house added on in 1856. The Hinchers and Tory Walker were nearly the only residents at the mouth of the river when the British landed marines onshore to forage for food during the War of 1812. Tying up the owners of a warehouse to prevent them from sending off an alarm, the British marines took their supplies, gave a receipt and left without harming the prisoners.

In another incident, the British ship entered into the river nearly to the Lower Falls where it evidently intended to again send marines to forage. A test shot fired by the British was misinterpreted by the handful of ragtag Rochester settlers who managed to set up a 40-pound cannon overlooking the river. The Rochester citizen returned fire though he had not received orders, but the British ship was out of range for the small American cannon. Colonel Isaac Stone

was so angry at the canoneer for alerting the British of their presence that he had to be restrained from attacking him with a sword.

The Americans once scared off a British ship that thought better of landing its marines, when what appeared to be scores of waiting American militia were actually a handful of Rochester's half-uniformed settlers who marched on the beach, disappeared into the woods, and reappeared in a continuous line, a seemingly endless number of soldiers.

Charlotte was a busy pioneer port and as the city grew its docks and warehouses grew busier. Two landings further upriver at Carthage and Hanford's Landing eventually took away some of the business, but it remained closely tied to shipping into the early twentieth century. Pleasure craft crowded the port and marinas. In the late 1990s Charlotte began to get a facelift including rebuilt streets and brick sidewalks and upgraded dock and harbor areas. In 2002 the 994-foot Colonel Patrick O'Rorke lift bridge will replace the Stutson Street Bridge that carries westbound travelers across the Genesee River from Pattonwood Drive to the Lake Ontario Parkway.

The Ontario Beach Park was refurbished during the Park Centennial in 1988. Period streetlights, a boardwalk and gazebo were built. The now century-old historic carousel carved by Gustav Dentzel was restored. Beach-goers walk the boardwalk and watch young people play volleyball, lie in the sun, build sandcastles or listen to the waves crash against the rocks. Some stroll out on the pier to the new lighthouse. Restaurants at the end of Lake Avenue serve lake-goers and the faithful residents tasteful food and popular Friday night fish fries. Abbots serves the popular local soft ice cream and yogurt to large crowds in season. On Wednesdays crowds gather at the beach to hear bands and philharmonics play through the evening. Bicyclists and strollers enjoy the music as it drifts in the breeze that cools Charlotte by as much as ten degrees compared to the city just six miles to the south.

River Street was once lined with busy bars that supported a rowdy nightlife. Today it is a quiet area. Beach Avenue boasts large beautiful houses that view the lake, while in walking distance of the beach other streets are filled with family homes, screened-in porches and backyards that often host barbecues.

In 2001 what may have been the oldest tree in the city was cut down when damage it sustained from two lightning strikes made it too dangerous to let stand. Pieces of the historic tree were preserved in area museums including nearby Charlotte-Genesee lighthouse which is today preserved by the Historical Society that bears its name.

Moving counterclockwise on the west side of the river is *Sector Two*, the upriver Maplewood neighborhood to the south of Charlotte. In the 1870s crowds attended harness races at Driving Park and watched baseball games played on the field inside the track. The Lower Falls marked the end of navigation from the mouth of the river at Charlotte. Schooners once carried goods and passengers to the landing there. Runaway slaves had boarded ships

Onlookers watch as the tall ship Bounty *sails into the harbor at Charlotte in the summer of 1997. Courtesy of City of Rochester*

A mounted patrolman watches over sun bathers at Lake Ontario Beach, Charlotte. Courtesy of City of Rochester

here or made their way to freedom in Canada. Frederick Douglass escaped to Canada in 1859 narrowly avoiding arrest following John Brown's attack on the arsenal at Harpers' Ferry, Virginia.

The Glen House was a popular restaurant where people could dine and dance, arriving by streetcar and being lowered by a fitful elevator or descending over 200 steps. Boaters arrived over the quiet waters on canoes or large passenger boats that carried them on day excursions. Near the peaceful restaurant were the water-powered factories on the brink of the Lower Falls. Maplewood Park along the west side of the river's bank was designed in 1888 by famous landscape architect, Frederick Law Olmsted. Today over 300 specimen roses attract visitors to a June festival. A hike/bike trail that crosses a pedestrian bridge to the eastside Seneca Park near the Seneca Park Zoo gives visitors a spectacular view.

Nestled in the heart of the Maplewood neighborhood are Nazareth Academy, Sacred Heart Academy and Aquinas Institute. An annual house tour invites visitors into many of the historic and renovated homes along the tree-lined streets. Just as it did more than a century ago, Lake Avenue offers convenient access to work downtown and shops nearby.

Sector Three centered on the west side of the Genesee River includes several of the most historic sections of the city including parts of Frankfort and what is now Edgerton, Lyell-Otis, Susan B. Anthony, Dutchtown, and Brown Square. Brown Square, originally set aside as a court house square, remains a neighborhood park in what was once Matthew and Francis Brown's 200-acre Frankfort tract. Blasting out a raceway from stone, workmen drew waterpower from above the High Falls, creating the most powerful industrial area in the Genesee River Valley. The Frankfort Tract joined the One Hundred Acre Tract to become a part of Rochesterville in 1817. Brown's Race was a bustling center of Rochester's water-pow-

ered industries before electricity untethered them from the river. The area remained a working industrial section into the twentieth century. The Platt Street Bridge that spanned the river at the falls carried vehicles between the east side brewery and Falls Field to industries on the west side. In the 1970s it was closed to vehicles and renamed Pont de Rennes after Rochester's first Sister City in Rennes, France. On the meadow below the bridge, Rochester Gas & Electric operated a coal gasification plant. Kodak's headquarters stands nearby on State Street at the head of Platt Street.

Sam Patch leaped from the brink of the Falls on Friday the 13th in November 1829, on the site of Parson's Sawmill. Trains still cross the river where once they slowed to point out to passengers where Sam Patch made his fateful leap. A factory built there later to manufacture steam gauges and railroad lanterns burned in a serious fire that claimed 29 lives as people jumped from windows to escape smoke and flames. Firefighters had difficulty reaching the island factory. Today the remains of the shoe manufacturer that replaced it, stands at the Falls.

Dutchtown was named for the German settlers who made the neighborhood their home in the mid- to late- nineteenth century. They brought with them skills in brewing, baking, woodworking, gear cutting and precision instruments. German language newspapers, school lessons and church services made the culture strange to Rochesterians, but the Germans quickly assimilated. Their arrival in the midst of the Temperance movement was untimely, as the brewery skills they brought with them increased the number of breweries from about five to fifteen in a short time. Still, all those breweries combined produced fewer barrels than Rochester's single High Falls Brewery today. Dutchtown is now a quiet neighborhood of small, neatly-kept homes.

The hike/bike trail along the Genesee River invites everyone to enjoy the outdoors. Courtesy of City of Rochester

The High Falls was the city's greatest source of industrial water power in the nineteenth century. The Gorsline Building on the right has been demolished to its foundation as an entertainment area. Courtesy of City of Rochester

While removing rubble from the burned-out Triphammer Mill at Browns Race, a bulldozer operator discovered the original wheel below the mill floor. It was restored and is displayed in its original wheel well inside the remaining stone walls. Courtesy of City of Rochester

The Susan B. Anthony House at 17 Madison Street anchors the neighborhood where she once lived with her sister Mary and next door to sister Hannah. Anthony worked for women's rights as well as abolition of slavery and temperance. Her sister Mary, was Rochester's first female school principal, having been a city schoolteacher for years. What is today Susan B. Anthony Square was first named Mechanics' Square, reflecting the occupations of workingmen of the neighborhood. Much of the architectural character of the frame and brick homes with fenced-in yards is preserved. Anthony often "marched" down the sidewalk to exercise and maintain the physical demands of her career.

Benches nestled among the gardens invite residents to stroll the concrete paths that criss-cross the park. A life-size statue of Frederick Douglass and Susan B. Anthony sitting at tea recalls discussions that must have taken place more than a century ago on civil rights and freedoms that we enjoy today. The pair met often until Douglass' death.

Across West Main Street are apartments and affordable homes recently built in a development named for the women's rights crusader.

The Edgerton neighborhood runs from Lyell to Driving Park and is hemmed in by the river and the old canal bed that is now the route of West Broad Street. The neighborhood was once the site of the Western House of Refuge, a girls and boys reformatory. When that state institution relocated to rural Rush, the site became Exposition Park which housed a museum and historical offices as well as exhibits. It was later named Edgerton Park.

A sprinkling of large homes are nestled among small two bedroom houses. The neighbors can stroll through Edgerton, Tacoma or Jones parks where gardens and benches invite a peaceful respite from the busy day. Children from the neighborhood often play, especially at Jones Square where once the early militia drilled and rugged baseball players "ripped the hide off the balls" and played without protective equipment.

Sector Three includes the Lyell-Otis neighborhood that stretches from the old subway bed where the old Erie Canal once flowed to the modern Canal where boats can be seen throughout the season. Lyell Avenue on the south and Driving Park on the north define this neighborhood.

Sector Four on the city's southwest side is bordered by West Main and the Genesee River. It includes today's neighborhoods of Mayor's Heights, Plymouth-Exchange, Genesee-Jefferson and the Nineteenth Ward. Businesses and small industries line some of the main streets while the neighborhood streets offer a variety of housing. The sector pulls together a diverse racial and cultural mix. While many homes are in need of repair, most have been updated and restored, including hardwood floors and trim as well as stained and leaded glass features that add character to the area.

Many are attracted to the original Sibley Tract homes of the Nineteenth Ward because of their beauty and size as well as their proximity to the

The Susan B. Anthony House and Museum now includes an educational center in the home of Ms. Anthony's sister, Hannah. Courtesy of City of Rochester

Genesee Valley Park and historic Erie Canal, the airport and expressway and the University of Rochester.

Sector Five includes the One Hundred Acre Tract, the nucleus of today's city of Rochester. While the first permanent settler lived on the site of today's Powers' Building at the Four Corners downtown, the oldest residential neighborhood was built by wealthy millers and industrialists.

Named Corn Hill after the fields of corn once grown there, beautiful mansions and carriage houses sprang up in their places. These entrepreneurs lived only a short distance from their businesses and overlooked the river that powered their mills and the Erie Canal that carried their goods in and out of the city. The downtown includes retail, business, banks, law offices, City Hall and the County Office Building which sits on the site of Colonel Rochester's chosen Court House Square. Some of the most important events in the city's history occurred in this Sector. The old Erie Canal passed through until 1919, after which its bed gave way to a more modern subway

Above: The Sam Patch *passes under one of three bridges designed by the firm of Frederick Law Olmsted when the Erie Canal was relocated to Genesee Valley Park in 1918. Courtesy of City of Rochester*

Below: The Corn Hill Festival is one of many neighborhood festivals that attract hundreds of people. Each festival is noted for its own attractions, arts, crafts and foods. Courtesy of City of Rochester

system. During urban renewal in the 1960s many of the old deteriorated mansions were torn down, but bold citizens moved into some of the homes and rehabilitated them with money and sweat equity. Where the neighborhood has been restored and is now the pride of the city, many of its residents could no longer afford to live in what are now desirable, historic homes. The community is further enhanced by recent development along the river where a new marina, condominiums and small retail shops and restaurants attract tourists and new residents to downtown.

New improvements also include riverbank parks at the aqueduct, walk/bike trails, historic markers and public docks at Corn Hill Landing that invite boaters and tourists to dine and shop at new businesses built among the newly-constructed apartments and condominiums. *Sam Patch*, the nineteenth century replica canal boat, carries a few thousand tourists and school children on the river and canal every season from May through October. Often, period actors retell the city's history through on-board skits.

A little farther north of the docks, the Community War Memorial with its newly-remodeled design, anchors the west side of the city. Historic markers inform downtown pedestrians of the city's rich history and point out the Broad Street bridge that once served as the second Erie Canal aqueduct.

On the east side of the river, development has boomed at Court and Broad Streets where several new buildings including Blue Cross/Blue Shield, Frontier Telephone, Clinton Square, Bausch & Lomb and the expanded Rochester Public Library have markedly changed the skyline of two decades ago. Bausch & Lomb's decision to build their international headquarters downtown sparked much new development.

Main Street was rebuilt with wide streets, new lights, a large accommodating Convention Center, sidewalks of paving stones and historic markers set on angled granite pedestals. The Main Street bridge was improved by the wrought iron rails of noted artist Albert Paley who also designed the gates at Village Gate and the beautiful metal sculpture depicting the Genesee River, placed by Bausch & Lomb in front of their downtown headquarters.

What was once the nineteenth century industrial hub is now the historic Browns Race Entertainment District at High Falls where refurbished old mills and factories house night clubs, restaurants, shops, offices and apartments. A museum in the nineteenth century Holly Pump Works (the city's downtown fire hydrant pump, now nearby), informs the public and students through interactive displays, exhibits and public presentations.

Sector Six on the city's southern end includes the neighborhoods of Swillburg, South Wedge, Ellwanger and Barry, Highland and Strong. Swillburg wears its name with pride today, though prior to its development as a residential neighborhood it was literally a gathering of pigsties where German and Irish farmers kept pigs fed on the swill and garbage they collected. The Highland Diner, an old-fashioned dining car restaurant, features a swill burger on its menu.

In the South Wedge, many popular restaurants and businesses make for a pleasant stroll through the neighborhood of neatly kept homes and apartments. Several small parks as well as a boat launch across the river from the new Corn Hill marina add to the neighborhood's appeal.

Named for the internationally-known nursery, the Ellwanger and Barry neighborhood now includes some of the city's finest architecture and cottage homes. Highland Park, the nucleus of the city's historic park system was created on 20 acres donated by Ellwanger and Barry in 1888. Today the enlarged Highland Park attracts thousands of people in May to the Lilac Festival where they see over 500 varieties of lilacs.

The Strong neighborhood offers young students and medical interns housing within walking distance of the University of Rochester and Strong and Highland Hospitals.

Near downtown, *Sector Seven* includes the Atlantic-University neighborhood referred to as the Neighborhood of the Arts, where comfortable homes are sprinkled among the Memorial Art Gallery, Visual Studies Workshop, George Eastman House, the city's public School of the Arts and Village Gate

The Vietnam Veterans Memorial at Highland Park brings people to honor and remember local soldiers who gave their lives during the Vietnam War. Courtesy of City of Rochester

Above: What was once an old factory, "Village Gate" has been transformed into a center for artists' studios, small restaurants and art shops. Located in the new University Avenue Arts area, the Visual Studies Workshop, the International Museum of Photography at George Eastman House, the city's School of the Arts High School and the Memorial Art Gallery are all located here. The gates were the work of noted sculptor Albert Paley. Courtesy of Studio America

Above: Nineteenth century residents commented that the river offered sanctuary and peace within the city's limits. Fishermen enjoy a beautiful day at the Lower Falls. Courtesy of City of Rochester

Left: Winter and summer Annie Mattingly offers Italian sausage, hot dogs, vegetarian burgers and snacks to downtown workers and shoppers. Her stand in front of the Rochester Public Library adds to the colorful, vibrant, urban atmosphere. Courtesy of Studio America

Square which draws artists' studios and shops. Pearl-Meigs, and parts of Monroe offer large, well-kept homes for single families and apartment dwellers. Park Avenue and Monroe neighborhoods offer unique shops and sidewalk cafes where the residents stroll from their homes and apartments summer and winter. Cobbs Hill and Upper Monroe neighborhoods include Cobb's Hill Park where one of the city's reservoirs displays a beautiful fountain. One of the most spectacular views of the city can be had from this hill. Many people walk around the reservoir and through the park. Cobb's Hill was the site of a pioneer clay brick factory, a World War II German prisoner of war camp and housing for returning American veterans. Lake Riley, today a popular pond, was once the western wide waters on the Erie Canal. Canal boat families often wintered in their boats.

East Avenue was the city's pride with large, private mansions and a wide street shaded by a canopy of trees. Many prominent businessmen including George Eastman made their homes on East Avenue. In the nineteenth century sleigh bells on horses jingled as people visited neighbors on holidays. Today East Avenue is the showcase for beautiful architecture in homes and condominiums.

Sector Eight includes expansive homes, large lawns and mature trees of the old Browncroft neighborhood that once included the Brown Brothers Nursery as well as the modest homes built when returning GIs traded their uniforms for their own home and a white picket fence. Homestead Heights and Beechwood neighborhoods offer many family-sized homes being remodeled and updated. Many businesses, shopping strips and small manufacturers line East Main Street. The Culver-Winton neighborhood is tied to the Culver merchants area by Merchants Road. A building-side mural reflects the character of the Culver-Merchants neighborhood. Residents walk to James Brown's Restaurant for a bite, Johnny's Smoke-free Irish Bar for a quiet drink with close friends or Calabrese's Bakery where they purchase bread or cakes and cookies to take home.

Sector Nine in the northeast portion of the city, is known simply by its post office designated zip code 14621. In this, and parts of Sector Ten, many of Rochester's successive waves of immigrants made their homes. Many of the city's older businesses and factories operate here among new start-up and support industries offering residents opportunities for employment. North Clinton, affectionately known as "La Avenida," reflects the Hispanic neighborhood's character including Hispanic restaurants and businesses.

The Rochester School for the Deaf on St. Paul Street at the river has earned a national reputation after more than a century teaching the deaf and the community about the hearing impaired. Farther north on the river is the Seneca Park Zoo at Seneca Park, one of the parks designed by Frederick Law Olmsted. Nearby Durand Eastman Park offers a view of the lake and the peace brought by the sound of crashing waves.

Rochester has always had a public market or two, but the oldest, built in 1905, now attracts bargain

The city's revitalized public market where people get bargains on everything from crafts and clothing to fresh farm produce and flowers. Public markets have been favorite city gathering places since its settlement. Courtesy of City of Rochester

hunters to its North Union Street location. North Marketview Heights and south Marketview Heights took their names from this public market. Fresh fruits and vegetables in season, fish and small animals, fresh baked bread and pastries as well as flea market items and clothing can be found there. Much of the old housing nearby has been replaced with new homes and developments.

The Upper falls neighborhood, included in *Sector Ten*, has been the home of waves of immigrants from the Irish neighborhoods through the Germans, Italians, African-Americans and more recently, Hispanics. Many of the Southeast Asians who also recently immigrated, live in the South Wedge. The city has attracted businesses and a major grocery store and has revitalized many of the neighborhood homes. In several places large urban gardens reflect the culture and hard work of the neighbors.

Rochester offers a neighborhood for every lifestyle. Many of the neighborhoods hold festivals and street fairs that allow the neighbors to get to know one another. They work together through their neighborhood associations to keep their community well maintained. Eastman's observation is as true today as it was a century ago—Rochester is a good place to live and raise a family.

The Genesee River attracted Rochester's first settlers and has remained the focal point of the city's planning through Rennaisance 2010. Kayakers take advantage of the rapids near the Broad Street Bridge in downtown Rochester. Courtesy City of Rochester

Colgate Rochester Divinity School near Highland Park in the summer of 1996. Courtesy City of Rochester

Chapter

13

Chronicles of Leadership

Cities are born in many places and grow for many reasons. They develop near harbors, rivers, and canals because of the waterpower; they become waystations on natural trails that are handy as commercial arteries; they grow in verdant valleys, which form fertile pastures for farmer's produce and livestock. Rochester was born and grew for many of these reasons and the character of its industry tells the story best of all.

The city was born on the Genesee River because water power was needed for its wheat mills; the wheat from the Genesee Valley was ground into the finest flour known in the United States at that time.

The Erie Canal was soon built; making it easier to transport flour from east to west; it also brought people and goods into Rochester from the east, and the city soon became America's first great boom town. As the decades advanced, artisans of many kinds came and stayed, They liked the little valley city and its citizens. They used their skills in many kinds of industries, some of which eventually replaced milling as king.

In almost every era in Rochester's history, one or two industries have grown to maturity and, assured of the region's prospering economy, have made the city renowned for a particular field of production. This began with the flour industry, and has continued with many others: flowers, seeds and shrubs, shoes, machine tools, pianos, men's clothing, optical instruments, photographic equipment and, finally, office copying machinery and electronics.

Modern Rochester enjoys a worldwide reputation for quality—particularly in its production of photographic equipment, optics, office copiers, and machine tools. These industries, together with scores of others, have helped forge a community outstanding for its industrial production, dedicated to education and culture, and famous for the success of its philanthropic organizations. Industry, which came first, has made all of the rest possible.

BAUSCH & LOMB

For 150 Years—Helping People See the Wonders of their World.

When John Jacob Bausch and Henry Lomb pooled their resources to open a small optical shop in the Reynolds Arcade building in 1853, they shared great confidence in the future of the Rochester community. They also held a fundamental belief that helping people to better see the wonders of their world would be a rewarding business in every sense of the word. Nearly 150 years later, Bausch & Lomb's success as one of the oldest continuously-operating companies in America is evidence that their confidence was justified and their business strategy was sound.

Commitment to new product development has been a hallmark of the company's operations since the beginning. But new product development has changed a lot since those early days. After starting their business selling optical goods imported from Europe, Bausch found a piece of hard rubber in the street and wondered if the material could be used for eye-

Bausch & Lomb's product portfolio comprises a broad range of products to fill every eye care need.

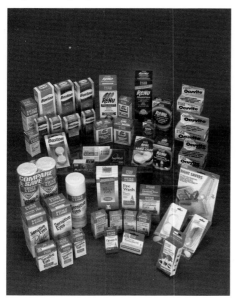

Company founders John Jacob Bausch (left) and Henry Lomb remained friends and partners throughout their lives.

glass frames. Experimenting on his kitchen stove, he ultimately created a process to mold the material, called Vulcanite, into eyeglass frames. The new frames were less expensive than gold-filled wire frames and more durable than those made of horn. This innovation revolutionized the optical business, making spectacles available for the first time to people who previously had been unable to afford the more expensive glasses of the day.

While Bausch was absorbed with growing the new business, Lomb enlisted in the 13th Regiment of New York Volunteers and went off to fight for his new country in the Civil War. After attaining the rank of Captain, he mustered out in 1863 and returned to Rochester to head the company's sales organization, while Bausch and his sons focused on research and manufacturing.

Early product introductions and patents earned by the company included microscopes, photographic lenses and camera shutters, binoculars and telescopes. World War I saw B&L expand to production of range-finders and searchlights for

military use, and by World War II the company was recognized as the leading producer of optical glass and instruments for government use. Ophthalmic and scientific instruments were the heart of the company's product line for decades.

Throughout the 20th century, Bausch & Lomb marked a number of significant achievements including the introduction of the classic aviator-style Ray-Ban sunglass; receipt of an "Oscar" from the Motion Picture Academy of Arts and Sciences for the development of the Cinemascope movie projection lens; introduction of the first soft contact lens; development of lenses used in the guidance systems for Polaris missiles, camera lenses that took the first satellite pictures of the moon; and telescopes used in the joint USA-USSR Soyuz-Appollo space mission.

Over the decades, as Bausch & Lomb prospered, the company renewed and reinforced its commitment to Rochester. As young immigrants, Bausch and Lomb never lost their affection for their native Germany—but they immediately and enthusiastically pledged their allegiance to the country and community that had become their home. Symbols of their early generosity still exist today. Lomb Memorial Drive on the Rochester Institute of Technology campus honors Henry Lomb's vision as a founder of the Mechanics Institute, the forerunner of today's R.I.T. The central building of the Rochester Museum and Science Center, Bausch Hall, sits on land donated by Edward Bausch. Today there are Bausch & Lomb buildings on the campuses of both R.I.T. and the University of Rochester. The downtown central library houses many of its important public services in a new Bausch & Lomb library building; the Bausch Street Bridge still carries traffic near the company's former factory site on St. Paul Street—where a monument to

Henry Lomb, dedicated by the city's German-American community, stands.

Even more significant, perhaps, than buildings and monuments, are two programs that have benefited the Rochester community for years.

Upon returning from service in the Civil War, Captain Lomb wanted to be sure that Rochester's children understood and appreciated the importance of good citizenship. In 1889, he initiated the Transfer of Flags ceremony in which exemplary students in each city school are designated as Standard Bearers and given responsibility to care for their school's American flag for the year. In recognition of their outstanding citizenship, each Standard Bearer receives a medal from Bausch & Lomb—a tradition which has continued for more than a century.

Believing that education, particularly in the sciences, is key to success, Bausch & Lomb founded

Integrated optical systems from Bausch & Lomb allow the ophthalmic surgeon to tailor surgical procedures to address the unique characteristics of each patient's eyes.

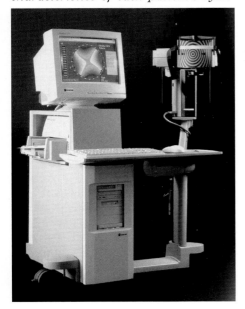

Bausch & Lomb's world headquarters building in downtown Rochester opened in 1995. Incorporated throughout the facility are masterworks by local artists and objects representative of B&L's global operations.

the Bausch & Lomb Science Award Program in 1933, to encourage and recognize academic achievement in science. Today, more than 800 schools around the country each present the Bausch & Lomb Science Award to their top science student, who then becomes eligible to receive financial scholarship assistance to study at the University of Rochester.

Bausch & Lomb also continues its partnership with the University of Rochester through a collaborative effort to advance scientific knowledge in the field of ophthalmology, and to establish Rochester as one of the nation's top eye care centers for research and clinical care. The company has made a multi-year, multi-million dollar commitment to recruit new academic and clinical research scientists; provide the latest in technology and equipment; develop new technology for vision care, correction and enhancement; and provide superior clinical care in ophthalmology for Rochester-area residents.

Today, Bausch & Lomb is the world's preeminent technology-based health care company for the eye, dedicated to helping consumers see, look and feel better. Its global businesses include contact lenses and lens care products, prescription and over-the-counter eye medications, and products for the ophthalmic surgeon. Led by Bausch & Lomb, the most respected name in eye care, the company's family of brands includes PureVision, SofLens66, Boston, ReNu, Technolas, Zyoptix, and Ocu-Vite. With annual sales of about $2 billion and approximately 12,000 employees worldwide, the company has operations in more than 35 countries and its products are available in more than 100.

Bausch & Lomb's corporate vision is to be number one in the eyes of the world. It's a vision that John Jacob Bausch and Henry Lomb would surely have endorsed. And it's a company of which they would certainly be proud.

BERGMANN ASSOCIATES

Preserving the buildings and spaces that make up a city's history requires care and sensitivity to the elements being preserved as well as to their present uses. So does creating structures that will become worthwhile parts of its future history. This has been the challenge gratefully accepted in Rochester by Donald Bergmann for more than four decades, and by Bergmann Associates for more than two. Bergmann, a structural engineer and urban planner, is principal in charge of the consulting architectural and engineering firm founded in 1980.

Bergmann Associates has been involved in maintaining, as well as turning to new uses, some of the oldest structures in Rochester.

Key among these are a number of bridges and right-of-ways associated with the original route of the Erie Canal. Bergmann cites as an example the Broad Street Bridge over the Genesee River, the only double-decker bridge in the area. Supported by stone arches, it was built in the early 1800s. When the canal was shifted away from the center of Rochester around 1944, the bridge became part of a trolley-line right-of-way and a street was built above it. The trolley followed the 40-foot wide abandoned canal 36 miles from

Canal Ponds Business Park.

Jonathan Child House, built 1835.

Broad Street to Lake Ontario.

In 1961, the eastern part of the route was co-opted for an expressway, while the lower level of the bridge and points north were converted for use by an industrial railroad connecting downtown buildings with the lake. In 1970, Don Bergmann and several of his staff were involved in an expressway alignment that included designing five new state-of-the-art concrete support bridges. Most recently, the firm did preliminary engineering for three miles of the expressway plus design of two large interchanges.

In the years that followed, the industrial railroad was gradually abandoned. In 1981, Bergmann Associates was hired to prepare a study examining putting the trolley back in place. That idea was voted down.

Even so, the structure has required continuous restoration, as have other similarly historic bridges in the area. "Court Street, Andrews Street,

Main Street and Broad are the oldest and most historic. They all have the stone arches, and we've done a lot of work reinforcing and restoring them as they moved through associations with row houses (along Main), parks and the farmers' market," notes Bergmann. For the similarly historic Ford Street Bridge, Bergmann has done three restorations over the years, including rebuilding its four towers.

Other structures related to the canal and to railroads such as the Erie and Lakawana came under Bergmann's care. These have included two major renovations of Veteran's Memorial Bridge, a huge arch bridge maintained by the State of New York, and redesign and construction work on the Old Erie and Lakawana freight house, finally torn down in 1996.

At the Rochester Harbor, Bergmann handled rebuilding of walls, renovation of bridges, parks and waterways, beach restoration including parking, access, and provision for a new restaurant and river boat bases. Plans in various stages include a new ferry system to Toronto, Ontario, Canada and a double-leaf rolling bascule lift bridge across the boat harbor. The bridge, replacing an old one at Stutson Street, would be the largest of its kind in the United States. Bergmann's role includes design of the movable bridge and two fixed approach spans, as well as machinery, control systems and power supply. The firm provided a complete vessel collision analysis, and designs for construction of a new arterial roadway, reconstruction of interchanges and a mainline parkway, and a new marina access drive with a municipal parking lot.

Standing as one of the foremost buildings, Bergmann has restored is the Jonathan Child House, built in 1835 for Rochester's first mayor and the husband of Nathaniel Rochester's daughter. It is a block from city hall and listed in the National Register of Historic Places, comprising with the adjacent Brewster-Burke House, the Jonathan Child National Historic District.

The Lodge at Woodcliff.

Broad Street Bridge.

Bergmann bought the house in 1987 to provide office space for its architecture, interior design, and site development groups. Restoring it became a glowing tribute to the use of fine old buildings in a modern world, as well as a demonstration of the firm's skills and respect for the past.

The resident groups, plus Bergmann's mechanical and electrical engineers, worked with the New York State Historic Preservation office to develop a comprehensive restoration program. They converted the twin front parlors, each with antique, cut-glass chandeliers and black and gold Italian marble fireplaces, into their formal conference room. The unused third floor was restored under strict guidelines to house the architectural services group, and the basement was structurally stabilized and remodeled as a survey area.

New infrastructure included a special lighting system that received an Award of Merit from the Illuminating Engineering Society. On the exterior, the five 30-foot tall Corinthian columns across the front portico were restored and repaired. This included replacing deteriorated metal and wood pieces of the ornate column caps with exact replicas made of fiber-

glass, repairing or replacing the column shafts, and designing new bases to prevent moisture from getting into the column interiors. The stucco covering the house was repaired and painted; color analysis achieved a close match with the original color. Other exterior work included repairs to the wooden cornice, restoration of the side porticos with their 11-foot tall Ionic columns, and a new northeast chimney.

Bergmann, needing more space, moved to other quarters in 2000, but the building remains a prime office site.

Similarly, the firm's engineers took offices in the former headquarters of the Pittsburgh-Erie Railroad Company in 1982. That building dates to the late 1800s when its southern wall was the northern wall of the rail line. Bergmann worked to preserve the building.

Bergmann's merger in 2001 with Handler Grosso Durfee + Associates (HGDA), a Rochester signature design firm, added to its capabilities to handle design intensive projects.

As for the city hall, which was a federal building before 1887,

Ford Street Bridge.

their HGDA staff restored it and designed an addition in 1982, taking great pains to make the two parts match.

Other historic Rochester buildings that HGDA has restored include the following:

• Stone Tolan Museum. This popular 120-year-old house, with its barn, was completely restored in 1986.

• Lawyers Cooperative Publishing Company, in 1982. The headquarters of the major publishing company was previously a horse harness factory. At its top is a 25-foot tall statue of Mercury, a downtown landmark rediscovered on the property during the renovation.

• The Powers Building, in 1991. Noted for its limestone and cast iron, the building consists of a core dating back to 1869 and several additions. Bergmann handled an interior and exterior renovation, including a new atrium and balconies.

When it comes to new buildings, Bergmann Associates provided project management, architectural and engineering services for the design of Rochester's new Public Safety Building, a 140,000-square-foot facility to house police and fire department operations.

It developed the master plan for a 300-acre parcel adjacent to the Erie Canal in the Town of Greece. Canal Ponds Business Park is a mixed-use development with offices, light industrial facilities, hotels, restaurants and recreational waterways.

"We have a very strong interest in older buildings and in developing public spaces," said Bergmann. This includes making spaces more usable, as he and the company have done at the University of Rochester, with infrastructure including walkways along the Genesee River and the pedestrian bridge at its bend. The company created parks from Cobbs Reservoir to the Finger Lakes, and handled major traffic studies, engineering work at St. Mary's Hospital, lock and dam work along the main barge canal, and library renovation.

The types of work Bergmann Associates does from its headquarters in Rochester is echoed by its offices in Buffalo, Philadelphia and Pittsburgh, Pennsylvania; Hoboken, New Jersey; Ft. Lauderdale and Jacksonville, Florida; Lansing, Michigan; and Toledo, Ohio. While its work originates in these largely Eastern U.S. offices, projects extend all the way to the West Coast.

The staff at each office provides full services to its clients and projects, drawing as appropriate on the abilities of the entire firm, which is closely linked by computer and communication systems. This structure has worked particularly well with larger clients that have facilities throughout the country. Bergmann serves them from the nearest relevant office, and when appropriate has based staff at their sites. The firm's multi-disciplinary capabilities provide complete planning and engineering services to clients in the commercial, institutional, retail, educational, and industrial arenas and to agencies at all levels of government.

The firm has grown to more than 330 people, and consistently ranks among *Engineering News Record's* top 500 Design Firms. Staff includes mechanical, electrical, industrial, structural, civil, water resources, environmental and transportation engineers, planners, architects and interior designers, who provide design and construction management of new facilities, additions and renovations, repairs, maintenance and operational improvements.

Teams also work in facilities management, master planning, landscape architecture, interpretive services, environmental assessments, geographic information systems, rail engineering, bridge design and inspection, CADD, visualization and computer animation.

Bergmann builds long-term client relationships by adhering to three fundamental principles: being uniquely responsive to their needs, commitment to excellence, and genuine care for employees. It fosters a creative and innovative approach. "Creative problem solving provides a constant challenge that develops leadership and pushes our staff to excel," the firm asserts. Its philosophy is to understand client cultures, policies, practices and goals, both in general and specifically to each project, and to maintain strong, constant communications. This results in designs that meet or exceed expectations.

CHAMBERLAIN, D'AMANDA, OPPENHEIMER & GREENFIELD

The law firm of Chamberlain, D'Amanda, Oppenheimer & Greenfield has been a presence in the Rochester community since its founder, Philetus Chamberlain, began practicing law in 1879. During his career, Philetus tried more than 5,000 criminal and civil cases. He was known for his commitment to his profession, his amazing skills in the courtroom and for the ability to effectively advocate for his clients.

Since its founding, the firm has continued in the tradition of Philetus Chamberlain. Today, the practice is general, with lawyers concentrating in the areas of litigation, insurance defense, business/corporate, plaintiff's personal injury, securities, tax, bankruptcy, labor, estates/trust, real estate and family law. Personal attention, broad experience, cost-consciousness, availability and expertise, as well as dependable, quality service are the hallmarks to servicing all clients. The firm's primary commitment is to the client and it does not stop at the end of each business day. Each lawyer is actively involved in the community, through positions in business organizations, educational institutions, legal organizations, and other community groups.

The name of the firm has changed many times in its history. Significant changes include Chamberlain, Page & Chamberlain, acknowledging the son of Philetus Chamberlain, Arthur, into the partnership in 1915. Francis J. D'Amanda joined in 1926 and, in 1937, upon the death of Philetus, the firm became Chamberlain, Page & D'Amanda. In 1963, it became Chamberlain, D'Amanda, Bauman, Chatman & Oppenheimer to reflect the addition to the partnership of Agnes L. Bauman, Arthur S. Chatman, Robert Oppenheimer and Louis D'Amanda, son of Francis. The final change occurred in 1984, when Stanley Friedman and Jerry

THE FOUR CORNERS

Offices of Chamberlain, D'Amanda, Oppenheimer & Greenfield since 1879

The offices of Chamberlain, D'Amanda, Oppenheimer & Greenfield have been at The Four Corners since 1879.

Greenfield joined. At this time, the firm became known as Chamberlain, D'Amanda, Oppenheimer & Greenfield.

Agnes L. Bauman was a pioneer in the field of law in Monroe County. She was a self-taught lawyer at a time when only two other women were practicing law in Rochester. Agnes was hired in 1923 as a stenographer for Chamberlain, Page & Chamberlain. When she applied, they were looking for two stenographers. "She told Philetus Chamberlain, 'Pay me one and a half times what you would pay two stenographers

and I'll do the work of two,' and she was hired," remembers Louis D'Amanda. "After about a year, though, she got bored. Mr. Chamberlain suggested she study law, and his son gave Agnes his lawbooks and notes. On the train to Canandaigua to answer the court calendar, she began to read a book entitled *Equity*. She told me she read the first page six times and didn't understand a single word. A gentleman also on the way to the courthouse asked, 'What are you doing little girl?' Agnes replied she was studying law. The gentleman said, 'Don't set your heart on it, little girl.' Right then she made up her mind that she would become a lawyer. When she went home, *Equity* was placed at the bottom of the pile of books. She read all the books, and when she finally came back to *Equity*, she understood what they were talking about. When she took the bar exam, there was a big betting pool in town as to whether she was going to pass the test. Agnes passed on her first attempt. She struggled in a man's world, but was never phased by it."

Three generations of Chamberlains, and the three generations of the D'Amanda family have inspired the warm and welcoming environment everyone experiences when they come in contact with the firm. Through the daily guidance of Edward C. Radin III, managing partner, Chamberlain, D'Amanda, Oppenheimer & Greenfield continues on in the tradition of its founders.

BLUECROSS BLUESHIELD AND THE EXCELLUS COMPANIES

More Than 65 Years of Service to our Community.

During the Great Depression of the 1930s, increased hospital costs, combined with widespread unemployment, led to the inability of many people to pay for hospital care. This, in turn, created a health care crisis for consumers and hospitals across the country.

The concept that people could pay a small contribution into a community fund that could be used to pay hospital bills was an idea that had been discussed for many years. In the 1930s its time had come. Thus, the Blue Cross organization was born with the intention of providing "hospital prepayment for pennies a day."

Through the work of many Rochester-area business leaders, health care organizations and groups, the Rochester Hospital Service Corporation, known commonly as Blue Cross of Rochester, was established in 1935. It was one of the first 10 plans in the nation. The first monthly premium was 65 cents for a single membership and $1.30 for family coverage. By the end of the first year, 18,000 contracts had been sold, and Rochester had the second largest plan nationwide.

The Blue Cross concept of prepaid hospital care proved so

BCBSRA called 41 Chestnut Street home from 1943 to 1984.

BCBSRA began as the Rochester Hospital Service Corporation in 1935, one of the first 10 Blue Cross plans in America.

successful that the need for a program that would also prepay surgical and in-hospital physician care became evident. Sponsored by the Monroe County Medical Society and local industry, Genesee Valley Medical Care, Inc., known commonly as Blue Shield of Rochester, was established in 1946.

Through the years, BlueCross BlueShield of the Rochester Area (BCBSRA) has grown to serve the health care needs of more than 70 percent of the greater Rochester community. The company has been recognized for its innovative approach to enhancing customer benefits, while also controlling costs. Its HMO plans have been consistently ranked among the best in the nation by *Newsweek, U.S. News and World Report,* and other leading consumer publications for both quality and customer satisfaction.

In the late 1990s, BlueCross BlueShield of the Rochester Area joined with BlueCross BlueShield of Central New York and BlueCross BlueShield of Utica-Watertown under the umbrella of Excellus, Inc., a non-profit holding company headquartered in Rochester. With its BlueCross BlueShield divisions sharing information

technologies and best practices in areas such as benefits management, information technology, medical policy, and claims processing, Excellus works to improve the quality of medical care received by its members and the health status of the entire community. At the same time, it holds administrative efficiency to national benchmark levels. By the year 2001, the Excellus companies had more than $4 billion in annual revenues and 6,740 employees, insuring 2.1 million people in 45 counties from Lake Erie to Lake Champlain, and from Pennsylvania to Canada.

In keeping with its mission of improving the quality of life in the communities it serves, Excellus not only offers health care coverage through traditional/indemnity, managed care, and dental products, but also provides many health care-related services through its subsid-

In 1973, The Joseph C. Wilson Center was the first Lifetime Health medical center built in Rochester.

iaries and affiliates. The Excellus Companies include:

• Lifetime Health, which was originally established as Genesee Valley Group Health Association (GVGHA) in 1973 as the first health maintenance organization (HMO) in New York state. Lifetime Health provides medical care through four medical centers and a number of community-based physician practices located throughout the greater Rochester area. Lifetime Health also provides urgent treatment for minor illness and injury through its AfterHours Medical Care program. Lifetime Health introduced the Rochester area's first family medicine practice for deaf and hard-of-hearing patients and Artemis Health, an internal medicine practice especially for women and staffed by female physicians.

• Genesee Region Home Care (GRHC), which provides skilled nursing, rehabilitation therapies, and assistance with personal care to more than 10,000 Rochester-area residents each year, helping them recover from illness or surgery. GRHC's hospice and palliative care programs continue to enhance its reputation as a caring and comforting service for the terminally ill and their families, and

Technology has evolved from manually typed, hand-processed forms to today's collection of 8,000 square feet of computer equipment helping to process 30 million claims per year representing $1.2 billion.

it offers an extensive array of bereavement support services open to the entire community.

• MedAmerica Insurance Company and MedAmerica Insurance Company of New York are wholly owned subsidiaries that specialize in long-term care insurance. Established by BlueCross BlueShield of the Rochester Area in 1987 as Finger Lakes Long Term Care Insurance Company, MedAmerica today is a national leader in long-term care insurance and is licensed in 48 states plus the District of Columbia.

• Excellus Benefit Services, a benefits consulting subsidiary, helps employers with actuarial, consulting, retirement and benefit administration services. It has offices in Rochester and Syracuse.

• RMSCO is one of the largest full-service third-party administrators of major, self-funded product lines such as health benefits, workers' compensation, property and casualty in the Northeast U.S. The company is based in Liverpool, New York, near Syracuse.

• Support Services Alliance (SSA) is a membership organization dedicated to group purchasing services such as health, dental, disability, life insurance and professional services for small businesses of 50 employees or less:

• Univera Healthcare, a Syracuse

and Buffalo-based health maintenance organization, joined the Excellus family in October 2001, making Excellus the second largest health insurance plan in New York state.

BlueCross BlueShield in Rochester has experienced tremendous growth since it began in the 1930s. The impetus for this growth has come from both members and employers. With support from Excellus, BlueCross BlueShield will maintain the strong local presence it has had for more than 65 years, and will remain true to its mission and the three timeless principles that guide the company:

• It is committed to being a non-profit health insurer.

• It exists to assure that as many people in our communities as possible have affordable, dignified access to needed, effective health care services, including long-term care.

• It recognizes the need, and responsibility, to reach out to all segments of the communities it serves, particularly the poor and the aged, in order to enhance quality of life, including health status.

DEWOLFF PARTNERSHIP ARCHITECTS

The mission of the DeWolff Partnership has always been to create stimulating and effective living and working environments while maintaining the highest degree of design and economy.

Carlton E. "Bud" DeWolff was born in Rochester, New York, to Edward and Lillian DeWolff. His father was an engineer and designer who worked on a number of WPA projects in Rochester in the 1930s; many of these projects were redesigned in the '80s by Bud DeWolff.

The DeWolff Partnership was founded in 1963, in Fairport, New York, by Bud Dewolff. In 1985, the firm moved to a historic six-story building in downtown Rochester, purchased by Mr. DeWolff, and has become the largest pure architectural firm in the Rochester

Carlton "Bud" DeWolff. Photo by Cris Maggio

University Hospitals of Cleveland Atrium. Photo by DOK Photography

area. His original partner was Robert Hallock, who is now retired. The other partners in the 60-person firm are John Hall, David Nichols, and Thomas Pavlock, who recently relocated to Cleveland to head DeWolff's new office in that city.

The firm has received countless architectural awards for its innovative design solutions, and for 14 consecutive years has been recognized as one of the top 100 architectural firms in the United States by *Modern Healthcare* magazine.

The DeWolff Partnership has also been named to the top 100 businesses in Rochester, New York, in five of the past nine years.

In 1954, after serving for four years in the Air Force during the Korean conflict, DeWolff entered the University of Illinois to study industrial design. However, he somehow got into the architectural registration line by mistake,

and upon reaching the desk, rather than go all the way back, decided not to switch lines. Thus, he became an architect by accident.

Mr. DeWolff attributes most of his success to his family, great partners, and a dedicated staff who appreciate being part of a successful national firm. He is not only proud of his firm's architectural and civic accomplishments but is most proud of his family, stating that they are much more creative than he is. His wife, Jean DeWolff, has headed the administrative and contracts departments of the firm and, as Bud states emphatically, "is one of the main reasons for the firm's financial success."

Darryl DeWolff, a talented industrial designer with two U.S. patents for designs for Kodak, joined the firm in 1994, and created a new marketing department. As director, he successfully created new marketing innovations and was responsible for bringing in well over $650 million of construction value in projects.

Curtis DeWolff, who holds seven Kodak patents in high speed digital imaging, is also an accomplished musician and composer, and as president of Graywolf Productions, produces audio-visual productions for radio and TV. He has had his music published on radio and TV as well.

Guided by his artistic vision, innovative mind, and enthusiasm for historic preservation, Mr. DeWolff designed the International Museum of Photography in Rochester, New York. Selected from an international search, DeWolff designed an underground structure—comprising two of the museum's three floors—which preserves the historic and aesthetic integrity of the stately mansion and magnificent grounds. With just one floor above ground, the new addition complimented the existing historic structure, and brought beauty and function

Blue Cross Arena, Rochester, N.Y.
Photo by Ken Pamatat

within the project's budget and scheduled programs. The museum has received numerous accolades and awards and is considered to be the world icon of photography.

"It is critical in architecture to be able to embrace architectural roots, to appreciate where we come from," says DeWolff.

Another notable project is the half-acre atrium at Case Western Reserve and University Hospitals of Cleveland. Steven Litt, art critic of the Cleveland *Plain Dealer*, called the DeWolff atrium "one of the great public rooms in Cleveland." DeWolff has since designed unique atriums for several projects, including a large healthcare complex for the Masonic Home in Utica, New York.

Other significant projects are the $41 million War Memorial expansion and the Clinton Square office building, both in Rochester, New York; and the $100 million Lerner Tower for University Hospitals of Cleveland, designed in collaboration with a Boston firm.

Perhaps most noteworthy is the national recognition the DeWolff Partnership has attained in the design of health facilities. With such prominent clients as the Johns Hopkins Hospital and Wilmer Eye Institute, in Baltimore, the firm has demonstrated its ability to meet client needs aesthetically and technically in highly-specialized environments. "In health facilities there is no room for inexperience or mistakes," says DeWolff.

Perhaps the most unique projects DeWolff has designed are three underground houses that have been published nationally. However, the most exciting project was his recent design and conceptualization of a multi-modal ferry terminal in the Toronto Harbor waterfront to provide fast ferry service between Toronto, Niagara, and Rochester, New York. This concept triggered the city of Toronto's 2000 waterfront development initiative.

Mr. DeWolff has had some notable experiences in his life. As student vice president, he picked up Frank Lloyd Wright at the train station and drove him to the University of Illinois in 1954. Being in the car alone with this legend was truly an experience. He also served as chairman of Land Use and Design, Vision 2000, Rochester, New York, 1990, to plan the future of the city.

Mr. DeWolff credits some of his success to three people—Dr. James Block of Baltimore; Andrew Wolfe, recently deceased, of Rochester, New York; and Doris Carlson, also deceased, of Rochester, New York. Dr. James Block, past CEO of Johns Hopkins Hospital in Baltimore, "very early saw my architectural abilities when he visited my radical 1969 design at the Voplex research and office facility in Perinton, New York. He was instrumental in creating opportunities to utilize my design talent in health care." Dr. Block brought dignity to health-

223

International Museum of Photography at the George Eastman House, Rochester. Photo by Richard Margolis

many discussions and intellectual teachings. She had a spiritual insight."

"They were truly innovative thinkers and I was blessed to be a part of their lives."

Mr. DeWolff was appointed by Governor George Pataki to serve as Commissioner to the Rochester–Genesee Regional Transit Authority, 1996-1998. He was appointed by Chancellor Posvar of the University of Pittsburgh to the University's Master Plan Committee in 1982, was a consultant to the Robert Wood Johnson Foundation, Princeton, New Jersey and was the design consultant to the National Planning Association in Washington, DC, 1976-1977.

Mr. DeWolff has also been active in speaking engagements on a variety of subjects, including health-care at Tulane University, New Orleans; the everyday utilization of the creative process at Syracuse University; and design and rendering at Cornell University, 1963.

What is ahead for Carlton "Bud" DeWolff? He wants to perpetuate the great work of his firm, to be carried to even greater achievements. Being an accomplished artist and renderer, he also is desirous to paint full time if or when he retires. He definitely wants to spend more time with his family.

DeWolff believes that architecture is the true chronological calendar of the past and the future, and sees no limit as to what the future can hold for his firm and Rochester, New York.

Appellate Division Fourth Department, Rochester, N.Y. Photo by Ken Pamatat

care through good architectural design.

Andrew Wolfe, former owner and publisher of the award-winning Wolfe Publications, "was astounding in his ability to write from his observations of life. We used to sit for hours at the historic Richardson's Canal House Inn, which he owned, and I was the architect who restored that 1790 structure. We talked about creativity, and created ideas such as lighting the 96-foot High Falls of the Genesee River in the middle of the city of Rochester." Mr. DeWolff has just completed a unique house for his widow, Vivienne Tellier Wolfe, and calls it the Living Wall House.

Doris Carlson, wife of Chester Carlson, the inventor of Xerography, "truly inspired me with our

DAVIDSON, FINK, COOK, KELLY & GALBRAITH, LLP

From Suite 1700 of the First Federal Plaza in downtown Rochester, peaceful views of the Genesee River and Lake Ontario are in sharp contrast to the bustle of activity inside the law offices of Davidson, Fink, Cook, Kelly & Galbraith, LLP. One of the first tenants in the landmark building, this highly-respected firm consistently proves their unwavering commitment to growing with their local, national and international clientele.

Founded as Beckerman & Davidson by S. Gerald Davidson and partner in 1968, the firm added Thomas A. Fink and Stuart M. Cook to the partner roster in the mid-1970s. The 1979 firm name of Davidson, Fink, Cook & Gates eventually gave way to Davidson, Fink, Cook & Kelly, evolving into today's letterhead in 1998 when Robert L. Galbraith, Jr. was welcomed to the team. With deep roots in Rochester—Davidson, Kelly and Galbraith are all native sons—the firm has grown to its current coterie of 15 full-time attorneys backed by a two-to-one support staff of 30 that occupy the entire 17th floor of their office building.

A highly selective firm, they have remained dedicated to General Civil Practice before all Courts in areas of Matrimonial and Family Law, Corporation, Construction, Mechanics Lien, Tax Assessment, Real Estate, Banking, Environmental, Land Use, Labor, Personal Injury, Education and Probate Law, as well as Bankruptcy, Negligence, Malpractice and Estate Planning. Several of the partners have been repeatedly recognized for their outstanding performance in *Who's Who in Practicing Attorneys, Who's Who in American Law* and *The Best Lawyers in America.*

Each of the partners has earned the respect of colleagues and peers through individual leadership in legal and community

Managing partners Walter Capell and Rob Galbraith.

organizations. Jerry Davidson served as past chairman and member of the Family Law Section of the New York State Bar; continues to serve as a member, Board of Managers for the New York Chapter of the American Academy of Matrimonial Lawyers. Tom Fink serves as a member, Panel of Arbitrators (Commercial) for the American Arbitration Association; and was president of Temple B'rith Kodesh. Rob Galbraith, past chairman of the Real Estate Committee of the Monroe County Bar, has served as member of the Executive Committees for the Real Property and Young Lawyers Section of the New York State Bar, as a member of the New York State Economic Development Council, and was recognized for his community acheivements in 1996 as one of Rochesters 40 under 40. Paul Kelly holds the position as president of the Genesee Valley region of the New York

State Trial Lawyers Association and Eugene T. Clifford serves as president of the Monroe County Bar Association. Gregory J. Mott and Suzanne Brunsting both have chaired the Family Law Section of the Monroe County Bar Association. Partners Stuart Cook and Walter Capell are active members of both the Monroe County and New York State Bar Associations.

Whether representing a local client, serving as counsel to an international corporation or conducting a hands-on seminar for students at the University of Rochester, the people of Davidson, Fink, Cook, Kelly & Galbraith, LLP have made a positive impact in the legal arena of upstate New York. When Jerry Davidson began practicing law in Rochester in 1957, it was a small town with just 500 practicing attorneys. Today it is a major metropolitan area of over one million people and 2,000 attorneys. The City of Rochester has reason to be justifiably proud of this seasoned firm dedicated to protecting and defending the rights of all its citizens.

EASTMAN KODAK COMPANY

It would be difficult to "picture" Rochester without Eastman Kodak Company. Quality and prosperity there would doubtless be—for Rochester has always supported progressive companies and industrial diversity. But the fact remains that in few, if any, other regions in America have a man, his company, and his city become so completely one. It is also doubtful that in any other region has one man's influence left an imprint that remains so alive, in so many places, for as long a period after his death.

One of the many things George Eastman did was to set a pattern for generous civic concern that others may follow, though perhaps none will ever match. He gave away his fortune where he felt it would do the greatest good for the greatest number, and Rochester has been and remains the chief beneficiary.

Few men leave two monuments. George Eastman left the evidence of his generosity and he left his company. The first influence remains in education, music and the good health of the community. The second—on the nation and the world—has been incalculable.

George Eastman did not invent photography, but he brought it to within the reach of every human being. He and his associates brought to the world, much earlier than might otherwise have been, the development of photographic science to further and improve personal satisfaction, industry, research, medicine, communications, entertainment, and eventually, space exploration.

When George Eastman died in 1932, the *New York Times* commented, "Eastman was a stupendous factor in the education of the modern world. Of what he got in return for his great gifts to the human race he gave generously for their good; fostering music, endowing learning, supporting science in its researches and teaching, seeking to promote health and lessen human ills, helping the lowliest in their struggle toward the light, making his own city a center of the arts and glorifying his own country in the eyes of the world."

Eastman Kodak Company's modern legacy is perhaps best described by Dr. Edwin R.A.

George Eastman, 1921.

Seligman in his introduction to Carl W. Ackerman's biography, *George Eastman.*

He writes, "So far as we know, Mr. Eastman was the first manufacturer in the United States to formulate and to put into practice the modern policy of large-scale production at low costs for a world market, backed by scientific research and extensive advertising."

Eastman pioneered to give his employees a proportional share in the success of his company, a practice that has improved the economy of the Rochester region beyond description. Quietly, and often anonymously, he gave away virtually all of his wealth—more than $100 million—to art, education, scientific and medical institutions to better the world condition and improve the lot of humanity. Two examples illustrate the magnitude of his generosity: his $51 million gift to the University of Rochester and the $20.2 million given anonymously to the Massachusetts Institute of Technology. Both institutions remain glowing testimonials to the wisdom of his decision.

But the history of Eastman Kodak Company can by no means be told only in terms of its founder. He surrounded himself with men of genius and foresight. His successors have built an enterprise so vast and successful that its sales are $14 billion and its net earnings over $1 billion a year. Eager for the improvement of its existing products and engrossed in the search for new products, methods, and technologies, Kodak spends more than $2 million each day on research and development alone.

Kodak remains, as it has been throughout this century, a world leader in imaging. Its product offerings span consumer and professional photography, medical diagnostic imaging, business information systems and digital and applied imaging.

Kodak is multinational in nature and operation. Its products are manufactured, distributed, and marketed worldwide, yet the company's headquarters in Rochester seem as natural a part of the landscape as the Genesee and the shoreline of Lake Ontario.

The Kodak influence extends far beyond its immeasurable contributions to the regional economy in terms of salaries and wages, taxes, and the purchase of goods and services. Its people contribute leadership to virtually every type of worthwhile human activity, while the company's generosity in support of the United Way, education, the arts, health agencies, and other areas of civic concern is cast in the mold fashioned by its founder.

It has been more than 120 years since young bank clerk George Eastman invented a dry-plate coating machine which changed the course of the infant photographic science and began the commercial production of dry plates in a Rochester loft.

Since then, the avenue that his company has followed is dotted with milestones in invention, innovation, production and distribution. They range from the production of the simple Brownie box camera to Neil Armstrong's use of 70mm Kodak Ektachrome film in photographing man's first walk on the moon. More recently, they have included success in expanding the popular field of digital imaging and the new field of info-imaging.

Indeed, it is a rare field of human or natural activity that is not in some way touched by what Eastman Kodak Company does and makes.

Flour, not film, was king in 1838 when Henry O'Reilly wrote of Rochester that, "in various departments of manufacture such as edge tools, carpeting, fire engines, cloths, leather, paper, pianos, etc., considerable energy is manifested." The manifestation of that energy has made Kodak and Rochester names known throughout the world. Of the more than $7.2 billion in Kodak sales outside the United States, more than half comes from products made in this country—and those mostly in Rochester.

Henry O'Reilly could not have envisioned today's Kodak. But then, neither could George Eastman, when he first brought photography to every fingertip.

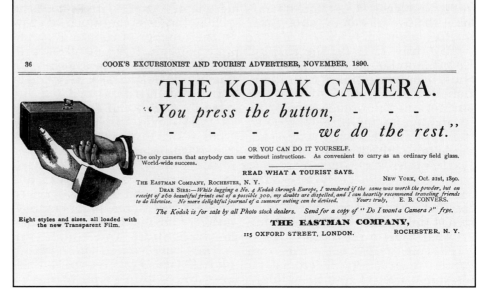

ELDREDGE, FOX & PORRETTI, LLP

Although Eldredge, Fox & Porretti (EF&P) was formed on July 1, 1979, its roots go back to the 1960s, when John O. Eldredge was a junior partner in Dye and Johnston, and P. Robert Fox was a senior accountant with the same firm. In 1968, Dye and Johnston was acquired by a national CPA firm and John Eldredge decided to join two other CPAs to form the firm of Aspenleiter, Doran & Eldredge. In conjunction with establishing the firm, John Eldredge acquired the practice of William Hallock, CPA, in Canandaigua, New York. A year later Bob Fox rejoined John Eldredge in his new firm.

During the 1970s, the nucleus of EF&P began to assemble at Aspenleiter, Doran & Eldredge. Robert N. Porretti, who started in public accounting with a national CPA firm, was employed as a senior accountant in 1972. That same year, Louis J. Camarella Jr. joined the firm directly from college. While he left a year later to earn his MBA and to work on the west coast for a year, he rejoined the firm in 1975. At the same time, two close friends graduated from college. Thomas F. Kelly joined the firm directly, while Timothy J. McNamara took a job in Ogdensburg, New York. Less than a year later, the two friends were reunited in Rochester.

On July 1, 1979, the firm of EF&P was created. The name was chosen because John Eldredge, Bob Fox and Bob Porretti were partners in the predecessor firm. In addition to the three partners, the firm started with nine staff members including tax manager Lou Camarella and senior accountants Tom Kelly and Tim McNamara. Almost immediately, the firm started its quiet, but steady growth. In 1980, Lou Camarella became a partner.

During the 1980s, the firm continued to prosper. Terrence P. McNamara and Craig S. Kellner, who had graduated from college in 1977, were among the early additions. The firm expanded so quickly that Craig was given the library as his office for a short period until new space became available. The firm acquired the practice of Robert Oliver, CPA, and expanded services to many of his clients. Tom Kelly and Tim McNamara were named partners in 1984. The philosophy of growth from within or through the acquisition of practices from other CPAs proved successful.

As time progressed, the partners recognized the need to acquire and develop special skills. David P. Veniskey, who had graduated from college in 1980, joined the firm in 1984 to provide it with a stronger tax background. In 1987, Terry McNamara joined his brother as a partner in the firm. James K. Leisner joined as a senior in 1983, becoming a manager in 1989. Craig Kellner and Dave Veniskey were named partners in 1988 and Jim Leisner was named partner in 1994.

EF&P started its second decade by acquiring the practice of Harold Parker, CPA. This acquisition has enhanced its presence in the suburbs and creates a broader foundation for a second decade of growth. Throughout the 1990s, the firm continued to grow in the number of clients it served and increased the services provided to individuals and a wide variety of businesses. Growth in the tax department created the need for additional expertise and in 1994 Kevin Hill joined EF&P from a 'Big Five' accounting firm. Kevin was admitted to the firm as a partner in 1998.

Eldredge, Fox & Porretti has always invested in new services to meet the increasingly complex needs of its clients. As highly-specialized audit and consulting services evolved in the early to mid-1990s, EF&P recognized the need to create a group to service the expanding area of forensic accounting and litigation support. StoneBridge Business Partners was formed in 1997 from a core of EF&P partners and staff and has grown in its relative short life to a nationally-recognized source for forensic accounting, investigative support, outsourced internal audit services and franchise audit services. Major corporations, among them some of the most recognizable brand names across the United States, have come to rely on StoneBridge as an independent resource for asset integrity preservation.

As the close of the century approached, EF&P moved to expand its area of operation, services, and diverse client base. It merged with Morga, Jones, & Hufsmith, a large firm in Canandaigua, interestingly, the home of the first practice acquisition by John Eldredge almost 30 years earlier. The head of MJH, Dennis Morga became a partner in the combined firm and oversees the Finger Lakes offices. MJH had grown on its own, expanding to the Geneva area with the acquisition of Jim Walters' tax practice in 1996. The Geneva office became a full-service business and personal operation the following year.

In 2000, EF&P ranked in the top 10 accounting firms and top five consulting firms by the *Rochester Business Journal,* and was recognized as one of the area's fastest growing private firms by being named to the prestigious Rochester Top 100 list. What started with a handful of friends has grown into one of the Rochester-Finger Lakes area's largest accounting and consulting firms. EF&P's dedication and commitment to its clients is exemplified in the corporate slogan, "Smart Answers to Tough Questions," and to the communities in which it operates by the high level of participation of EF&P staff active with community service organizations.

Today's Eldredge, Fox & Porretti bears little resemblance to its original form. The Rochester area is served from the main office in Brighton's Corporate Woods and satellite offices in Webster and Brockport. The Finger Lakes region is served from the Canandaigua office and satellites in Geneva and Penn Yan. EF&P's client base reaches all segments of the Greater Rochester and Finger Lakes economy—from construction and real estate to healthcare and professional practices, from government, school districts and not-for-profit organizations to farms, vineyards and wineries, from retail businesses to commercial printing operations, and from high-tech start-ups to transportation, and thousands of individual clients. Services range from traditional audit, accounting and tax services to financial and estate planning services, valuation and cost segregation studies, and wide range of business consulting activities. EF&P draws great pride and motivation as a participant in the Rochester-Finger Lakes economy.

From left to right, James K. Leisner, Dennis A. Morga, Louis J. Camarella, Jr., Robert N. Porretti, P. Robert Fox, David P. Veniskey, Terrence P. McNamara, Timothy J. McNamara, Craig S. Kellner, and Kevin C. Hill.

GALLO & IACOVANGELO, LLP

Louis J. Gallo had been practicing law as a sole practitioner for 13 years when Frank B. Iacovangelo met him shortly after graduating from law school in 1965. "We formed an association," says Frank. "We shared office space and helped each other out on cases. It worked so well that we formalized the relationship in 1971 and became partners." Frank's brother, Bernard, joined the partnership a few years later, and together they built the foundation of what has become a true Rochester, New York success story.

Throughout the next two decades, the Gallo & Iacovangelo law firm developed a concentration in corporate investments as well as residential and commercial property transactions. Particularly with Frank and Bernard's growing personal experience in real property investment and development, the firm became generally regarded as one of the preeminent sources of real property law expertise in the Rochester community.

Michael J. Ringrose joined the firm as an associate in 1986 and became a partner in 1992. Mike now heads the firm's Residential Real Estate Department, and he has overseen thousands of transactions assisting clients in buying and selling their homes.

At an early age, Mike developed a profound respect for the law and a keen understanding of the hard work necessary to be a successful lawyer. His father was a practicing attorney and is now the Oneida County Surrogate's Court Judge. His grandfather served as a judge of both the Surrogate's Court and the State Supreme Court. With a degree in accounting, Mike is uniquely qualified to counsel clients in business transactions and real estate matters, as well as in drafting wills and general estate planning.

Mark Hollenbeck also became a partner in 1992, and now heads the Mortgage Lending Department.

Michael J. Ringrose and Frank B. Iacovangelo.

"The coordination of mortgage closings has become more and more demanding as our lender clients have expanded to regional and national levels," says Hollenbeck. "We are committed to sound customer relations with a personal touch, despite regionalization."

Frank Iacovangelo credits Louis Gallo with the firm's philosophy concerning client service. "Lou Gallo treated each client like they were his only client, with a singular focus on their needs and interests. It was the way he lived, the way he practiced law, the way he did business," recalls Frank. Louis Gallo, meanwhile, says that Frank was the moving force behind the growth and success of the firm. "Frank had the vision for building a firm with attorneys who would specialize in areas of practice. He had unbridled energy and he wasn't afraid to take the chances you have to take to build a law firm."

Those two founding philosophies have served the firm and the community well. The attorneys of Gallo & Iacovangelo, LLP have adhered to the values of the founding partners despite the fact that the firm has grown from a two-attorney partnership to the 11th largest law firm in Rochester, New York. As the firm developed through the 1980s and into the 1990s, the need to broaden its areas of concentration became more and more critical. "With the number of clients we had coming through our doors for real estate transactions and general business advice we naturally became a more full-service law firm," says Frank. "Our clients needed us more often for wills, estate planning and administration, for family law matters, and most particularly, to represent their interests in litigation."

In 1995, the firm recruited Joseph B. Rizzo, a local product who had been litigating cases in the New York City area, to further develop and manage the firm's Litigation Department. "I was intent upon moving back to Rochester, and the firm needed litigation support," says Joe. "We had a natural fit." Joe immediately expanded Gallo & Iacovangelo, LLP's expertise in personal injury litigation, and in a few short years had obtained millions of dollars in recoveries for the firm's injured clients.

In addition, Joe brought significant experience in insurance and municipal law matters, and defending municipal entities in the Rochester community quickly became a primary concentration of the firm's Litigation Department. The firm's clients include counties, cities, towns and villages, as well as public authorities, school districts and other special districts, offering full-service representation in whatever capacity required. Gallo & Iacovangelo, LLP has also become known as one of the most effective law firms in the upstate New York region in the defense of police liability claims. In 1999, David D. Spoto joined the firm and has since become a partner. Dave had previously served as an assistant district attorney for Monroe County, and his skills in the area of criminal law translated well into the defense of police and police agencies. "Gallo & Iacovangelo, LLP is an ardent supporter of our local police departments and it is our distinct privilege to advocate on behalf of law enforcement clients," says Spoto.

Joe Rizzo's father had attended school with Frank and Bernard Iacovangelo at Aquinas Institute and St. John Fisher College. Joe becoming a member of the part-

Left to right: Current partners Joseph B. Rizzo, Michael J. Ringrose, Sandra G. Wilmot, Frank B. Iacovangelo, Anthony B. Iacovangelo, Mark S. Hollenbeck, Michael A. Polozie and David D. Spoto.

nership really marked the beginning of a new generation of young attorneys at the firm. In fact, Frank's son Anthony B. Iacovangelo, and Lou Gallo's daughter Sandra G. Wilmot, were soon to become partners and key members of the firm's Real Estate Department, reaffirming the sense of family upon which the firm was built and remains dedicated to. Anthony and Sandra are instrumental in continuing the levels of service, dedication and passion that the community has come to expect from Gallo & Iacovangelo, LLP's real estate practitioners. "In a way, Gallo & Iacovangelo has always been a family business," Frank reflects, "and I try to mentor our young attorneys like I would my own family."

"Frank has taught me so much about the practice of law," says Joe Rizzo. "When I arrived from Manhattan, I had already litigated some major cases and I considered myself to be a pretty sound legal technician. But Frank focused my attention on the business of law and on how to truly communicate with my clients." Mike Ringrose echoes these sentiments. "Frank took me under his wing from day one," he says, "preparing

me for the day when I might be needed as a manager."

Indeed, as of October 1, 2001, Michael J. Ringrose was elected as only the second managing partner in the firm's history, and Frank Iacovangelo, for one, couldn't be more pleased. "My time to run the business of the firm is coming to an end," muses Frank. "It's time for Mike and the younger attorneys to drive the firm into the future, and I'm very confident that the future management of Gallo & Iacovangelo is in capable hands." Frank's time and efforts these days are dedicated to a thriving legal practice, as well as to his duties as the public administrator in and for Monroe County, a position to which he was appointed in January 2000 by Monroe County Surrogate Edmund A. Calvaruso.

Together, the attorneys of Gallo & Iacovangelo, LLP look forward to their continued growth and success into the new century, and to perpetuating the values upon which the firm was founded in dedicated service to the people of the Greater Rochester, New York area and beyond.

Litigation department members Joseph B. Rizzo, John M. Munro, David D. Spoto and Bryon W. Gross.

DR. KONSTANTIN FRANK VINIFERA WINE CELLARS

Konstantin Frank, a Ukrainian war refugee who also held a Ph.D., didn't exactly suspect what great things lay ahead for his family as he toiled at menial jobs like dishwashing and sweeping floors in New York.

In a plot that could have been lifted from a Hollywood melodrama, Frank had a great idea—a radical one, really—that European vinifera grapes, the world's finest, could thrive in New York's Finger Lakes. In fact, he had written his thesis on growing vinifera in a cold climate.

This was heresy in the wine world during the 1950s. The experts said the delicate European vinifera could not survive, much less excel in, New York's harsh winters. A world-class wine would never emerge from the Finger Lakes, according to these experts.

So Frank, the penniless immigrant who once ran the Soviet Union's vineyards, did what he had to survive. When he visited Cornell University, home of a preeminent wine research facility, his theory fell on deaf ears.

As luck would have it, it was at a wine conference in 1953 where Frank met Charles Fournier of Gold Seal, then the premier winery of New York. Both men spoke French, and Frank "bent Charles' ear with talk of making wines from the varieties of Europe," says Fred Frank, Konstantin Frank's grandson and now the president of the company.

It worked. "Fournier literally hired Dr. Frank on the spot and made him director of research at Gold Seal," adds Frank. "From floor-sweeper to director of research in one day, without ever having the resources to prove his theory correct."

But the gamble worked. After a few years of working at Gold Seal, developing French-style champagnes for the company, Dr. Konstantin Frank established his own winery, bonded in 1962.

"It took the industry 20 years before they considered him the future to follow," says Fred Frank. "Now we have a renaissance going on, to say the least." Dr. Konstantin Frank Vinifera Wine Cellars Ltd. is not only regarded as producer of the best of the Finger Lakes wines, as evidenced by international awards in recent years, they have also gone where no New York wine has ever been before, to the White House and the prestigious New York Athletic Club, among others.

"I open doors, I break the ice, and make New York state wines more acceptable," says Willy Frank, Konstantin's son and Fred's father, who is now chairman of the company.

Visionary Konstantin Frank died in 1985. Since then, Willy Frank has exhibited his own daring streak, turning his father's company from a research facility into a profitable winery, by hiring a cadre of French-trained winemakers, buying the best French oak barrels to age the wine, and selecting only the dozen or so best of the 60 vinifera varieties his father had grown on the slopes overlooking Keuka Lake.

Today the company employs 14 people full-time at its Hammondsport winery, where there are 60 acres under cultivation, and a handful of part-time workers and seasonal employees. Its sister winery, Chateau Frank, produces sparkling wines and has 29 acres under cultivation. Chateau Frank, like the best French champagnes, ages its sparkling wine underground in stone cellars—a departure from the rest of the American wine industry.

But just as important to Willy Frank as making his company grow was bringing New York wines into the competitive arena worldwide. By all accounts, he has done so. The respected *Wine Spectator* has called Willy Frank the leading vintner fighting for recognition of New York's wine industry.

"The proof is in the pudding," says Fred Frank. "We are able to supply consistency year-in and year-out. That's what the wine consumer is looking for and why there is so much loyalty among our customers." As evidence, the Frank wine business has grown an average of 20 percent a year since 1993.

The greatest tribute to the vision of Konstantin Frank and the business acumen of his son and grandson, may be found on the slopes overlooking Keuka and Seneca lakes. There, where wine experts said the European vinifera could not live, Rieslings are produced that rival those made in Germany, Alsace and Austria; Pinot Noir grapes match up with the best of the French red burgundies; and Chardonnays and Cabernet Sauvignons stand up to the French champions.

Just like Konstantin Frank said they would.

GEVA THEATRE

Geva Theatre is Rochester's leading professional theatre and the largest theatre in New York State outside Manhattan. It began humbly in 1972, when a group of theatre supporters and city officials organized the Genesee Valley Arts Foundation (adopting Geva as its shortened name) and has grown steadily into one of Rochester's most highly respected not-for-profit organizations.

The first public activity of the fledgling theatre was a 1973 Saturday morning workshop for children, which was followed by a series of lunchtime plays. By 1976, from its home in the old Rochester Business Institute building, Geva was ready to offer its first full season of theatrical productions. The season played to an intimate group of just 700 subscribers. When the RBI building was scheduled for sale, Geva sought a permanent home. In 1982, Geva bought and renovated the Naval Armory (built in 1868) at the corner of Clinton Avenue and Woodbury Boulevard. The 552-seat Mainstage opened its doors in 1985, and through the years it has consistently delighted theater-goers with everything from musicals to reinvigorated American and world classics.

Built in 1868 as a New York State Arsenal, the building that Geva Theatre now inhabits has served as a Convention Hall, a concert site, an office building and a myriad of other roles.

Geva Theatre, as it looks today.

In 1999, Geva continued to grow, transforming a large rehearsal space into the intimate 180-seat Nextstage. The Nextstage specializes in fresh, contemporary theatre, including world premiere plays by cutting-edge young playwrights. It also houses Geva Theatre's Big Theatre for Little People, which mounts fully-produced original plays for young people in grades K-8. All of Geva's productions are created and rehearsed in and for Rochester. It draws upon the talent of the actors, directors, designers and writers from around the country who are shaping the American theatre scene.

Several well-known Broadway and small- and big-screen actors have spent time at Geva. Samuel L. Jackson made his Geva debut during the 1977/1978 season in *A Raisin in the Sun*. Scott Bakula was at Geva for *Keystone* in 1980/1981. Robert Downey, Jr. and Bill Pullman both graced the Geva stage during the 1982/1983 season (the former in *Alms for the Middle Class*, the latter in *Ah, Wilderness*).

Joanna Gleason performed in 1983/1984's *A Hell of A Town* and Josh Brolin did a series of play readings at Geva from 1990 until 1993. The 2001/2002 season's East Coast Premiere of *House and Garden* attracted the talented Karen Ziemba, who won a Tony Award for Best Actress in a Musical for *Contact*.

In addition to serving the Rochester community through its Mainstage, Nextstage and Big Theatre for Little People productions, Geva Theatre also offers a wide variety of educational, outreach and literary programs. Each year, emerging playwrights are featured in the American Voices and Hibernatus Interruptus play readings. The Regional Playwrights and Young Playwrights Festivals highlight local and area artists of all ages. Geva also recently forged an educational alliance with SUNY Brockport and established a Fellowship Program in Acting and Directing.

From the Mainstage to the Nextstage to the classroom and beyond, Geva Theatre is an active member in the Rochester community, offering a multitude of opportunities for audience members to get into the act.

GLEASON CORPORATION

In 1874, nearly 10 years after he founded The Gleason Works, William Gleason was credited with the invention of the bevel gear planer. This revolutionary new machine opened enormous possibilities for power transmission technology in the post-Civil War industrial expansion. Over a century later the company, still headquartered in Rochester, has become the clear leader in the world marketplace of power transmission technology. Still focused on the core technology that gave it birth, the company continues to develop, refine, apply and expand this gear knowledge to keep a world on the move. Gears produced on Gleason machines insure smooth power transmission, making it possible for automobiles to run, trucks to deliver, airplanes to fly, power tools to fix, ocean tankers to sail, oil rigs to produce, tractors to harvest and even roller

Original Gleason plant at Brown's Race in 1865.

coasters to roar. From the back roads of China to the superhighways of California, virtually anywhere that there is a need for the smooth transmission of motion, there are gears produced by Gleason technology.

Today the company's name is

legendary in the gear world as it celebrates its 136-year anniversary. From a small shop in Brown's Race on the banks of the Genesee River, Gleason Corporation has exploded its reach with a manufacturing presence on three continents.

Gleason machines, products and services are found in over 50 countries throughout the world. Annually, Gleason products are sold to customers in over 35 countries. It's unique global position is due in part to the vision of Kate Gleason, the oldest daughter of William Gleason and great aunt of the current chairman and CEO, James S. Gleason. Kate's contributions to Gleason Corporation's success were impressive. In 1880, at age 14, she was the Company's bookkeeper. By 1890 she served as the secretary-treasurer and also as its chief sales representative. In 1893, at the age of 27, she traveled unescorted to England,

Original bevel gear planer, first sold to John T. Noye, Buffalo, October 27, 1874 for $1,500 and restored in 1929.

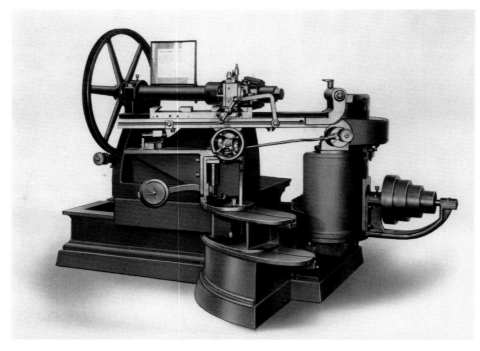

Scotland, France and Germany to market the products of The Gleason Works and establish a firm international footing. She succeeded and returned home with orders from some of the most prestigious companies in Europe. Since then Gleason Corporation has held steadfast to this course of pursuing overseas markets.

Technical dominance in its core technology has been the major focus throughout the years. In the early 1900s, James E. Gleason, eldest son of William, was the principal inventor of new bevel gear machines that produced gears in half the time, with increased accuracy. This technical leadership continues today with Gleason holding hundreds of patents in the U.S. and abroad. Under the current direction of Jim Gleason, great grandson of the founder, the company has continued to introduce new products that revitalize gear technology

and dominate the industry. In the last decade the acquisition of two international companies—The Pfauter Group and the Hurth Company—both world leaders in complementary areas of gear technology, has resulted in doubling the size of the Gleason Corporation and the scope of its product offerings.

In addition to its dedication to technological excellence, the Company has focused on building long-term relationships with customers by providing complete support from instruction in gear theory and assistance in gear design, to optimization of equipment for gear production and customer training. Gleason Customer Technical Support Centers are located in many areas of significant customer concentrations to insure rapid response to customer needs. This passion to serve and understand the customer has been its credo since the late 1800s when

The present location of Gleason Corporation at 1000 University Avenue.

Kate Gleason made her inaugural marketing voyage overseas. Major customers include leading companies in the automotive, aerospace and aircraft, truck, recreational vehicle and power equipment industries.

From its modest beginnings in 1865, Gleason Corporation has grown to be a truly global enterprise and yet remains a significant factor in the history and economy of Rochester. As to the future, Jim Gleason says, "We are committed to remaining the unquestioned world leader in all aspects of gear production and technology and will continue to achieve this by offering the broadest array of superior products and services to our customers."

HARRIS CORPORATION, RF COMMUNICATIONS DIVISION

One summer's day, Bill Stolze was sitting in chief engineer Elmer Schwittek's office.

"Elmer, how would you like to start a business?" said Stolze.

To his amazement came the reply: "I would."

The next day, the two met at a hot dog stand two miles away from their employer—a place they figured no company executives would find them. Through subsequent conversations over hot dogs at Schaller's in Irondequoit, they became determined to reach underserved communications customers around the world by building and selling a long-range, two-way radio.

Schwittek brought in his assistant, Roger Bettin. Stolze soon called upon Herbert VandenBrul, a young attorney, to handle financing and legal matters. With an initial investment of $5,000 each, the four founded RF Communications. That was in 1960.

Today, as part of Harris Corporation, Harris RF Communications Division is widely recognized as a leading supplier of secure radio

The new millennium has taken the world from analog to digital, multitasking techniques and concepts. In the same vein, RFCD expands into the 21st century, offering digital-based communications systems that connect the battlefield with the office.

Chet Massari, president, Harris RF Communications Division.

communications products, systems and networks for voice and data communications to military, government and commercial organizations worldwide.

Its parent company, Harris Corporation, is an international communications equipment company focused on providing product, system, and service solutions. The company provides a wide range of products and service for commercial and government communication markets such as wireless, broadcast, government, and network support.

"Harris has expanded its RF Communications business by adding hand-held radios, higher data rate products, VHF/UHF multiband systems, and tactical networks," said Chet Massari, president, Harris RF Communications Division. "This expansion, combined with the use of commercial technologies that allow the company to provide many off-the-shelf solutions, has positioned Harris to serve an expanding international market for two-way radios."

Often, countries must standardize their communications equipment to join NATO, and they are selecting Harris' radio equip-

ment to get the job done. Harris anticipated this need for inter-operable communications equipment with the introduction of a family of tactical radios capable of transmitting voice, data, still image and video in the shortest possible time. The key to this radio family is a common, software-based, digital platform that meets the increasing need for integrated communication systems. This highly-successful approach for the 21st century has allowed Harris RF Communications to secure extremely valuable, multi-year defense contracts all over the world.

"To succeed on the battlefield in this century, fighting forces require reliable, communications," said Massari. "By applying our world-leading HF communications technology to new VHF and multiband tactical digital radios, Harris RF Communications in Rochester is meeting that future demand today."

With such a keen eye to the future, Harris RF Communications has never lost contact with its past. At the turn of the century, the division celebrated its 40th anniversary by welcoming back all four founders to reflect on their achievements.

"Shortly before we formed RF Communications, it was a question as to whether or not to stay in Rochester due to perceived economic advantages elsewhere," said co-founder Stolze. "But we liked the area too much to leave, and I have never regretted that decision."

The founders originally set up in VandenBrul's Park Avenue basement and began building a radio prototype. For six months they labored.

Two weeks after officially launching RF Communications, the Securities and Exchange Commission approved their stock issue and they sold 150,000 shares at $1 each. Because they were oversubscribed three-to-one, the stock immediately began trading

at $2. Four subsequent RF stock sales were approximately $5, $9, $17, and $27 a share.

The first official RF Communications office opened in a vacant beauty parlor on Merchants Road. Within two years, rapid growth moved operations to a portion of the division's current headquarters on University Avenue.

At his previous job, Stolze ran a department of 40 people. At RF Communications, he wrote all the brochures, rang doorbells, demonstrated radios, and traveled around the world supporting independent sales agents. He frequently walked up and down the halls of the Pentagon dragging a radio behind him. The founders worked harder than the competition, and due to their company's small size, could make decisions on the spot.

Several companies had similar products on the market, but RF Communications made superior radios by building in features the others lacked. For example, they put in six channels rather than four.

Underdeveloped countries with unreliable long-distance telephone systems were among the

Above: RF Communications founders Roger Bettin, Bill Stolze, Herbert VandenBrul and Elmer Schwittek.

Below: In 1963, Harris began manufacturing a new SSB transceiver system intended for military and sophis-ticated commercial applications. Known as the RF-301 Transceiver, it was extensively used by the U.S. Navy late in 1967 during the Vietnam War.

first target markets for the fledgling company. One big customer was the Bank of Mexico. It would take them a day or two to place a telephone call from one branch to another, so they preferred Harris radios.

Another strong market was Nigeria, where their agent, Chief Abeola, sold tens of millions of dollars of RF Communications (and later, Harris) equipment. He used to visit Rochester regularly, and once attended RF's annual picnic with his four wives.

The young founders' personalities were reflected in their no-nonsense policies. The board of directors never voted on anything, instead resolving conflicts by discussion. Each founder received an equal paycheck.

"Once a year, we might have a conversation about salary over lunch and somebody would say, 'Hey, we had a pretty good year, how about a raise?' and someone else would say 'Five G's?'" recalled Stolze. "End of discussion. That was very important. Small companies have enough problems without the senior executives arguing about compensation."

In 1968, annual shipments for the company reached $18 million and it was determined that much strength could be added by an association with a larger company. As a result, RF Communications merged with Harris-Intertype Corporation in early 1969. In the subsequent years, the RF Communications Division has supplied equipment to the U.S. government, every branch of the U.S. military, NASA, and to government agencies in more than 90 countries.

"One of the most satisfying aspects of leading this company in the new century is the knowledge that our founders' original entrepreneurial spirit, innovation and appreciation for Rochester's tight-knit community is alive and well with employees today," said Massari.

HIGH FALLS BREWING COMPANY

High Falls Brewing Company was formed in December 2000 and is the successor company to the Genesee Brewing Company, which traces its roots back to 1878. High Falls brews and packages 14 brands of beers and ales, including Genesee Beer, Genny Light, Honey Brown Lager, Genesee Cream Ale, Michael Shea's Irish Amber, and 12 Horse Ale. It is also a major contract brewer and has produced under contract such well-known brands as Sam Adams Boston Lager, Mike's Hard Lemonade, and Smirnoff Ice.

The Brewery has been situated on the banks of the Genesee just beyond the High Falls since the late 1800s. At one time, Rochester boasted over 12 breweries with five of these breweries on St. Paul Street along the river. The young city's location near good and plentiful water, hydropower, and easy transportation to markets, along with a strong German immigrant population, made Rochester a hotbed of brewing activity.

High Falls Brewing Company is the proud brewer of the Genesee family of products and specialty beers such as J.W. Dundee's Honey Brown Lager.

The brewery was founded on the banks of the Genesee River in 1878. It now encompasses 28 acres and has a capacity of 3.5 million barrels.

Today, those assets continue to be important to High Falls, which is now the fourth largest brewer in the United States. With a brewing capacity of 3.5 million barrels, High Falls distributes its products in 37 states. Despite enormous consolidation in the industry over the past 20 years, High Falls has survived as an independent brewery in large part due to the consistent quality of its products and a dedicated and experienced staff of brewers and production personnel who take great care and pride in their work.

Like the river, the beer flows in many places—from a keg at a family reunion on a hot August day to a tap at one of Rochester's sophisticated nightspots. For more than a century, the company's label has been a Rochester icon.

The new management team at High Falls is committed to building upon the tradition of quality

238

inherited from the Wehle family, which operated the brewery from the first days after the end of Prohibition to the sale in December 2000.

In 1933, Brewmaster Louis Wehle purchased the company and began a tradition of excellence that continues today. Wehle believed there was nothing more important than brewing beer with a clean, crisp, cold-aged taste—a taste that was consistently good, glass after glass. He began brewing beer at a single location and today the company remains at its original site overlooking the High Falls of the Genesee River. Tom Hubbard, chairman and CEO of High Falls Brewery, has reiterated the brewery's commitment to these brewing traditions. "The Genesee/High Falls portfolio of brands have survived the onslaught of national brewers' media campaigns because of one essential fact—our brewmasters make excellent products day after day. And, they have been innovators in the industry creating such popular new brew styles such as Honey

Genny Light's new packaging compliments the best tasting light beer brewed in America.

Brown and Michael Shea's Irish Amber. The fact that our brewmasters have been selected to produce, on a contract basis, some of the country's most popular brands in their respective categories is testimony to their skills and capabilities."

High Falls Brewery's portfolio of brands have garnered multiple awards from national beer festivals, including silver medals for Honey Brown and Michael Shea's at the Great American Beer Festival in 2001. The reintroduction of 12 Horse Ale, a top fermented ale which uses the original yeast strain brought over from England in 1933, has been popularly received in Rochester and the surrounding area. And the company plans on introducing new products, which appeal to the changing consumer taste profiles. Howard Jacobson, chief marketing officer, says, "Our goal is to have our consumers connect to our products because of their excellent taste, innovative packaging, and creative marketing. We have a superb group of distributors supported by an experienced and energetic sales force. We are determined to succeed as a quality regional brewer."

A part of High Falls' mission is to be a good community citizen, and in 2001 it sponsored the very popular and enthusiastically received "Horses on Parade" community art project. Over 160 life-size fiberglass horses were

J.W. Dundee's Honey Brown Lager was introduced in 1995 and is now sold in 37 states.

decorated by a group of talented local artists and were displayed from May through August throughout the community.

High Falls Brewery is a private company owned by a group of managers and outside investors. Its mission is to delight its customers with outstanding beverages, services and innovation, and to have all of its stakeholders "toast to mutual growth!"

239

HILLSIDE FAMILY OF AGENCIES

What is known today as the Hillside Family of Agencies began in 1837 as the Rochester Female Association for the Relief of Orphans and Destitute Children. The association members—who included the wives of many influential Rochester businessmen and church leaders—were dedicated to caring for the city's orphans.

Little did these women know that their founding efforts would grow to become a nationally recognized integrated system of care, serving thousands of families and children each year, with dozens of programs and multiple service sites throughout the state.

In the first year, 46 children were served in a small rented cottage on Corn Hill. Renamed and incorporated as the Rochester Orphan Asylum in 1839, the organization constructed a larger facility in 1844 at Hubbell Park. Throughout the rest of the 19th century, this facility and the organization's efforts grew in response to the needs of area children. Orphans were still admitted, but also children in crisis whose families struggled to provide for them.

The Infants' Summer Hospital of Charlotte (now Crestwood Children's Center) was founded in 1885 in pitched tents along the shores of Lake Ontario. It would not be until 1913 that the Hospital would move to a building on Beach Avenue.

Young children from the Rochester Orphan Asylum (now Hillside Children's Center) attend kindergarten in one of the "cottage" style buildings built on the Asylum's campus on Monroe Avenue.

Even a devastating fire on January 8, 1901, could not stop the spirit of service that drove the leaders of the Rochester Orphan Asylum. That tragic fire destroyed more than half of the Hubbell Park building, and killed 29 children and three staff members. The Rochester community grieved for the terrible loss of life and put their full support behind rebuilding efforts.

In 1905, the Rochester Orphan Asylum moved to a 30-acre location on Pinnacle Hill (what is now the Monroe Avenue headquarters of Hillside Family of Agencies). The new location was built as an innovative cottage system to reflect the changing theories in caring for children. Efforts were focused on keeping troubled children within the parental home or family unit, with the entire family receiving necessary services. When a family's situation made this impossible, the child would be removed from the home and housed in an institution. At the Rochester Orphan Asylum, the cottages created a home-like environment within the boundaries of the institution.

To reflect the shift from providing a home for orphans to caring for "dependent and neglected children," the Rochester Orphan Asylum changed its name in 1921 to Hillside Home for Children. Another name change came in 1940 when Hillside Children's Center was adopted and a goal set: "For every child, a fair chance for the development of a healthy personality."

This goal took on an international aspect during World War II when Hillside and Eastman Kodak Company combined efforts to help the children of Kodak employees in England. Between 1940 and 1942, 156 British children were brought to the Rochester area by Kodak to safeguard them from the war in their home country. Hillside assisted in placing these "Kodakids," as they were called, with the families of local Kodak employees or in foster homes for the duration of the war.

As the years progressed, Hillside continued to grow and change to accommodate the needs of more children, including those with more difficult problems. In 1965, Hillside broadened its mission to helping "dependent, neglected, learning disabled, emotionally disturbed, socially maladjusted, and delinquent" children. The importance of the family was recognized, including the need to reunite children with their families whenever possible. As Adelaide Kaiser, director of Hillside Children's Center from 1949 to 1969, said, "No matter how good a job we do, we can never make up to a child what he loses by not being with his parents." Kaiser and others began to create programs and life skills classes to prepare children to return to society, either in biological family homes or in foster or adoptive family homes.

During the 1970s, Hillside Children's Center experienced great growth. The institution began its conversion to a residential treatment center and reopened its campus school, which had been closed since 1931. In 1976, the emergency shelter and crisis-counseling program began, providing a safe haven for children and youth in times of desperation. A day treatment program made it possible to keep more children with their families while providing them with the services they needed.

In 1996 a new parent organization, Hillside Behavioral Health System (HBHS), was formed in order to provide services more efficiently and effectively. Hillside Children's Center and Hillside Children's Foundation served as partner affiliates.

A new affiliate, the Wegmans Work-Scholarship Connection, was acquired later in 1996. Founded by Wegmans Food Markets in 1987 as a mentoring program to improve the graduation rate within Rochester City Schools, the program was named one of President Bush's "Thousand Points of Light" in 1991. Renamed

Hillside Family of Agencies' headquarters is located on Monroe Avenue on 30 acres of land that was bequested to the Rochester Orphan Asylum in 1902 by Mrs. Laura B. Adams.

New York State Governor George Pataki, and then Texas Governor George W. Bush, visited Hillside Family of Agencies' Monroe Avenue Campus in October 1999 to recognize the accomplishments of Hillside Work-Scholarship Connection (HW-SC). Pictured here are (left to right): Governor Pataki; Annette Gantt, HW-SC executive director; Chris Knowlin; HW-SC graduate; Erica Grandberry, HW-SC graduate; and Governor Bush.

Hillside Work-Scholarship Connection, the program continued its focus on helping youth stay in school, achieve academic success, and earn their high school diplomas through a web of support provided by school-based youth advocates and worksite mentors. Since its inception, HW-SC has consistently helped more than 85 percent of participating students to graduate from high school and gain acceptance into college—a statistic that demonstrates the effectiveness of this cutting-edge program.

In 1999, Hillside Behavioral Health System added to its family when Crestwood Children's Center and Crestwood Children's Foundation affiliated with it. Founded in 1885 as the Infants' Summer Hospital of Charlotte, Crestwood's specific mission is to provide comprehensive mental health services to culturally diverse children and adolescents who have serious emotional, behavioral, or mental

disorders. Like the other members of the Hillside family, Crestwood provides these services in partnership with families.

Hillside Family of Agencies was adopted as the system name in December 2000 to better represent the diversity of services provided by each affiliate. Today, Hillside Family of Agencies is not only one of Rochester's oldest family services organizations, but one of the most innovative and well respected. Hillside affiliates provide a full range of services, including home and community-based programs, non-secure detention, residential treatment, day treatment education, foster care, emergency services, outpatient mental health services and customized services. In locations throughout Central and Western New York, Hillside employees are dedicated to building better futures with children and families.

HICKEY-FREEMAN COMPANY, INC.

"Keep the quality up" was one of Jeremiah G. Hickey's favorite sayings. The phrase was used often by Hickey and his two partners Jacob L. Freeman and George A. Brayer, when they founded Hickey and Freeman Company in 1899. At that time the clothing business was the largest industry in Rochester—totaling more than 100 individual businesses and competition was fierce. Today, however, Hickey-Freeman is Rochester's only clothing manufacturer, causing some biographers to cite Jeremiah Hickey as a typical American success story.

The current name, Hickey-Freeman Company, Inc., came as a result of a merger in 1908 with the Beckel-Baum Company. The plan was to specialize in making quality clothing with an overriding emphasis on hand craftsmanship. This idea bucked tradition in the ready-made clothing industry, but the new partners believed that the economy could support a much larger proportion of fine clothing and, if costs could be reduced by large-scale operations, the firm might very well spread the gospel of quality clothing from coast to coast. They were right on both counts.

When describing the suits that would soon become the industry standard, J.G. Hickey used to say that a well-made garment "feels old when it's new and looks new when it's old." Understated elegance became the preference of many businessmen, and by the early 1900s business was booming for the company.

In 1912, Hickey-Freeman erected a building at its present-day location. All work could now be done under one roof, enabling the firm to take a great step toward its quality ideal. And, as a constant reminder that quality is forever the watchword and perfection is the continuing goal, "Keep the Quality Up" was imprinted on all the girders in the new factory.

But even this story is not without setbacks. Both World Wars and the Depression caused scarcity of materials and economic hardships. However, management stuck with the policies that made the organization successful—"Uncompromised Quality"—and emerged time and again as the leader in the manufacturing of men's tailored clothing. The company's clothing is now sold in more than 500 retail stores in this country, and it has a license agreement with a quality apparel manufacturer in Japan for manufacture and distribution in that country.

Today hand tailoring, which is essential to the integrity of every Hickey-Freeman garment, is enhanced by modern technology to ensure a comfortable and better fitting garment—continuing its heritage as the premier clothing house in the United States.

In keeping with the quality standards set by Hickey-Freeman, an exclusive luxury sportswear collection was created and introduced in 1988. By naming the line after the 20th century sports legend, Robert Tyre Jones (Bobby Jones), assured the success of the collection. Jones' accomplishments in his short golf career include the "Grand Slam" in 1930, designing the Augusta National Golf course in 1931 and founding the Master Tournament. The Bobby Jones Sportswear Collection offers exquisite fabrications, refined styling, and understated elegance. Bobby Jones is distributed to fine retail stores and golf shops throughout the world.

The founding officers of Hickey-Freeman, circa 1924. Standing, Jacob Freeman and seated, J. G. Hickey.

Buttonholes, including lapel button holes (shown below), are hand sewn at Hickey Freeman, with long-wear linen thread over a fine, twist-free gimp.

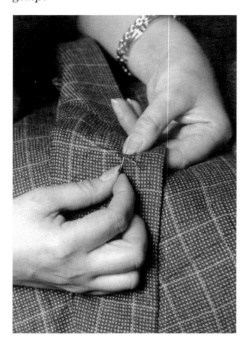

HOME PROPERTIES

Home Properties, the 10th largest apartment company in the United States, is a real estate investment trust (REIT) which owns, manages, acquires and rehabilitates apartment communities in the Northeast, mid-Atlantic and Midwest. The exceptional performance of Home Properties and its predecessor company over the past three decades has supported growth well beyond its roots in Rochester, New York. Today, from its headquarters in downtown Rochester, the company operates approximately 300 communities in 12 states consisting of 50,000 apartment units—homes to more than 75,000 residents.

Home Properties' predecessor company, Home Leasing Corporation (HLC), was founded in 1967 by identical twin brothers Nelson and Norman Leenhouts, who continue to lead the company today as co-CEOs. They began their real estate careers by purchasing single-family homes in the Rochester suburbs, which they then leased, primarily to young families who could not afford a down-pay-

Founders and co-CEOs, Norman (left) and Nelson Leenhouts.

ment on a home. These residents were given an option to purchase their homes, with a portion of the rents applied to the purchase price. More than 50 percent of these residents exercised their purchase option, eager to have the opportunity to own their own homes. The culture of enhancing the quality of life of Home Properties' residents that began in those early days continues today.

By the 1970s, Home Leasing Corporation began to focus on the multifamily residential property business. During the decade, HLC acquired or constructed 1,039 apartment units. It also became active in commercial real estate, developing Brighton Commons and Churchville Commons, as well as converting the famous Aeolian Piano Factory in East Rochester into the highly-

successful Piano Works office and retail complex. These projects firmly established Home Leasing's expertise as a property manager.

During the next decade, Home Leasing continued to acquire apartments and develop commercial projects, including the construction of Clinton Square in downtown Rochester, which today houses the company's headquarters. The planned community of Gananda also evolved with the completion of homes, a championship golf course and industrial/office facilities. While upstate New York remained its prime location, HLC began to extend its geographic territory, acquiring an apartment complex and shopping center in Ohio.

A milestone was reached when Home Properties of New York, Inc. was formed to continue and expand the multifamily property ownership, management, acquisition, development and marketing operations of Home Leasing. In August 1994, Home Properties completed its initial public offering, raising more than $100 million. It was listed on the New York Stock Exchange under the ticker symbol HME. At that time, the company owned 16 multifamily residential properties containing 3,991 apartment units; all but one were in upstate New York.

Since its inception as a public company seven years ago, the company has grown more than 10 times in size. It now operates over 50,000 apartments with capital of more than $2 billion and continues to grow. Focusing on the future, Home Properties remains committed to building on its proud history of creating value for shareholders and enhancing quality of life for residents while preserving its unique culture and expanding its leadership role in the multifamily REIT industry.

Home Properties' headquarters at Clinton Square in downtown Rochester.

LECHASE CONSTRUCTION

Raymond F. LeChase was born in 1913 to Giacomo and Civita LeChase in Rochester, New York. LeChase started working as a water boy at the age of 14 for A. Fredericks & Son and rapidly became a superintendent. He married Rachel Palumbo in 1943, and a son, Raymond Wayne was born a year later. Following Wayne's birth the LeChases had two daughters: Eleanor and Gloria.

In 1944, Raymond LeChase founded LeChase Construction Company to fill the demand for local construction work during World War II.

His beginnings as a businessman were modest. He personally drove workers to job sites, while Rachel handled payroll and accounting. LeChase's first major project, a $90,000 contract was for Kanty Paper Company, a production center for assembling paper boxes, located on Carter Street in Rochester, New York.

In 1967, Raymond LeChase, Inc. was formed following Raymond's disposition of all interests in LeChase Construction Company. The motivation for forming Raymond LeChase, Inc. was a result of his son Raymond "Wayne" LeChase's decision to emulate the family's construction tradition established by his grandfather and father. As a practicing attorney, Wayne proved to be an invaluable asset in the firm's continuous and progressive growth.

Upon succeeding his father in 1981, Wayne LeChase, a former attorney with LaDuca, Offen & LeChase, oversaw a nine-fold increase in volume in the next six years. This explosion included LeChase Construction's first project outside Monroe County, a $26.5 million medium security correctional facility in Marcy, New York. The expansion was out of necessity, as the amount of available construction work in Rochester and Monroe County

Raymond F. LeChase, founder.

was insufficient to maintain the company's solid team of managers and tradesmen.

LeChase's continuing expansion includes the opening of offices in Corning, NY; Charlotte, NC and Tampa, FL. LeChase is also an emerging force in the international construction community, with projects in Canada, Brazil, and the United Kingdom.

World-class workmanship and exceeding customers' expectations, along with positive, long-term relationships with customers and employees, has enabled LeChase to generate $200 million in construction projects in 2000 and an estimated $320 million in 2001.

The company has completed numerous construction and reno-

vation projects and takes great pride in its successful involvement in all of its projects. They include St. Mary's Church; the University of Rochester Medical Research Facilities; Rochester City Hall; Colgate Divinity School; Rochester Chamber of Commerce; Seneca Park Zoo; OakHill Country Club; Blue Cross/Blue Shield Headquarters; Bausch & Lomb; Paychex; and the Hillside Children's Center, as well as several facilities at Eastman Kodak Company and Xerox Corporation.

The Company's greatest asset is its employees. LeChase believes that the dedication, interest, loyalty and hard work of key personnel and the "success culture" shared by all members of the company have and will continue to motivate and provide the inducement necessary to maintain a controlled and successful growth.

LeChase Construction investments are not restricted to its own operations. They believe in taking responsibility for improving the quality of life in its community.

LeChase continues to be a community leader supporting United Way, Otetiana Council of the Boy Scouts of America, Association for the Blind and Visually Impaired, St. John Fisher College, Junior Achievement and various scholarship programs for at-risk youth and many other not-for-profit organizations.

After nearly 60 years in business, Raymond LeChase Sr. is not one to sit back and enjoy retirement. At 88, LeChase, still chairman of the board, wakes up at 5:30 a.m. each day to have breakfast with his wife Rachel before leaving for the office.

LIBERTY PRECISION INDUSTRIES

It has been nearly 80 years since Liberty Tool & Die Corporation was established in a loft on Court Street in Rochester, with meager savings and indispensable credit extended by a used machinery dealer. In the course of those decades, Liberty, like the many companies it serves, has grown and changed with the advancement of technology.

Charles F. Hallick Sr., founded Liberty in 1922, choosing its name in keen appreciation of the freedom for enterprise, which exists in America. A Hungarian, Mr. Hallick had lived in Germany, where he learned his trade well. He was joined by another German toolmaker, Karl Fuchs, in the late 1920s. Mr. Fuchs soon became Hallick's general manager and right-hand man, as well as a key player in Rochester's manufacturing growth and the future of Liberty.

The success of the company over the decades was due in large part to the immense skill and capability of Liberty's employees. Many were European immigrants or sons and

daughters of immigrants who used their skills to design and build some of the most precise and reliable components and machines manufactured. By consistently combining skill with advances in technology Liberty has grown over the years to be one of the most respected builders of manufacturing systems in the country.

After Charles Hallick Sr. passed in 1966, his son Charles F. Hallick Jr. took over operations of the company until 1988 when, due to poor health, he sold the company to Karl Fuchs. Fuchs, who had been Liberty's general manager through 1947, had left Liberty to start his own manufacturing company, Alliance Tool Corporation. After building Alliance into one of the largest tool and die companies in the country, Fuchs merged Alliance with Gleason Works (a large local

The company's state-of-the-art manufacturing facility is located in this 100,000 square-foot building on South Winton Road.

manufacturer) and retired. After being called by Hallick Jr. in 1988 Fuchs agreed to acquire Liberty and help continue the growth and innovative spirit of the company.

Liberty is currently run by Douglas Woods, grandson of Karl Fuchs. Mr. Woods, who has been the head of the company since 1992, has focused on its core area of expertise in flexible machining systems and machining systems integration. Together with a strong management team and skilled employees Mr. Woods has built Liberty into the largest machining systems company in Rochester.

Liberty's current lines of flexible machining systems have been widely accepted in the marketplace. Current customers include DaimlerChrysler, General Motors, Eaton, Delphi, Honda, Nissan, Alcoa and TRW. Liberty's machining systems can be found in customer facilities throughout the United States and Europe.

To accommodate Liberty's growth the company has expanded from its first manufacturing facility on Water Street to its newest 100,000-square-foot facility on Winton Road. The new facilities allow Liberty to service more customers and larger customer programs. The typical machining system orders have grown tenfold over the last few decades, from $500,000–$1,000,000 to $5–$10 million.

This rotary transfer machine was designed and built for Daimler-Chrysler to machine steering knuckles for the PT Cruiser.

MACO BAG CORPORATION

Maco converts laminates into bags and pouches. It has been turning sheets made of combinations of nylon, polyethylene, foil, nylon, polyester and their precursors into custom-purposed flexible packaging for more than 60 years.

Maco Bag Corporation is a family business with deep roots in the Rochester area. Its three divisions serve niche markets with demanding needs. It has built its reputation by designing and producing unique bags for difficult applications. They can be leak proof, light proof, or antistatic. They also can be custom printed. Its five-sided, three-dimensional bags are used for lining containers, covering valuable equipment during shipping, and a wide variety of other applications. It packages millions of pounds of adhesives for customers each year using release-coated films.

Maco's niche markets include imaging, medical, dry toner applications, industrial chemicals, food products, electronics, and the military.

As part of its decades-long participation in the imaging market, where its largest customer is

Maco Bag Corporation at 711 Rowley Road in Victor.

Eastman Kodak, Maco's products wrap imaging films and papers. For these products, the packaging must protect its contents from heat, moisture, and light. So much as a pinhole in a package can let in light thus damaging the film.

Because of such demands, quality systems are essential to Maco's processes. Certified as ISO 9000 compliant, Maco has an in-depth assurance program to prevent mistakes during the converting process and detect flaws before the product reaches the customer. If a movie director is setting up a complex and costly scene, the result will not be ruined by damaged film, because there are no irregularities in Maco's package.

Each of Maco's other niches has unique applications using distinct materials. For example, clean, dust-free, leak proof bags and pouches for the medical market are made from such raw materials as linear-tear films and autoclavable extrusions. Customers in this area have included the American Red Cross, Johnson & Johnson, and Exxon Chemical.

Electronics clients, including Xerox, Kodak,

and Scott Aviation, want packaging products with superior antistatic or conductive properties, such as reusable cushion bags, zip closures, and antistatic shrouds. Maco uses pink antistatic film, black conductive film, nickel metallized/antistatic film laminations, and antistatic cushioning products to meet these needs.

Maco traces its history back to 1929 and the MacDonald Advertising Company. It was founded by Stuart MacDonald, who was born in 1909 and is still part of Maco's daily life. The advertising company specialized in billboards and counter displays for such clients as Kodak and a number of breweries.

In 1939, MacDonald was called to take a physical in case there was a military draft. He was fine, and realized he was liable to be called to fight if he remained in advertising. While he wanted to support the war effort, he did not want to leave his young family. From contacts his agency worked with he identified the military's need for bags to hold airplane parts, food products and other necessary goods. He started his manufacturing operation to fulfill these needs, calling it Maco, short for MacDonald Advertising Company.

Maco's first packages were waterproof sacks made from kraft paper coated with asphalt and used by the military on the open seas. At the time, the company operated out of a barn behind

Maco Bag operator Rhonda Ives keeps watch on a Ttarp automatic flat-bed die-cutter.

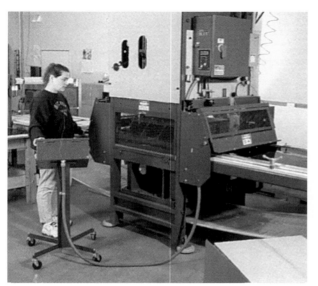

J. Stuart MacDonald, founder of Maco Bag Corporation.

MacDonald's home on Ardmore Street in Rochester.

After the war, Maco made bags for such companies as Remington Rand, Xerox, and Kodak. The packaging activities strengthened while advertising activities slackened and disappeared. "We did some advertising for a while, but the bags worked out better for us," MacDonald recalls.

In 1966, Scott Miller, who was married to MacDonald's daughter Susan, came to work at Maco. In due course, their three sons also joined the company. It grew rapidly.

"Going into bags turned out to be an excellent decision," MacDonald says. "The manufacturing business has provided a legacy for my grandchildren that advertising could never have offered."

Needing more space, the company moved its operations in 1975 to Scottsville, on Main Street, and in 1980 to its current location in Victor. The Maco Bag Division at that location now has 40,000-square-feet for production.

In addition to manufacturing, Maco has an in-house research and development team and laboratory personnel who work with customers to create imaginative solutions for their challenging packaging needs. They may use existing products or design an entirely new package to meet requirements.

For custom bags, Maco's capabilities include leak proof seals, duplex double walls, in-line die-shape sealing, heavy-gauge side seals, tape closures and printing in up to six colors. The bags can be made of high-density and rubber-modified high-density polyethylene; low-density and linear low-density polyethylene; co-extrusions, release-coated, antistatic, conductive and nylon films; and cellophane.

The company makes pouches for vacuum and moisture barrier needs and die-sealed custom shapes. Machines produce sizes up to 48 by 120 inches. There are stand-up pouches and zip-closure pouches, and materials can be film-to-foil, paper-to-foil and film-to-film laminations; adhesive and extrusion laminations; military specification materials, and metalized film laminations.

Its variety of die cutting equipment gives Maco leading-edge sheeting and slitting capabilities that routinely produce parts requiring tolerances of less than 0.006 inch. It offers design and development services and finished products of virtually any size or shape, with no minimum quantity. It applies its die cutting capabilities to high-and low-density polyethylene to 0.03-inch thick, polyester, kraft paper and chipboard, and all types of laminations.

In 1993, Maco opened a new division—M.C. Pac (short for Maco Contract Packaging). M.C. Pac, with some 20,000-square-feet of production space, is also in Victor. It converts pre-made roll stock into pouches and bags for specialty uses, and then puts the product in them. Dedicated staff and modern equipment handle out-sourced as-

At work next to a Maco-designed 48-inch servo controlled pouch machine are: left to right, Vice President of Engineering Scott Miller Jr.; Executive Vice President James McRae; Operator Dave Mason; and Production Manager Craig Miller.

sembly and packaging projects for many different clients.

M.C. Pac provides imaginative solutions for difficult packaging applications, and custom designs processes for the most demanding assembly challenges. Services include taping, labeling, folding, gluing, bag loading and kit assembly.

In 1997, Maco went international, opening its Miller Packaging Division in Guadalajara, Mexico. This brought the Maco Group's total production space to 80,000-square-feet. Miller Packaging makes, assembles, inventories and distributes a total scope of packaging products for a range of companies in Mexico's niche markets.

Today, the three divisions share recognition as a knowledgeable and responsive manufacturer of high-quality, flexible packaging.

THE METALADE GROUP

The original company, Metalade Inc. was founded in April 1968 by a group of 18 former employees of a sheet metal fabricator known as the William J. Meyer Company. The Meyer Company had been sold in 1967 to Yawman & Erbe Company of Rochester, and the new owners decided to consolidate the Meyer operations into the basement of the Y&E building in downtown Rochester. The Meyer employees were not happy at the prospect of moving from the newly-built factory in suburban Henrietta, to the basement of an old building in the city.

The idea to start a new company was actually born on the Meyer Company shop floor by a group of employees who presented the idea to Robert Ade, the executive vice president of Meyer Company. Mr. Ade had been with the Meyer Company since 1945 after his return from World War II, and was well respected in the job shop sheet metal field. Mr. Ade liked the idea of starting a new company, and agreed to be its president; hence the name of the new company became "Metalade,

Richard F. Groth, co-founder of Metalade.

Inc." In addition to Mr. Ade, the officers of the new company were Richard Groth, vice president of sales; Robert Gage, vice president of manufacturing; Helen Schult, treasurer; Otto Stingle and Carl Rittler, vice presidents. The company was capitalized by selling stock to all of the employees, plus some outside investors.

The company started out in 5,000-square-feet of leased space in the rear of a screw machine shop. The shop had a 20-foot-high metal ceiling, and the only separation from the 13 screw machines was an eight-foot plywood wall. The original office was 10 feet by 30 feet for four people. The working environment was not very pleasant during the first three years, but it was overcome by the pride of ownership amongst the group. By 1971, the company had grown enough that they moved into a new 12,000-square-foot building on Metro Park. A 10,000-square-foot addition was completed in 1977, as the company continued to grow.

Mr. Ade retired in 1978, and Mr. Groth took over as president. Mr. Stingle and Mr. Rittler also retired, and were replaced as officers by Theodore Strang and Hans Papproth who had been with the company from the beginning. In 1982, the company moved into its current headquarters in a 57,000-square-foot building located in Henrietta, NY, with sales revenues of $3.5 million. The company acquired a plating and painting company in 1987 known as Stuart Oliver Holtz and began operating it as the Finishing and Assembly Division of Metalade, Inc. In 1991, Metalade acquired a company in Erie, PA, known as Ervite Corporation. Ervite was a 150,000-square-foot fabricating plant with 100 employees. By 1992, the combined revenues of all three locations were in excess of $20 million, and it was decided to

Corporate headquarters and fabricating plant in Rochester.

separate the three locations into separate companies. The fabricating plant became Metalade NY, Inc.; Ervite Corporation was renamed Metalade PA, Inc.; and the Finishing and Assembly Division remained Metalade, Inc.

Metalade PA continued to grow over the next four years when Digital Equipment Corporation in Massachusetts awarded them a very large contract for rack mount cabinets. The contracts expanded over the next two years, and Digital requested that Metalade PA open an assembly and warehousing operation in Salem, NH to support the "just-in-time" manufacturing philosophy they had adopted. Metalade PA leased a 20,000-square-foot building located two miles from the Digital Equipment Northeast Manufacturing plant in Salem. By 1999, Metalade PA was producing over 10,000 cabinets per year for Digital, who by that time had been acquired by Compaq Computer Corporation. In addition to the tremendous growth in Pennsylvania and New Hampshire, Metalade NY in Rochester had decided to open a small fabricating shop in Sanford, Florida to better serve some major customers in the Orlando area.

Finishing and assembly plant in Avon, New York.

Metalade fabricating operation in Orlando, Florida.

In 1997, Metalade leased a 15,000-square-foot building in Sanford that became known as Metalade FL, Inc. Metalade FL acquired a fabricating shop in Sanford in 1999 that was a captive shop owned by Datamax Corporation, a manufacturer of bar code label printers. Metalade FL moved its small operation into the former Datamax shop, and became a total of 55,000-square-feet with 100 employees. With five different locations, "The Metalade Group" as it became known, had grown to over 350,000-square-feet with 500 employees and total annual revenues of $50 million.

In late 1999, Compaq Corporation decided to close their Salem, NH manufacturing plant, and move the product to Texas and California. Although Compaq was anxious to have Metalade PA establish remote sites similar to New Hampshire in Texas and California to support the product shift, Mr. Groth decided it was in the best interest of the company to focus on the East Coast customers. In early 2000, Metalade PA was sold to one of the largest enclosure manufacturers in the world, APW Corporation. Due to the demand for powder coat painting by their customers, Metalade NY opened a new powder coat finishing plant in East Avon, NY, and consolidated all of their finishing operations there. By 2001, the Metalade Group consisted of the fabricating plant located in Henrietta, NY, the finishing and assembly division in Avon, NY, and Metalade FL, Inc. in Sanford, FL, with annual revenues of $20 million.

Over the 33-year history of the company, all of the original 18 employees had retired, with the exception of Mr. Groth, who along with his wife now owns the companies. Mr. Groth attributes the wonderful success enjoyed by the companies to the tremendous dedication and hard work of the employees over the years. Mr. Groth currently dedicates most of his time to the operations in Florida, where he now makes his home, while Executive Vice President Mr. Richard McKay is managing the Rochester and Avon operations.

Metalade has always had a "passion for pleasing the customer" philosophy, which has been the cornerstone of its success.

MONROE COMMUNITY COLLEGE

The time was right for Monroe Community College. It was 1960, the dawn of the decade of empowerment. Nationwide, a scattering of community colleges was just beginning to take root. For thousands of men and women previously excluded from higher education, a publicly-funded, two-year institution in their own community offered exciting new opportunities for growth.

In Rochester, the seed was planted one afternoon with a single phone call to County Manager Gordon Howe. "Listen, Gordon," said Carl Hallauer, president and chairman of Bausch & Lomb. "I've just seen the community college down at Corning. Monroe County's got to have one of those." Hallauer soon had the ear of Governor Nelson A. Rockefeller and, within a year, Monroe Community College was born.

Monroe Community College opened its doors in the fall of 1962 in the former East High Schood on Alexander Street. Demand was so high, it took only a few years to outgrow that site; the College moved to its Brighton location on East Henrietta Road in 1968.

By the time MCC opened for business in September of 1962, it had been embraced by hundreds of families whose sons, daughters, husbands and wives had long desired an affordable college in their midst. It had likewise been championed by the Rochester business community, whose success depended on a steady supply of well-trained employees, and by the Monroe County Legislature.

The fact that 410 Alexander Street, the old East High School, had been condemned by the city as a fire hazard was no deterrent. With the "can-do" spirit that came to define MCC, the College had its first campus.

It was Monroe County that provided the land for the new Brighton Campus. For years, the property on East Henrietta Road had been the site of a pig farm. By 1968, however, it was transformed into a carefully designed, if still quite dusty, new home for MCC.

It was a roll-up-your-sleeves attitude that would build MCC into the largest community college in Upstate New York. MCC became the fastest growing of the 30 community colleges in the state, increasing its enrollment during the '80s by more than 41 percent. Such growth, however, put a severe strain on the physical plant and in 1991, MCC announced plans for a second campus to handle the load. Named in honor of long-time and highly-respected Trustee E. Kent Damon, the Damon City Campus opened in 1992.

In 1997, MCC opened its Applied Technologies Center, a $6.4 million state-of-the-art training facility for some of the fastest growing industries in the country. There, approximately 1,000 students, many of them employees of Rochester area businesses, now

Monroe Community College returned to its roots in 1992 with the establishment of the Damon City Campus in downtown Rochester. Floyd "Bud" Amann, executive dean of the Damon City Campus, Dr. Alice H. Young, chair, Board of Trustees, and Dr. Peter A. Spina, president, unveil a portrait of the campus' namesake, E. Kent Damon, longtime MCC trustee, Xerox executive and community leader.

gather to learn the latest methods in precision tooling and machining, automotive technology, and heating, ventilation and air conditioning.

"The spirit of an institution is developed first by those who come to teach," says Dr. Alice H. Young, a founding trustee and MCC Trustee Chair Emerita. "Their dedication to the betterment of this institution and to this community has given MCC its national reputation for innovation."

In the 21st century, Monroe Community College is internationally-recognized for the quality of its programs and its commitment to innovation. One of only 20 institutions that constitute the board of directors of the League for Innovation in the Community College, MCC is frequently looked to as a leader in the community college movement. Locally, MCC is the college of choice for students across the demographic spectrum and a "front-and-center" player in meeting the unique needs of Greater Rochester.

THE NORMAN HOWARD SCHOOL

The founders of The Norman Howard School had a specific purpose in mind. They wanted to provide their learning disabled children (LD) with an educational program that would help them make progress in learning. They wanted that education to be provided in Rochester, so that the children could benefit from the support of their families. Up until 1980, if parents were exploring options outside of the public schools, the only choice was to send their children to boarding schools specializing in educating students with LD.

In 1975 Bill Hoskin, Madeline Roeding, and Shirley Cass set out to establish a day school that would deliver comprehensive curriculum for girls and boys diagnosed with learning disabilities from the Rochester area and surrounding region. Mr. Norman Howard, head of the Gow School in South Wales, provided inspirational leadership in establishing the school that bears his name.

The Norman Howard School (NHS) was granted provisional charter by the Board of Regents of the University of New York in 1978. In 1980, NHS embarked on its mission to deliver programs designed to address individual learning needs and to advance understanding and awareness of LD in the community. Occupying a rented classroom and office in the Oakview School in West Irondequoit, NHS opened its doors to six students. The School made two moves as it grew in the late 1980s: one to a location on Helendale Road in East Irondequoit and a second one to the Brookside School, owned by the Brighton Central School District. In 1995, NHS acquired a former church located in Henrietta and moved to its permanent home.

A major hurdle was crossed in 1984, when the Board of Regents granted NHS an absolute charter. In 1990, NHS received New York

Outdoor education is an integral part of the curriculum at the Norman Howard School.

State Education Department accreditation as a special program, which meant that school districts could place and pay the tuition for approved students.

The educational program at NHS comprises a combination of remedial work with strategy instruction relevant across all the content areas. The School utilizes a neurodevelopmental model, training teachers to pinpoint the areas of competence and areas in need of improvement. NHS adopted The Wilson Reading System, an Orton-Gillingham based, multi-sensory remedial reading program, in 1995. Performing and fine arts encourage individualized learning and offer a means for students to express what they know. Adaptive technology software and Internet access provide alternative oppor-

tunities for learning, work production, and creativity.

NHS is a thriving program in demand by many western New York students needing a specialized approach to learning. The School serves nearly 190 students from more than 44 school districts and 10 surrounding counties. NHS remains a day school, so some of these students are bused in from great distances. Two-thirds of all students are sent to NHS to learn to read and all students receive a period per day dedicated to reading. As a designated NYSED 12:1:1 program, student to teacher ratio in the classroom is effectively low.

NHS supports community education and awareness of learning disabilities by hosting speakers throughout the year and offering these presentations to the public. In addition, NHS fosters community collaboration by exploring and implementing new models of education for students with LD with area public and private schools.

OPTICAL GAGING PRODUCTS, INC.

Many of the products people use every day are made possible by a company most people do not know. From headquarters in Rochester, New York, Optical Gaging Products (OGP®) produces dimensional measurement systems manufacturers rely on to meet their quality requirements. Thousands of OGP systems are in use around the world, measuring parts as diverse as fuel injectors for the automotive industry, razor blades for personal care, and coronary stents for cardio-vascular surgery. Virtually any manufactured part that has a dimensional drawing is a candidate for measurement by an OGP system.

OGP provides "Precision for People." It offers precision for the company that uses OGP systems to manufacture high quality parts and also for the operator of the OGP machine who depends on its accuracy for making the right decisions about the manufacturing process. And ultimately, for the

The Optical Gaging Products facility in Rochester, New York houses all the company's engineering, marketing, and manufacturing departments. In addition, the company has facilities in Tempe, Arizona; Germany; and Singapore.

Edward C. Polidor, founder and retired CEO of Optical Gaging Products shown demonstrating an optical comparator, circa 1948.

end-consumer of those parts who expects quality from his or her investment in that company's products.

The history of Optical Gaging Products starts in 1945 with Edward C. Polidor. OGP's story is actually a woven history of a few companies—some that owned OGP and others owned by OGP. They included ESD (Engineering Specialties Division of the Universal Engraving and Colorplate Company)—the original company founded by Mr. Polidor, PGI (Projection Gages, Inc.), and Automation Gages. Throughout the history, the Polidor family has been at the helm.

Optical Gaging Products' history is full of individual accomplishments and collective pride. A family spirit has always been an important part of OGP's success. Nothing shows this better than the dedication of its employees and sales representatives as expressed by their longevity with the company. Plaques line the walls of the main conference room citing employees with 20 and 30 years of service. Several of the company's independent sales representatives have been with the company continually since the 1950s.

The influence of Rochester is an important aspect of the company's history. Rochester, New York is known as the "World's Image Center," because of such well-known companies as Eastman Kodak, Bausch & Lomb, and Xerox. It was Eastman Kodak that started OGP on the path it has followed ever since. As the exclusive distributor for Kodak's Contour Projector product line, OGP embarked on its mission to provide precision dimensional measurement equipment for manufacturers everywhere. Since that time OGP has advanced the technology, producing optical comparators that are recognized as the best that money can buy. In addition, the technology evolved to video measurement, now the largest part of OGP's business, and a market where OGP is recognized as number one.

From day one, OGP's products have been noted for their ease of use. In the spirit of precision for people, a goal of the company has been to make technically-advanced measurement technology available to and usable by the people who need it, without sacrificing the necessary precision and accuracy in the process. An early example is its Projectron™ product, the world's first automatic edge detection system for the company's optical comparators. With Projectron, almost any user could get measurements that used to rely on the expertise of a seasoned operator.

In the late 1970s, OGP's direction was passed on to Ed's son Tarry, a graduate engineer from Norwich University and MIT. Under his strong technical leadership, OGP continued its history of innovation in dimensional measurement, while successfully steering corporate strategy through competitive and economic obstacles.

A breakthrough product that more than any other has defined what OGP is most noted for today is the SmartScope®. Introduced

One of the early OGP Contour Projectors®, the Opticom Qualifier™ 30. OGP continues to offer a full line of contour projectors for customers who rely on this proven technology, now incorporating electronics and software for automatic measurement. As a result, these new systems reduce training costs, and increase productivity.

in 1991, this compact benchtop video measurement system brought a formerly expensive, high technology capability to the majority. At half the price of comparable systems, and with features such as a color camera, zoom lens, and friendly MeasureMind® software, it was an immediate success. SmartScope exemplified the company's goal of bringing precision measurement to the people, and continues to do so today, now with more than 10 models under the SmartScope banner.

Today OGP has sales of more than $50 million and employs more than 250 people. The company's systems are in use around the world. With its software available in a dozen languages, OGP continues its effort to provide precision measurement without the need for complex, formal training. More and more of the skill necessary to get high quality measurements is being designed into the products themselves, reducing the demands on the operators, and improving productivity.

The companies in the history of Optical Gaging Products changed yet again in 2000 with the formation of a new parent company. Quality Vision International (QVI)

One of OGP's latest products, the SmartScope® Quest 650, is a fully-automatic measuring system that integrates several technologies to give it capabilities formerly available only in a number of separate instruments. Based on video measuring technology, its patented TeleStar™ optics offer superior resolution, while tight integration of laser and touch probe sensors allow Quest to measure a wider range of critical features to even tighter tolerances.

was founded by the management of OGP as an umbrella company for OGP and associated companies. As the new millennium gets underway, those associated companies include Quality Vision Services (QVS) to provide service to the family of companies; QSoft, a software development company that caters exclusively to QVI companies; and View Engineering, a manufacturer of in-process measurement systems. The need for precision measurement continues as manufacturing tolerances get tighter—all in the effort to continually improve quality. OGP and its sister companies intend to continue the mission of providing the measurement tools needed by manufacturers to meet these demands.

PENFIELD FEDERAL CREDIT UNION

Founded on the premise of "people helping people" the credit union movement's natural progression to today grew out of the concept that people pool their money, allowing them to make loans to one another. This process offered neighbors a way to succeed, in turn building a prosperous community.

What is a credit union? A credit union is a cooperative, not-for-profit financial institution organized to promote thrift and provide credit to its members. They are member-owned, controlled by individuals who join them. In fact, the board of directors is comprised of members, who serve their elected terms on a volunteer basis. Because they are not paid for their services, earnings from the business flow back to its members in the form of higher dividends on savings and lower rates on loans, with fewer associated fees. It is a system designed to benefit the membership as a whole, rather than a select few.

During the 1960s credit unions were beginning to pop-up in educational circles. Penfield's founders met with the president of West Irondequoit Teacher's Federal Credit Union, embracing the concept of "people helping people."

Everyone loves a parade! PFCU earned national acclaim as the first place winner of the CUES Golden Mirror Award for their participation in community events throughout 2000. Here, employees and their children march in Perinton's July Fourth parade.

Circa, mid-1970s, PCFCU's main office just inside Len's Den.

They wholeheartedly believed in this grassroots opportunity to develop an alternative to the impersonality of commercial banks while providing low cost financial services to fellow employees. In February 1969, in the home of teacher Dick Dennison, Penfield Central Federal Credit Union (PCFCU) was born, chartered to serve the employees and their families of the Penfield Central School District.

PCFCU's Charter membership consisted of President Richard Dennison, Vice President Richard Piccirilli, Treasurer William Leo, Secretary Phyllis Sleight and Director Hiram Korpeck. Committee members were Fred Beerse, Gary Lazenby, Donna VanHoover, Richard French and F. Gordon Shay, representing all departments of the school district. Officers and committee members, impassioned by their cause, served without compensation. Today, all charter members remain active in PFCU.

According to former President/CEO Len Szumiloski, one of the founders' greatest hurdles was to convince people that a credit union was different from a bank and that being an owner/member of their credit union was far superior to being a customer of any bank. During PCFCU's first three months in operation 200 school district employees and their family members joined the credit union, putting their faith and finances in this new not-for-profit, member-owned venture.

With expansion in mind, PCFCU's charter was amended to include four private schools in Fall of 1980—Our Lady of Mercy High School, St. Joseph's School, Harley and Allendale-Columbia Schools. Employees of these institutions were looking to join a credit union, feeling it would be more pragmatic to align with a pre-existing one, rather than create theirs from scratch.

The year 1983 saw more changes for PCFCU. In April, BOCES #1 Monroe Federal Credit Union merged with Penfield. By joining forces, the combined credit unions could offer additional services to their members, better effecting economies while growing the credit union's membership base.

Expanding to include other groups, it became clear that a name change was necessary. In March 1984 the board of directors voted to seek a charter change to officially drop "Central" from their title. Penfield Federal Credit Union (PFCU) is the name that identifies the credit union today.

Penfield Federal Credit Union experienced steady growth over its 32-year history. To accommodate this growth, PFCU has had several homes, literally, throughout their history. Beginning in Dick Dennison's house, then moving to Don Sowinski's, the first few years saw transactions taking place in three presidents' homes. Most notably, however, was during the mid-1970s, in former President/CEO Len Szumiloski's den. As the story goes, members waiting to be serviced, took a place in Len's den. While waiting their turn, Len & Molly's children entertained members by reading stories or playing games before bedtime. Proudly, the credit union remains a family tradition with many relationships formed in that den still strong today.

In the early 1980s PFCU's membership outgrew its down-home surroundings and moved to the Denonville Middle School in the heart of Penfield. With membership rising to over 14,000 members, the building could hold no more. So in 1995 PFCU, with over 150 schools, social service agencies, small businesses and community groups offering credit union eligibility to their affiliates and family members, built their

present location at 2520 Browncroft Boulevard in Penfield.

With assets at $69 million, 1997 marked a year of transition, ushering in Ron Oleston as the new president/CEO. With his vision for the future, Ron catapulted PFCU into the new millenium bringing technological advancements while maintaining the top-notch standard of personal service PFCU is noted for.

PFCU's vision for the future is simple: "We will be our member's first choice for financial services by creating an experience that cannot be duplicated."

With increased membership comes increased responsibility to provide a full-range of financial services while maintaining the highest level of member satisfaction. In Spring 2000, PFCU celebrated the opening of its first branch, in Perinton, to accommodate the more than 185 eligible groups. By September 2001, under Ron's direction, PFCU's assets increased to over $89 million.

The motto "People Helping People" is probably best characterized though a story related by Len Szumiloski. A young man approached Len during his term

Penfield Federal Credit Union's present location at 2520 Browncroft Boulevard, near the corner of Creek Street in Penfield.

as president/CEO. He thanked him for saving his life. Taking the young man's statement as a figure of speech, Len responded appropriately. The gentleman soon made himself clear. Life had taken a bad turn. He had been unemployed until the job that qualified him for the credit union. Other areas in his personal life were in disarray. He had applied for a loan with PFCU without much hope of his request being granted.

PFCU granted the young man's request. From that day forward, he vowed to turn his life around. What Len didn't know was, years earlier while applying for his loan, the young man before him had been on the verge of taking his life.

As the years pass, leadership changes, and technology advances. But what remains constant is the commitment of Penfield Federal Credit Union's role in its member's personal stories. People helping people.

PHOTIKON CORPORATION

Photikon Corporation was founded in 1989 by James D. Condon and John W. Fitzpatrick. Photikon, meaning "light image" in Greek, seemed to be an appropriate name for this innovative new company.

Jim's background was mainly in sales and distribution; he had spent over 10 years selling components to the imaging industry. John was an engineer with Xerox Corporation for 10 years and was instrumental in the development of the Organic Photoreceptor Belts (OPC) used in Xerox high speed copiers. John also held many patents for his work with toners and developers.

Condon had founded Engineering Sales Consultants (ESC) in 1986. ESC was primarily a distributor of hard-to-find components used in copiers and printers. With the emergence of the remanufacturing industry, came new opportunities in toners and developers. These opportunities brought John Fitzpatrick and Condon together, and soon John became a partner in ESC.

From left to right: Mark Condon, executive vice president, Jim Condon, president, and David Kurty, vice president and general manager.

While still operating from Condon's basement the company grew through product sales and consulting contracts.

In the summer of 1988 Jim and John met with Frank Cantor, manager of OEM sales for IBM. With the fast growth of remanufacturing there was an opportunity to sell organic photoreceptor belts. In January 1989 Photikon was founded and a contract was signed with IBM to supply OPC web material to Photikon. With John's belt manufacturing expertise, a contract manufacturer was set up in Boulder, Colorado.

The business operated out of Condon's basement until 1992, when Photikon moved into a 1,500-square-foot office and small manufacturing area in Fairport, New York.

Scott Gosert joined the company in 1992 to manage ESC. ESC was bought out by Photikon in 1993 and Scott became an employee of Photikon, as well as a stockholder. The company began to remanufacture belt-type OPC cartridges for some large OEM's and remanufacturers.

In 1993 David Kurty was added to the senior staff and became a stockholder. Kurty had an extensive background in operations from Bausch & Lomb and Schlegel Corporation and was responsible for organizing the company into a state-of-the-art operation. The company continued to grow and add new products such as fusers, developers and cleaners for the remanufacturing industry. OPC belts remained the company's main focus and by 1994 they were manufacturing 10 different belt products. Photikon became known worldwide as the only independent OPC belt manufacturer with customers in the U.S. and Western and Eastern Europe. With the objective of manufacturing niche products Photikon continued to grow and be profitable.

In 1994 John Fitzpatrick retired and was put on a five-year consulting contract. John worked on special product development

Photikin world headquarters.

Manufacturing area w/opc film sensitive-lighting.

Compatible printer and copier consumables remanufactured by Photikon.

projects until his death in 1997. Late in 1994 Mark Condon, Jim's son, joined the business. Mark came from an extensive marketing and sales background with Eastman Kodak and Harris Corporation. Mark took over as sales manager and new business development. With significant growth by the following year, Photikon had to move again—this time to a 9,000-square-foot office and manufacturing facility.

In 1995 Photikon formed its first Board of Advisors. The roster included: Jim Condon, chairman; Dave Kurty, secretary; Bill Vick, treasurer (retired co-founder of General Dynamics); Mike Murray (retired vice president and general manager of Kodak Copier Division); Bill Fowble (senior vice president of manufacturing, Kodak); and Jim Wemett (owner of ROC Communications). The Board of Advisors was primarily formed as a mentoring system for all key managers. This group of talented individuals was a key element in Photikon's success over the last seven years. Today Jim, Dave and Mike are still on the

Board and Mark Condon (treasurer), Joe Marino (retired vice president of manufacturing, Xerox) and Ron Kosmider (president, Printer Components, Inc.), make up the 2001 board.

In 1997 Photikon achieved the Rochester Top 100 Privately-Held Companies Award. Photikon has also received awards for hiring people with disabilities.

In 1998, with over 20 employees Photikon needed more space to grow. Not finding adequate space in the area Condon decided to build a new facility. With help from the Monroe County Industrial Development Agency, the Town of Perinton and local banks, a 17,000-square-foot building was constructed at 100 Photikon Drive in Fairport, New York.

A state-of-the-art building was finished in September 1998 with offices, high production lines, product development and quality labs. Production capability increased 35 percent and product quality increased to 98 percent. Today, with over 30 employees Photikon, continues to grow at a rate of 15 to 18 percent each year.

THE PIKE COMPANY

When he was a small boy, John Barnabas Pike crossed the Atlantic from Holland with his parents, sailed up the Hudson, and crossed New York State by packet boat on the Erie Canal to Rochester. Here the elder Pike, a carpenter, settled shortly before the Civil War. John followed his father's trade and as a young man in 1873 became a carpenter contractor.

John B. Pike's first general headquarters was on Minerva Place in downtown Rochester, where the firm produced fine millwork to be installed by its carpentry division. Early in the 1900s, the second John Pike, John Derrick Pike, designed a building for the company office and mill at One Circle Street in Rochester. This remained the headquarters of John B. Pike & Son, as it was directed by John D. Pike's son-in-law, Thomas F. Judson, chairman and chief executive, and, president and chief operating officer. John

Eastman International Museum of Photography archives world famous photographs.

Corning Incorporated Riverfront Expansion to existing World Headquarters, Corning, N.Y.

Derrick Pike died in 1975 at the age of 91; until the age of 89, he had attended to business daily.

In 1985, Thomas F. Judson, Jr. established The Pike Company to continue the tradition started by John B. Pike. Today he serves as chairman and chief operating officer.

The Pike name is identified with scores of structures across New York State and throughout the Northeast, and in the coastal regions of the South—on churches and factories, schools and libraries, colleges and hospitals.

Its first project of significant size was the original Stromberg-Carlson plant, built on Carlson Road on the city's East Side about 1911. Since then its accomplishments have been little short of staggering. Pike's historic construction experience includes the architectural gem, McKim, Mead and White's Rochester Savings Bank, the Rochester Museum and Science Center, Asbury First Methodist Church, the Finger Lakes Race Track, Midtown Plaza, and Kodak's Riverwood Marketing Education Center to name a few.

By the early 1980s, Pike was identified with bridges and highways, marine projects and hard rock tunnels, from Maine to the Florida and as far west as Vancouver, B.C. Other pioneering civil projects included a hard rock tunnel for Niagara Mohawk at Oswego, process equipment work for the Monroe County Resource Recovery Facility, construction of nine bridges on Interstate Route 590 from Scottsville Road to the Lehigh Valley Railroad, a bypass for the Canandaigua Southwest

Arterial Highway, and numerous other projects throughout the East.

In the world of construction, the name Pike has come to mean integrity, craftsmanship and a commitment to doing the job right the first time. With a reputation for company values such as these, its no wonder that Pike has constructed and managed scores of structures across New York State and throughout the Northeast, Midwest and the coastal regions of the South.

Recently, Pike has completed projects for Rochester Institute of Technology, University of Rochester, Xerox and Monroe County. Last year, the company completed two major Rochester renovation projects: Xerox Square Tower's interior multi-floor renovation and Rochester Institute of Technology's Residence Halls project. Currently, Pike is working on the second phase of the Monroe County Hall of Justice and is constructing the Monroe County Jail.

Asbury First Methodist Church, 1955, the pattern for laying exterior limestone developed on the job.

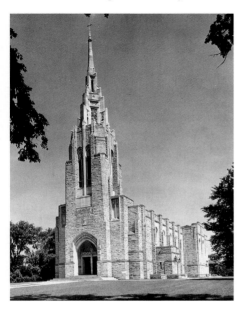

Interior of Rochester Savings Bank, 1928, designed by McKim, Mead and White, Architects.

While remaining solidly in the business of constructing buildings, Pike began to penetrate more and more into the nonbuilding construction arena. Since the 1940s, the company became a leader in construction management while the concept was still new to many. The nature of construction management enables Pike to work closely with client and architect, from budget to ribbon cutting.

The versatility of The Pike Company has been as significant as the vast size and importance of many of the projects it has seen to conclusion. It is safe to say that no other Rochester company in its field and few in the entire Northeast have left so many enduring memorials and such solid, visible, everyday, useful evidence of the skills of its engineers, artisans, craftsmen, and laborers.

The Pike Company's history is a legacy of construction excellence. But instead of being content with the past, the company continues to look ahead. Now in its fourth generation of family leadership, Pike is consistently meeting new challenges in all phases of work, always with the uncompromising philosophy of doing the job right the first time. Today, Judson reflects on future endeavors, stating: "With our depth of experience, Pike is an ideal strategic partner to help its clients grow their businesses."

ROBERTS WESLEYAN COLLEGE

Roberts Wesleyan College traces its roots to the Civil War era, a time when America was forced to confront critical social, political, religious and educational issues. The College's founder, Benjamin Titus Roberts—a contemporary of Frederick Douglass and Susan B. Anthony—was an active leader in seeking just and ethical resolution of those issues.

Ralph Waldo Emerson's assertion that "an institution is the lengthened shadow of one man" describes well the relationship between Roberts Wesleyan College and its distinguished founder. B.T. Roberts forsook a promising career in law to answer a call to Christian ministry, and then gave up the tempting path of comfortable ministry to contend for important but unpopular matters of principle. In short, Roberts Wesleyan College's motto, "Education for Character," reflects both her founder's mission for the institution and his own essence as a man of character.

Born in 1823, from his youth B.T. Roberts was a champion of causes and reforms vital to his day, most of which have prevailed since his death in 1893. He was a firm believer in labor rights and argued fervently for the farmer; consistently advocated for the rights of women, even when such a position was unpopular in his own movement; promoted temperance; stood in opposition to slavery; and argued for free seats in the house of worship. He was a founder of schools and advocated universal education.

For his stands against what he perceived as unacceptable compromise with moral principle in a variety of issues, B.T. Roberts was expelled from the Methodist Episcopal Church. This action was reversed a half-century later when the Genesee Conference of the Methodist Episcopal Church vindicated his character by restoring his parchments to his son, Benson H. Roberts.

The arch, built in 1926, symbolizes the college's connectedness to church and community.

Unbowed in his commitment to the issues and values he had championed, Rev. Roberts was chosen to be the first bishop of a new denomination, the Free Methodist Church. Subsequently and independently, he also founded Chili Seminary, an educational institution to prepare well-educated young people to become the servant-leaders of high character, of which he believed America was in so great need.

B.T. Roberts' life and vision are honored in the ongoing vitality of Roberts Wesleyan College and its educational philosophy that says, in part: *Academic pursuit is strengthened by the College's historical Christian concern for the communication of human values and the development of the whole person. Its curriculum and co-curriculum are designed to foster awareness and development of one's potential, sensitivity to the rights and needs of others, and the integration of living, learning, and faith. Through membership in a community of learners, students are encouraged to cultivate the knowledge, skills, and attitudes that prepare them personally and professionally for life-long learning, creative leadership, and service to God and society.*

Roberts Wesleyan College is a vital part of Rochester's exceptional mix of educational opportunities. A coed liberal arts college with an enrollment of more than 1,800 students, a Christian world-view, and a tradition of excellence dating back to 1866, Roberts offers some 40 undergraduate programs, plus Master of Education and Master of Social Work degrees and a Master of Science degree in Organizational Management. Northeastern Seminary on the Roberts campus offers Master of Divinity and Master of Arts in Theology degrees. Innovative undergraduate offerings at Roberts include adult degree-completion programs in Organizational Management and Nursing. In addition to regional accreditation by the Middle States Association of Colleges and Schools, Roberts Wesleyan enjoys professional accreditation by the National Association of Schools of Music; the National Association of Schools of Art and Design; the National League of Nursing; the Council for Social Work Education; and the Association of Collegiate Business Schools and Programs.

Roberts Wesleyan has two primary focuses, one inward and one outward: to maximize the value of each student's college experience and to address appropriate educational needs of the community. Roberts' community-minded approach is reflected in such activities as establishment of undergraduate and graduate degree programs designed around specific community needs; development of college-community orchestra and theatre programs; construction of athletic/recreation and fine arts complexes for community as well as college use; development of College

The Roberts Cultural Life Center has brought art, music and theatre to Rochecster's west side since it opened in 1996.

With enrollment having climbed from 600 to more than 1,800 students since 1981, Roberts Wesleyan College's recent history is a study in the potential of visionary planning, effective marketing, development, budgeting and educational delivery. Consequently, vigorous progress has become one of the College's primary characteristics.

Since 1981, Roberts Wesleyan College has:
• Increased student enrollment from 600 to more than 1,800 students,
• Built an endowment to $12 million,
• Conducted three successful capital campaigns producing major campus expansion,
• Launched five graduate degree programs, including those of Northeastern Seminary,

• Achieved national professional accreditation in five academic concentrations,
• Completely computerized the campus,
• Developed an on-line management degree program,
• Balanced the budget for the past 20 years,
• Secured funding sources which will eliminate all but self-amortizing debt by the year 2002, and
• Developed College Greene, Inc., an 87-acre retirement community adjacent to campus.

The past two decades represent one of Roberts Wesleyan College's most extensive eras of development and expansion. The College is a vital institution today because of individuals committed to its mission and future. This includes not only a dedicated faculty and staff, but also the many individuals, corporations and foundations who embrace Roberts as a valuable part of the community and generously provide resources for the College to grow and expand its quality service to students.

Carpenter Hall, built during the Great Depression, was named for Adella Paulina Carpenter, dean of women for 40 years.

Greene, a college-related retirement community; and increased involvement of faculty as professional resources for the community.

As a "college of the community," Roberts Wesleyan has continually sought to meet the real educational needs of the citizenry it serves since its founding just a year after the Civil War ended. Initially operated as a pre-college academy, the institution became a junior college in 1945 and a four-year college in 1949. The College entered the field of graduate education in 1992. Northeastern Seminary was established on the campus in 1998 and is already recognized as one of the largest graduate level seminaries in upstate New York.

ROCHESTER GAS AND ELECTRIC CORPORATION

While never becoming a household word, the name Thomas W. Yawger pops up often in the history of Rochester Gas and Electric Corporation. The young man had to be jittery that early morning in 1888, reporting for his first day of work at Edison Electric Illuminating Company.

The new Edison power plant was where the Rochester Community War Memorial is today. The young man was told he'd be working there 12 hours a day, seven days a week with no holidays. To be available for emergencies in off-hours the company set him up with a free bed and washing basin right there at work. The usual emergency came when the nearby Lyceum Theater energized electric footlights. Yawger had to scramble to adjust the voltage so that the lights for other customers wouldn't dim too much.

Energy was bustling in Rochester and so was invention. Just down the road from Tom that morning another young man was pushing feverishly to get a new product on the market. It was a hand-held roll-film camera that would bring the wonders of photography to everyone. Just push the button, and his company would

do the rest. George Eastman had already decided on a name for his product—one that would become a household word—Kodak.

In 1888, electricity was still a novelty around Rochester. It had been only eight years since a small electric dynamo driven by the flow of the Genesee River cranked out the first power here to light 10 electric arc lamps in the Reynolds Arcade Building.

Forty years before that, in 1848, Rochester Gas Light Company built a gas plant that lit 10 streetlights and 80 homes. More

gas companies sprung up as this new fuel replaced whale oil and invisibly delivered the fuel directly to the appliance in homes and businesses.

Five separate power companies and three gas companies would serve different customers in Rochester toward 1900. It really made sense to combine them into one company. The economies of scale and removal of redundant energy systems would not only work better for the customers, but for the communities and investors, as well.

Through a series of mergers and acquisitions, Rochester Railway and Light Company collected all the energy companies under one roof in 1904. In 1919, Rochester Railway and Light Company was renamed Rochester Gas and Electric Corporation, and continued to power Rochester's significant share of the American Industrial Revolution.

In 1936, Yawger wrote, in one of his many accounts of the role of energy in Rochester, "It lifted the burdens of millions of people and gave new and vital impetus to industrial progress." This was a city of rapid growth and invention—from optical visionaries John Jacob Bausch and Henry Lomb, who partnered in 1855 as Bausch & Lomb, to George Eastman's Kodak and later in the 20th century to Haloid Corporation that brought xerography to the world as Xerox Corporation. They became global companies that nurtured the establishment and growth of hundreds of other businesses and institutions in the Rochester area—all relying on RG&E for consistent electric, gas and steam energy.

Keeping pace with rapidly growing energy demands was RG&E's job, and still is. Post World War II escalation of prosperity, population, and productivity demanded a doubling of electric energy capacity every 10 years. Sprawl to the suburbs exhausted the capabilities of Rochester-based manufactured gas. Pipelines

were built to transport natural gas from the fields far south right up to RG&E customers in communities beyond Rochester.

Power plants were planned and built to meet all the increased energy needs. Beebee Station was built on the banks of the Genesee in downtown Rochester amid the ovens that manufactured gas. Russell Station on Lake Ontario added coal-fired generating units from 1948 to 1957.

As early as 1947, RG&E was studying the potential that could come from nuclear fission. It was a long and politically bumpy road over the next 20 years until 1970, when the R. E. Ginna Nuclear plant went into commercial operation, nearly doubling RG&E's electric capacity at that time. In 2000, the Ginna plant not only remained one of the top-ranked nuclear plants in America, but became the longest-operating one as well.

The logic that drove the local mergers of separate energy companies at the onset of the 20th century prompted a similar move entering the 21st. The idea to deregulate the energy industry and offer consumers a choice of energy suppliers gave rise to the consolidation of energy operations on a regional and national level.

RG&E negotiated a five-year deregulation plan in New York State in 1996. The plan worked exceptionally well, reducing electric costs to customers while promoting energy choice. Agreements to deregulate natural gas had already been made.

While retaining its regulated business of producing, delivering and selling energy, RG&E created and acquired unregulated energy companies that compete for business among customers both inside and outside of its service territory. In 2000, RG&E shareholders formed RGS Energy Group, Inc., a holding company overseeing the RG&E regulated business and the unregulated Energetix subsidiary and its subsidiaries, as well.

In 2001, RGS Energy Group shareholders approved a merger proposal between RGS and Energy East Corporation. Just as consolidation had worked well in the early 20th century for consumers, employees, shareholders and communities, so too can it work now.

RG&E, now providing electric and gas energy to more than a million people in its 2,700-square-mile territory, has been at the leading edge of Rochester history spanning three centuries. But it's always the people who make history, not companies. RG&E's history is rooted in the generations of dedicated people who worked with energy and communities here since 1848.

Tom Yawger went on to become head of RG&E electric operations and a noted energy author. He died in 1954—still an active employee—66 years after reporting for work that first day in 1888.

RG&E. Always At Your service.

RG&E people make it all work. Thomas W. Yawger, RG&E electrical pioneer.

ROCHESTER INSTITUTE OF TECHNOLOGY

Internationally-recognized as a world leader in career-oriented and professional education, Rochester Institute of Technology (RIT) has been setting an innovative standard since 1829, when Colonel Nathaniel Rochester became the first president of the Rochester Athenaeum. In 1891, the Athenaeum merged with Mechanics Institute, which had been founded by a group of business leaders to instruct in "drawing and such other branches of studies as are most important for industrial pursuits." In 1944, recognizing the increasingly specialized professional nature of its programs, the university adopted the name it holds today. Since then, RIT has continued to evolve as a university that is innovative, forward-thinking and responsive to the changing needs of industry, its community and the world.

Since moving in 1968 from downtown Rochester to a 1,480-acre campus in suburban Henrietta, RIT has expanded its student population significantly and added numerous academic programs. RIT

RIT's campus covers 1,480 acres and has won awards for its architecture.

today enrolls nearly 15,000 full- and part-time undergraduate and graduate students in more than 360 career-oriented and professional programs. The student population draws from across the United States, and includes over 1,200 international students. The university's cooperative education program is the fourth oldest and one of the largest in the world.

RIT's academic portfolio covers a broad range of disciplines, and the university is particularly renowned for its expertise in imaging, computing and information sciences, photography, and education of the deaf. As a teaching university with a strong interest in applied research in targeted fields, RIT is committed to preparing students for successful ca-

reers in a rapidly changing world. Many of its academic programs are unique and enjoy a worldwide reputation, including the nation's first undergraduate programs in software engineering, information technology, and microelectronic engineering and the world's only Ph.D. program in imaging science. The university's unusually diverse spectrum of programs includes telecommunications, computer engineering, computer graphics, photographic illustration, biomedical photography, biotechnology, bioinformatics, printing management, art and design, and international business. RIT has also been at the forefront in using distance learning technology to expand educational opportunities for individual learners and to address the education and training needs of its corporate partners.

The newest of RIT's eight colleges is the B. Thomas Golisano College of Computing and Information Sciences. Typical of RIT's visionary approach to career education, the College was established in 2001, in anticipation of the exploding worldwide demand for information technology professionals. In its initial year, more than 3,000 students were enrolled in computer science, information technology and software engineering. The National Technical Institute for the Deaf (NTID), established in 1965 by an act of Congress, provides comprehensive technical and professional programs for nearly 1,100 deaf and hard-of-hearing students. The other colleges at RIT are the College of Applied Science and Technology, College of Business, Kate Gleason College of Engineering, College of Imaging Arts and Sciences, and College of Liberal Arts. In 1997, RIT established the American College of Management and Technology in Dubrovnik, Croatia, offering programs in hospitality and service management to help rebuild the economy in the

The newest of RIT's hundreds of programs include a focus on microsystems. Here, students learn about microlithography, which plays a crucial role in next-generation computer chips.

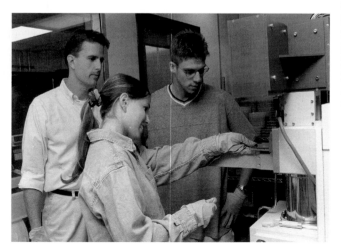

Early ceramics technology at RIT: 1909 instructor Frederick Walrath works alongside a student at Rochester Athenaeum and Mechanics Institute's Department of Applied and Fine Arts. Today, RIT's ceramic studies are a part of its School for American Crafts. Courtesy, Archives and Special Collections, RIT.

region. The American College joins the U.S. Business School in Prague, Czech Republic, in expanding RIT's reach to overseas programs.

RIT is the home of one of New York State's Strategically Targeted Academic Research (STAR) Centers, called the Information Technology (IT) Collaboratory. A partnership with several major corporations including Global Crossing, Frontier, Corning, Kodak and Xerox, along with the University at Buffalo and Alfred University, the Center's research is focused on four areas—microsystems, photonics, remote systems and high-bandwidth telecom networks. The STAR Center exemplifies RIT's role in contributing to the economic growth and vitality of the region and to the state of New York, a key part of RIT's mission throughout its more than 170-year history.

RIT's Chester F. Carlson Center for Imaging Science, named after the inventor of xerography, is also a key resource to industry and government for expertise in imaging and related sciences. The Center is a partner in the New York State Center for Advanced Technology in Electronic Imaging Systems whose mission is to conduct research in the field of electronic imaging, leverage these results for economic advantage to the state and the nation, and contribute to U.S. efforts to retain world leadership in imaging, document processing and telecommunications.

RIT's Center for Integrated Manufacturing Studies (CIMS) also contributes to the university's economic impact. Its mission is to increase the competitiveness of U.S. manufacturers through applied technology and training. Headquartered at CIMS, the National Center for Remanufacturing and Resource Recovery (NCR[3]) is the world's leading center for the development and transfer of technology in remanufacturing and product life-cycle design.

For the past decade, *U.S. News and World Report*'s poll of college presidents has ranked RIT as one of the nation's leading comprehensive universities. In the 2002 edition, RIT ranked fifth among the top regional universities in the north and tied for first in academic reputation. RIT's graduate photography program has consistently been ranked as first in the nation.

RIT contributes significantly to the educational, economic and cultural foundations of the Rochester community. It has grown and expanded to meet the emerging needs of area industries, and at the same time has broadened its role in responding to technology and workforce needs nationally and globally. Its academic and applied research programs have contributed to Rochester's reputation as a stronghold of technology and innovation.

Dating from its earliest days, the leaders of RIT have understood the key role that universities play in stimulating economic growth. The long tradition of partnering with industry and government to address emerging needs allows the university to claim its place as the "university of choice in a technological world."

Telecommunications technology connects to high-powered career programs at RIT, many focusing on management. Information technology, computer science and software engineering are also among top choices.

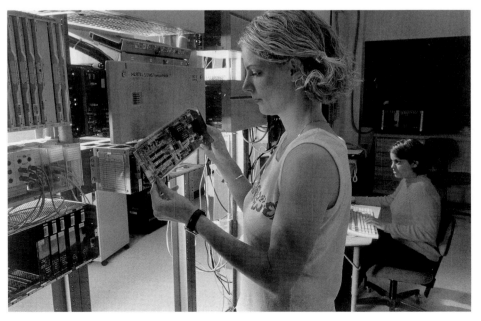

THE ROCHESTER MIDLAND CORPORATION

Entrepreneurship has played an important role in the history and growth of the United States since the invention of the cotton mill and the steam engine. The spirit of invention and new ventures was certainly alive and well in Rochester, NY in the late 19th century, when George Eastman developed the Brownie Camera and launched a revolution in photography. Technological innovations were appearing with increasing frequency, and a number of other companies were founded during this time, including the Genesee Brewing Company (1878), The RJ Stasenburgh Company (1886-pharmaceuticals), and Garlock Sealing Technologies (1887). Shoe and button manufacturing as well as flour processing were also booming industries in Rochester during and after the Civil War.

Two young and ambitious occupants of a boarding house in Rochester were also keen to start their own business during this exciting period of change and promise. Daniel N. Calkins and C.P. "Percy" Crowell believed they could

Company CEO and chairman of the board, Harlan D. Calkins.

Daniel Calkins, center, and C.P. Crowell, right, with their wives and a friend at the Chicago World's Fair, 1893.

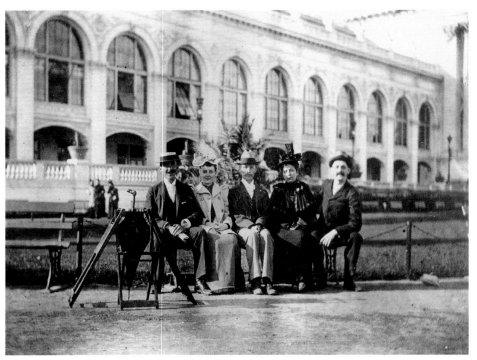

do (and earn) more than their day jobs could offer them, and in 1886, they began to spend evenings in the boarding house attic, cutting out components for baby shoes and children's moccasins by hand. Local women were paid on a piecework basis to sew and finish these shoes manually, and the fledgling business operated under the name of the Calkins & Crowell Company.

Two years later, The Aromatic Disinfecting Company of Philadelphia decided to sell its Rochester operations. With the proceeds of the sale of some property they had bought a year or two earlier, Calkins and Crowell purchased this business, which manufactured, sold and serviced disinfecting appliances for public restrooms. At the time of the purchase, there were about 600 such units installed primarily in hotels, restaurants and saloons between Rochester and Albany, New York.

In 1894, two more partners joined the company, and in 1897 the business was incorporated under the name of the Rochester Germicide Company. By now they had a fluid formula of their own and a total capitalization of $8,000. The shoe business was discontinued in 1895, and Calkins continued to hold down two jobs, now as a bookkeeper for the Crescent Flour Mill in addition to Secretary-Treasurer for Rochester Germicide. He also began developing a new fluid delivery system. The new unit was patented in 1898, and in January 1900, Calkins joined the company full time for $15.00 per week plus commissions.

In succeeding years, equipment and materials were further improved, related products manufactured, and regional sales offices opened. By 1907, Rochester Germicide was making hand soaps, floor cleaners, disinfectants, and insecticides, while warehousing and selling these products in Boston, New York, Toronto, Chicago, Pittsburgh, and Cleveland. In 1910, a new factory was built at 16 Dowling Place, which required two later expansions (this site is now in the center of the High Falls Brewing complex). In 1914, Daniel Calkins and twelve other manufacturers founded the Chemical Specialties Manufacturers Association, which is still in operation today as the Consumer Specialty Products Association (CSPA).

An important diversification opportunity occurred in 1927, when the Johnson & Johnson Company appointed Rochester Germicide as the exclusive distributor for vending machine sales of the "Modess" brand of sanitary napkins. With the bulk of its sales force already focused on the original restroom deodorization service, plus hand soaps, disinfectants and related products for sanitation and building maintenance, this was a natural fit for the growing company.

In the mid 1930s, the company developed a new fluid delivery system to replace the "Calkins Machine," and began using the name "Sanor®" for both the unit and the fluid. The Sanor name was later trademarked, and is still in use today.

A Rochester Germicide sales rep and trusty companion around 1897.

Rochester Midland's headquarters in Rochester.

Another milestone in Rochester Germicide's history came in 1946. By then, the company had outgrown the Dowling Place factory. In January 1947, the firm moved to its present location at 333 Hollenbeck Street, where it housed manufacturing and warehousing, shipping, R&D, and corporate administration offices.

The company's leadership also changed as the century progressed. In 1937, Daniel Calkins became chairman of the board, a position he held until his passing in 1950. His son, Harlan F. Calkins, an attorney with Harris Beach & Wilcox, was subsequently elected chairman and remained so until he passed away in 1962. Willard B. Eddy, who had begun with RGC in 1918 as a sales representative, was named president in 1937, and chairman in 1962. Eddy worked for the company for an astonishing sixty years, culminating as honorary chairman in 1979. H.J. Chamberlain, who also had a long and successful career with the company, served as

president from 1965 to 1979, and also as chairman from 1979 to 1983.

The company's current Chairman and Chief Executive Officer is Daniel Calkins' grandson, Harlan D. Calkins. He began with the company as a sales representative in Detroit in 1958, after his graduate work at the Harvard Business School was interrupted by the draft in 1955. Following assignments as a branch manger in Indianapolis and Boston, H.D. Calkins was recalled to Rochester in 1970 to serve as the company's Vice President of Corporate Development. In this role he led several of the company's acquisition efforts as Rochester Germicide moved to become a truly national organization. Calkins became President in 1979 and Chief Executive in 1988. The company continues to be a family enterprise, as two of Harlan's children, Bradley and Katherine, are also actively involved in the business as Vice Presidents of Marketing and Corporate Development, respectively.

One of the key acquisitions in the 1970's was that of the Midland Laboratories Company of Dubuque, Iowa. This was one of the largest acquisitions in the company's history, and enhanced its product line, sales force, customer base and geographical coverage significantly. Reflecting the evolving nature of the business and the important role of the Midland Labs acquisition, the company changed its name in 1980 to the Rochester Midland Corporation.

Since 1980, the company has undertaken a number of initiatives to diversify its product lines, but has maintained a consistent emphasis to stay close to its core business of specialty chemicals and related services for industrial and commercial use. New divisions have been created in the areas of food processing sanitation, water treatment, and industrial/manufacturing applications, with each of these targeting specific market segments. Acquisitions have continued, including Industrial Chemical Laboratories in 1991, Clark Paper in 1998, and Protecto, Inc., in 2000. Meanwhile the original Sanor product line, along with the Institutional and Personal Care Divisions have grown and strived to keep pace with the numerous changes in the sanitary supply industry. The company also has a fast growing International division, which serves some 70 countries, plus

A food plant sanitation worker applies one of RMC's foaming cleaners.

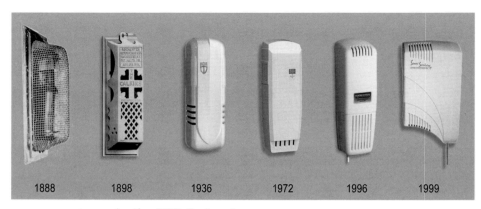

1888   1898   1936   1972   1996   1999

Evolution of the original disinfectant unit through today's models.

newer ventures in the UK, Ireland and South Africa. RMC's Canadian subsidiary, Rochester Midland Limited, has also contributed significantly to the company's growth since its origins as a branch office in Toronto in the early 1900s.

A key component of RMC's strategy today is its leadership in the field of environmentally preferable chemical products and related programs. As awareness of chemical sensitivity and safety issues continues to grow, RMC's Green Building Housekeeping Program and innovative new product development efforts will become increasingly important to the way the world looks at its work and public space environments.

In 2000, Rochester Midland unveiled a new corporate logo, website, and identity to better communicate the company's focus and the trend toward supplier consolidation. The strategy is summarized in the tag line: *Creating Integrated Solutions for Human Health, Industrial Productivity, and the Workplace Environment Since 1888.* The company's strategy is straightforward—to provide the best quality products and top-level service possible, while helping its customers achieve better cost savings, productivity, and safety.

It's not all about the bottom line at RMC. For thirty years following the death of Daniel Calkins, the company donated generously to the Rochester community through the D.N. Calkins Memorial Fund.

Since 1990 the employees of the company have been ranked among the highest in the area in terms of per capita giving to the United Way of Greater Rochester. More recently, the company and its employees have contributed funds, products, and/or time to various charitable organizations, including the Al Sigl Center, Highland Hospital, The Humane Society, and Food Link.

In 2000 the company formed a special relationship with Big Brothers/Big Sisters of Rochester. Led by the company's president Mike Coyner, several RMC employees participated in a first ever round-the-clock relay run covering the entire length of the Erie Canal. Including a lead donation from RMC, the participants raised over $40,000 for this essential organization. Building on the success of this event, in 2001 RMC sponsored the first annual RMC Labor Day Erie Canal Run, a 5K race that drew close to 140 runners. The event both started and finished in the scenic Genesee Valley Park, and earned over $13,000 for BB/BS. More community involvement is certain to follow as the company continues to stress its core values. There's little doubt that Daniel Calkins would be proud of what his successors have accomplished and the kind of company Rochester Midland has become.

ROCHESTER SCHOOL FOR THE DEAF

Carolyn Perkins has long since faded from local memory. She was a pretty and winsome child more than 100 years ago, born to affluence—and also born to deafness. Her great good fortune—and that of a great many youngsters ever since—was the deep concern of her parents for her education.

Today, hundreds of people with deafness live useful and rewarding lives because Mr. and Mrs. Gilman Perkins were people of perception, purpose, and persistence. Thanks largely to their efforts, the Rochester School for the Deaf was founded in 1876. Over the years, it has been nurtured by the devotion, generosity, and concern of many members of the Rochester community.

Situated comfortably on its 8.5-acre campus on St. Paul Street, the Rochester School for the Deaf is much more than a group of buildings housing classrooms and the most sophisticated modern teaching aids. It has been designed to overcome the unique communication barriers erected by deafness, with a staff trained to give young people, from infancy through the high school level, the maximum opportunity to succeed. That they have succeeded in large numbers attests to the soundness of the school's program and the skill and dedication of its staff.

The curriculum of RSD, a New York State certified school, is consistent with the course offerings in most public schools. Classes are small and highly individualized. The school maintains a close working relationship with the public schools, thereby ensuring the best possible educational placement for each deaf or hard of hearing student.

The school also preserves close ties with many college research programs in the teaching of deaf students. The school maintains a deep commitment to the general welfare of deaf people in the greater Rochester area, with its

A small college campus atmosphere pervades the Rochester School for the Deaf, where classes are small and highly individualized.

staff members participating in activities ranging from early childhood programs to job placement.

The Rochester School for the Deaf is a non-profit, state-supported, coeducational institution. Its 25-member board of directors provides the overall direction for programs administered by Superintendent Harold Mowl. It also takes an active role in ongoing school activities and often assumes fund-raising responsibilities, as the school continues to depend on private contributions to carry on its many programs. The personal commitment and dedication of these board members, past and present, is one of the keys to the school's success and national reputation. In 2001, the Rochester School for the Deaf is celebrating 125 years of continuous service to deaf and hard of hearing children.

The Rochester School for the Deaf is dedicated to the development of the total child. Many of its students go on to higher education, while others directly enter the labor market as self-supporting contributors to society. The school develops the young person scholastically, socially, athletically, and philosophically. No school at any level of education can claim to do more.

The school provides a full range of educational services from infancy through the high school level. Many students go on to higher education or enter the labor market with marked success.

ST. JOHN FISHER COLLEGE

To understand the present, one must understand the past, and the past is where St. John Fisher College's strong traditions were nurtured and grew into the college it is known as today.

In 1937, the Basilian Fathers of Toronto, Canada assumed direction of Aquinas Institute, a Catholic high school for boys in Rochester. Their charter stipulated that no other religious order or congregation could establish a college for men within a 50-mile radius of Rochester for 15 years. That 15-year period would expire in 1952.

It was then that the seeds of what would become St. John Fisher College started growing in the hearts and minds of two great men. These men were the Most Reverend James E. Kearney, then Bishop of Rochester, New York, and Father Hugh Haffey, a Basilian priest from Toronto who taught at Aquinas Institute. Bishop Kearney was keenly aware that Rochester had a fine Catholic high school for boys (Aquinas Institute); excellent Catholic high schools for girls; and a fine Catholic college for girls, Nazareth College, run by the Sisters of St. Joseph. Alas, there was no Catholic college for men.

In 1947, at the invitation of Bishop Kearney, the Basilian Fathers purchased the present site of St. John Fisher College, at the juncture of Fairport Road and East Avenue. The original 70-acre location (now 136 acres) was geographically distinct from Aquinas Institute, which was desirable in order to create the image of separation from the high school. Yet its proximity to Nazareth College, a growing college for women on East Avenue, was also advantageous for the potential exchange of professors and academic programs between the two colleges.

In 1947, fund-raising began for the new college, with a $1,047,236 goal set for the campaign. Such an

Kearney Hall today.

amount was unheard of in the late 1940s in Rochester, but the Basilian Fathers were confident that between the parishes and Rochester business and industry, the goal was achievable. In the name of the Archbishopric of New York, Cardinal Spellman presented Bishop Kearney with a check for $25,000 to officially open the fund drive. In the end, the Basilians topped their goal by 18 percent, when Bishop Kearney announced in 1948 that the fund drive had in fact netted $1.2 million.

Thus, in 1948, through the combined efforts of civic leaders, the Rochester community at large, the Basilian Fathers, and Bishop Kearney, St. John Fisher College—the "College on the Hill" — was borne out of the community's desire to provide its young men with a traditional education in the humanities, social sciences, sciences, and business. The goal was to create an educational environment that would enable Fisher graduates to succeed in life, and to help strengthen the fabric of the Rochester community.

In June of 1949, ground was officially broken for the new institution. In 1951, beginning with just one building on campus, the original 120 men in the class of 1955 began forming the traditions and customs that would make

Fisher the college it is today.

Guided throughout the years by the educational philosophy of the Basilian Fathers, the College continues to emphasize liberal learning for students in both traditional academic disciplines and in more directly career-oriented fields. In keeping with the openness that is characteristic of its Basilian heritage, Fisher welcomes qualified students, faculty, and staff regardless of religious or cultural background. Fisher's commitment to individuals from varied backgrounds and with differing educational needs reflects both its emphasis on lifelong learning and its direct involvement in the community.

The College, which became independent in 1968 and coeducational in 1971, now teaches nearly 3,000 men and women programs of study built on a solid core curriculum. Today, Fisher offers 24 undergraduate majors and 12 graduate programs.

The Basilian motto, "Teach me goodness, discipline, and knowledge," continues to capture the College's traditions and values. To that end, the College has twice been named to the John Templeton Foundation Honor Roll for Character-Building Colleges. This places Fisher among a select group of colleges and universities in the United States recognized by the Foundation for innovation and leadership in promoting character development among their students.

In the Fall of 1998, in honor of the College's 50th anniversary, the Board of Trustees approved a multimillion dollar building project—the most ambitious improvement and expansion program in the history of the College. At that time, the College was experiencing record enrollment, attracting students from across New York State, and the curriculum was expanding to meet the changing needs of the marketplace. It was also a time to look back and acknowledge all that had made the College successful and to look to the future and guarantee that the College was providing its students with an academic and technology-rich environment. A new spirit, a new momentum, and a new pride are building at St. John Fisher College. The im-

Spring of 1999—Groundbreaking for Fisher's new stadium. From the left: R. Wayne LeChase, then vice-chair of the Board of Trustees; Dr. Katherine E. Keough, president of St. John Fisher College; and then Chair of the Board Charles Constantino.

provement and expansion program has accelerated that spirit and has brought Fisher to new heights as an academic institution. However, Fisher is still a caring community that emphasizes important life values: respect for every individual, a belief in service to others, and a commitment to lifelong learning.

For over half a century, St. John Fisher College and the Rochester community have enjoyed a successful partnership. The College's 15,000 graduates, many of whom

Unveiling a portrait of Bishop Kearney by the artist John C. Menihan. To the right are Bishop Kearney and Father John Murphy, first president of St. John Fisher College.

hold leadership positions in the public and private sectors throughout the Rochester area and beyond, have benefited from the opportunity to gain a quality, advanced education based on traditional academic values. But Fisher strives to develop the whole person—to teach young adults to be successful members of society, to provide for themselves, to look for ways to help in their communities, and to enrich the world in which they live. Looking at its impressive list of alumni, it's clear that Fisher has succeeded.

Chronology of Presidents:
The Very Rev. John F. Murphy, C.S.B. 1950-1958
The Rev. Charles J. Lavery, C.S.B., 1958-1980
The Rev. Patrick O. Braden, C.S.B., 1980-1986
William L. Pickett, Ph.D. 1986-1996
Katherine E. Keough, Ed.D. 1996-Present

271

SEAR-BROWN

Throughout nearly five decades of change, Sear-Brown has been a steady force in the design and construction of Rochester's buildings and infrastructure. From its origins as a small six-person civil engineering firm on downtown Rochester's Broad Street, to a place among the top 100 design firms in the nation, Sear-Brown has remained committed to the growth of Rochester and Monroe County. This 1,000 plus person, multi-discipline firm

Bradley J. Harmsen, AIA, President.

has successfully launched a national practice from the strong community roots forged in Rochester.

In 1955, Thomas Sear, P.E., L.S., a specialist in site planning, established a sole proprietorship for the practice of engineering. Eight years later, Mr. Sear formed a partnership with Robert Brown, P.E., a municipal engineer. Sear-Brown's initial years were marked by steady growth in the civil and site engineering and land surveying disciplines. The firm's growth in many ways mirrored that of the community. Engineers were deeply involved with major urban

renewal programs that defined the 1960s and 1970s. New expressways, roads and bridges to accommodate an increasingly mobile population, water and sewer systems that complied with more stringent environmental regulations, more recreation facilities and expansive residential subdivisions to house a burgeoning suburban base defined the era. As Rochester grew, it always found a trusted partner in Sear-Brown.

During the 1980s, Sear-Brown continued to expand its services, transforming into a truly full-service company through the addition of architecture, mechanical, electrical, environmental, structural engineering and landscape architecture. At the same time, Sear-Brown launched a geographic expansion throughout New York State to better serve state clients such as the New York State Department of Transportation.

Throughout the decade, Sear-Brown worked with Roch-

Sear-Brown was a design consultant for Frontier Field, greater Rochester's outdoor sports facility.

ester-based developer Wilmorite, providing site engineering, landscape architecture and transportation engineering for the hottest concept in commercial development—the regional mall. Today's Irondequoit Mall, Marketplace Mall, and Greece Ridge Center represent just a few products of this successful collaboration. During the late 1980s transportation

Michael A. Triassi, P.E., CEO.

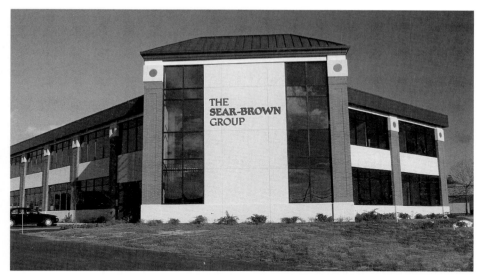

Sear-Brown designed and built their corporate headquarters in 1998.

Original founder Tom Sear (left) reviews drawings in the 1970s.

Park, Frontier Field, the Seneca Park Zoo and the Greater Rochester International Airport. While maintaining a full roster of local projects, Sear-Brown launched a nationwide expansion, establishing more than 20 offices in eight states. With clients such as Corning Incorporated, CVS/Pharmacy, Wyeth-Ayerst and the World Bank, Sear-Brown's national, and international, reputation continued to grow. During this time, the firm also added a construction

Sear-Brown provided space planning, facilities design and engineering services for the renovation of Monroe County CityPlace in downtown Rochester.

planning emerged as a major urban/suburban issue. In response, the firm developed an award-winning team of planners and engineers to assist communities struggling with these complex and costly issues.

In the 1990s Sear-Brown's impact on the local landscape continued. Area work included architecture and/or engineering for a diverse base clients and projects, including Xerox, Eastman Kodak, the "Can of Worms" reconstruction, Rochester Science

division to provide fully-integrated project delivery services from planning through construction, to clients.

The success of this Rochester-based company is attributable to many factors. Chief among them is a commitment to employee ownership and the focus on client collaboration and technical quality and innovation which ownership fosters. Sear-Brown's leaders remain committed to the Rochester community which has been so instrumental to the firm's success.

SAUCKE BROS. CONSTRUCTION COMPANY, INC.

William Henry Theodore Saucke was born on St. Patrick's Day in 1898. At the age of 17, his father died, leaving him with his mother, five younger brothers and two younger sisters. With the help of his brothers, William kept the family together. His education was interrupted but later completed at night school.

In 1920, at the age of 22, Mr. Saucke started William Saucke Builder and Contractor. He built houses and did carpentry work on churches and small buildings, primarily as a subcontractor. In 1922, Herbert Saucke joined the company. The brothers work expanded and increased. In 1928 Walter Saucke joined his brothers and formed a corporation called Saucke Bros. Construction Company, Inc.

As the company grew, the brothers decided to branch out, and true to the name, became general contractors, completing entire projects. They saved enough money to see them through the Depression, and after it was over, built schools, commercial buildings and churches. The company expanded and became known for the quality of its work.

In 1948, upon returning from

Genesee Brewery tank storage building, 1965.

William H. Saucke.

World War II, Walter sold his interest to his two younger brothers, Elmer and Carl. Elmer was a civil engineer who had graduated from Rensselaer Polytechnic Institute and Cornell University. Carl was an architect graduating from Syracuse University. With the addition of the brothers, the company grew, continuing to specialize in school construction. In 1956 Herbert retired, followed by Elmer in 1972.

The company's growth slowed. In 1976, William died. Soon after, Carl retired. William's three sons, William, Robert and Raymond, were all working for the company at the time. They bought the business, and with fresh ideas expanded their work into larger projects. The continuation of work for the Genesee Brewing company, a client embarking on a major expansion, helped greatly. Saucke Bros. was the only general contractor to do work at the Genesee facilities and the Genesee Country Village in Mumford, New York. Saucke Bros. was instrumental in constructing a 55-building village including a 15,000-square-foot art gallery.

The company continued to prosper. In 1988 Robert retired and William and Raymond decided to diversify into property management and development.

The company purchased the Auditorium Theater and Masonic Temple Complex and changed the name to the Auditorium Center. The company developed over 100,000-square-feet of office space in the complex and operated the 2,500-seat theater.

The company constructed, owns and leases buildings for the Carrier Corporation, Lac De Ville Medical Center, Kodak Polychrome Graphics in Victor and many other properties. They also built a world headquarters for Monroe Muffler in Rochester, and various shopping center interior stores throughout the Northeast, as well as warehouse facilities for Kodak Polychrome Graphics in California and Georgia.

The company still competes for private and public sector projects. Among the company's current projects are a $5 million addition and renovation of the Avoca High School to be completed in 2002; a new firehouse in Hornell, New York; a bus garage in Rushville, New York; and renovations to the 152-unit Amber Court Facility in Horseheads, New York.

Over its 81-year history Saucke Bros. has completed such projects as a dormitory and lecture hall for the University of Rochester; dorm buildings and renovations for the Rochester School for the Deaf; and 65 public schools in the State of New York. Private work includes the Brightonian Nursing Home; Marine Midland Bank branch offices; The Defender Photo Co. (later called DuPont); Rapidac Machine Company; Macy's Department Stores; Genesee Brewery; The Genesee Country Museum; Kodak Polychrome Graphics; Fairport Methodist Church; St. Thomas Moor Rectory; North Baptist Church; and others. The company's policy of quality and satisfaction has always been upheld by close personal contact with every project and by the owners.

SCJ ASSOCIATES, INC.

SCJ Associates, Inc. may have been born out of necessity but it grew into a worldwide company out of dedication and determination.

In the beginning it was indeed a necessity for three local Rochester residents who found themselves faced with seeking new positions after their previous employer closed their division's doors. Now, 31 years later, the necessity still exists, but it is by SCJ Associates' customers, who rely on the company to produce quality electrical and mechanical design and manufacturing services.

In January 1971, former General Dynamics Corporation engineers Thurlow "Suds" Sutherland and Norman Johnstone and program manager John Corryn joined together to form SCJ Associates. Each partner brought with him years of experience and professional skills that would create a firm foundation upon which their company could be based.

Out of their small, 1,000-square-foot office on the east end of Brighton–Henrietta Townline Road, the three partners set out to secure clients and establish their business. It wasn't a coincidence that General Dynamics was their first customer to sign on; the three former electronics division employees had been known for their hard work and ability to achieve successful results.

SCJ owner and CEO Suds Sutherland.

In mid-1971, the emerging company purchased the shares of Norman Johnstone, creating an equal shareholding partnership for Sutherland and Corryn.

As the country grew and changed in the 1970s, SCJ Associates evolved into a viable company by providing turn-key engineering and manufacturing services to meet its customers unique needs. It was during this time that SCJ established strong relationships with the Ritter Company, General Railway Signal (which is now known as Alstom), Rochester Products (now known as DELPHI), Rochester Institute of Technology, Coherent Radiation, Pulsa-feeder and the United States Navy, among others.

SCJ management and staff.

The growth of SCJ's business opportunities created the need for a larger working space. The group decided a move was in order, so they relocated to a 2,400-square-foot office near Winton Place. In just one year, 2,100 more square feet were added to the space.

The 1980s brought even more growth, but not just to the client list. John Sutherland, the son of Suds Sutherland, joined the firm as a machinist in 1987, introducing a new generation to the firm. Also, SCJ's active account roster expanded to add Mobil Chemical, Kodak, Xerox and the local University of Rochester.

In 1988, Suds Sutherland purchased the shares owned by his partner and became the sole shareholder and owner of SCJ. That same year, David Sutherland, Sud's youngest son, joined the firm working in various departments to learn the business. He is currently the company' controller.

Entering the nineties, the need for more space for the established but still growing company was needed. The third move was made to the current location on Commerce Drive in Henrietta.

Progress also meant more positive change as the company added Lockheed Martin, Kayex, Veeco, MOOG and 100 other companies to its expanded account base. SCJ also brought Teresa Sutherland into the fold of family business. She currently holds the position of sales manager.

Today, three decades later, this strong and productive local company has equipment operating in China, England, France, Australia, the Netherlands, Brazil, Canada, and Mexico, among other countries. A worldwide business may have grown out of an immediate need, but it has evolved into a well-founded multigenerational business in Rochester, New York.

TREVETT, LENWEAVER & SALZER P.C.

Trevett, Lenweaver, & Salzer, P.C. is a law firm located in Rochester, New York that provides legal service to the Genesee Region in Upstate New York. It was founded in 1926 by Oscar Brown of Baldwinsville, New York.

Formed as Brown and Zurett, the Rochester firm was one of three affiliated firms in Upstate New York founded primarily to serve the legal needs of various insurance carriers. Through the 1940s and '50s, the firm numbered among its client base over 25 major insurance carriers. Over the years members of the firm distinguished themselves in the courtroom and in the leadership ranks of the trial sections of the state and national bar associations. Three of its recent partners have served as presidents of the Monroe City Bar Association.

In the 1960s and '70s, the firm's client base expanded to include other major areas of practice. The membership of the firm grew to include trial practitioners whose specialties are plaintiff's personal injury litigation, criminal defense, family law, commercial litigation and administrative and regulatory hearing representation.

The firm has also developed a full-service residential real estate department, representing mortgage lenders, homebuilders and homeowners alike. More recent additions to the firm's membership have enabled it to expand into corporate work and tax litigation, as well as municipal law.

The firm continues to expand, yet seeks to provide its range of legal services to its clients in a cost effective manner. That type of representation is made possible by a team of partners, associates, paralegals and staff dedicated to producing a work product that meets the needs and the budgets of the clients of Trevett, Lenweaver.

Litigation is the foundation of the firm's practice and it members

Karl L. Salzer, Esq., managing partner.

practice before all courts, state and federal, as well as regulatory and administrative bodies.

Trevett, Lenweaver attorneys are acknowledged as leaders in the ranks of personal injury trial practitioners at local, state and national levels. Included in the firm's institutional clientele are Kemper Insurance Group, Erie Insurance Co., NY Central Mutual Insurance Co. as well as self-insureds such as Wilmorite & Genesee Management. Various large manufacturers have chosen Trevett, Lenweaver to handle their litigation needs in the Upstate area including John Deere, Hobart, Piper Aircraft, General Electric and the Manville Corporation. The firm's practice areas

have expanded to include litigation on behalf of injured persons, as well. A mainstay of the firm's practice has been and continues to be personal injury litigation.

From the automobile accident case, to the mass toxic tort claim, all cases receive the thorough attention and preparation necessary to maintain a strong trial posture. Trevett, Lenweaver's cumulative expertise includes the trials of very diverse matters such as complex product liability, aviation law, employment law and professional malpractice matters. The firm is involved in commercial construction disputes and toxic tort claims as well.

Commercial litigation is actively practiced at Trevett, Lenweaver. Members of the firm are currently handling commercial matters such as employment discrimination, labor law and not-for-profit corporation matters, in addition to state blue sky law violations and share holder and real estate syndication disputes. State and federal tax litigation is currently supervised by a firm member who is a former prosecutor for the Internal Revenue Service.

Numbering in its membership three former criminal prosecutors, Trevett, Lenweaver offers to the Rochester community seasoned criminal trial practitioners supported by a strong staff of associates and paralegals necessary to properly attend to the task of defense of persons accused of crimes.

Trevett, Lenweaver possesses a very active appellate practice. The firm's attorneys appear before all appellate courts at both the state and federal levels.

The attorneys of Trevett, Lenweaver currently represent a number of municipalities in the Rochester area. The firm also numbers among its clientele two Upstate counties. Trevett, Lenweaver is attuned to the growing area of municipal litigation including civil rights, violation claims, planning and zoning decision disputes and personal injury actions against municipalities. Among its institutional clients is a long list of law enforcement associations. Legal practice in this area of the law is unique, and the firm's experience and reputation command a loyalty of the majority of law enforcement groups in the region.

The firm is heavily involved in the burgeoning area of environmental law and litigation. Members have managed the defense of mass tort claims based upon exposure to hazardous substances and have advised municipalities concerning their duties to comply with many new environmental laws and regulations.

Trevett, Lenweaver offers a complete range of real estate services to its clients; individuals, corporations and institutions alike. The firm represents mortgage lenders as well as home builders and homeowners. An experienced staff of paralegals complements the firm's ability to perform the detail-intensive tasks involved in real estate practice.

The firm offers to its clientele legal services involved in adoptions, matrimonial concerns and divorce and custody proceedings. Trevett, Lenweaver is in an advantaged position to handle contested matters because of its trial capabilities.

Also offered to its individual clients is Trevett, Lenweaver's ability to assist in the planning and administration of estates. Various Trevett, Lenweaver attorneys appear regularly on estate matters in the Surrogates Courts of New York and the firm counts among its members a veteran practitioner of the New York State Estate Tax Bureau.

Rounding out its ability to fully serve its clients' legal needs is an active practice devoted to matters concerning the small business or closely-held corporation. Whether performing a simple incorporation, merger, or devising a tax avoidance strategy, Trevett, Lenweaver is able to attend to the legal matters which affect the small business owner.

Standing, from left: Clark J. Zimmerman, Esq.; Peter A. Jacobson, Esq.; Joseph G. Interlichia, Esq., Jon P. Getz, Esq.; Karl F. Salzer, Esq.; James C. Gocker, Esq.; Thomas N. Trevett, Esq.; Richard M. Doyle, Esq.; James M. Valenti, Esq.; Louis B. Cristo, Esq.; Kenneth Bersani, Esq.; and Thomas E. Lenweaver, Esq.; Seated, from left: Lawrence J. Andolina, Esq.; Cynthia Constantino Gleason, Esq.; Simona Lapadat, Esq.; Nicole L. Black, Esq.; and Robert E. Brennan, Esq.

UNIVERSITY OF ROCHESTER

The University of Rochester was founded in 1850 at the urging of local businessmen who foresaw that the booming "Flour City" warranted an institution of higher education mirroring Rochester's aspirations as a major metropolis. Today it is a nationally recognized private research university whose programs in arts, sciences, engineering, medicine and health care, music, and other fields are counted among the best in the country. The University retains its local focus as a provider of world-class health care, as a community resource for premier cultural offerings, and as a top local employer.

The University early on established its ethos of providing a topflight education on a personal scale, maintaining that approach as it has grown from a small, regional college in the second half of the 19th century into a true "university" early in the 20th. With an enrollment of about 8,660 students (undergraduate, graduate, and professional), the University provides the educational opportunities of a national research university while deliberately maintaining an intimate, collegial environment.

Largely due to the campaigning of renowned Rochester suffragist Susan B. Anthony, the University admitted women in 1900, becom-

A number of academic programs at the University—including those in music, optics, medicine, business administration, engineering, political science, economics, and nursing—have achieved national prominence.

Home to the College (the University's core programs in arts, sciences, and engineering), the River Campus also is home to the Margaret Warner Graduate School of Education and Human Development and the William E. Simon Graduate School of Business Administration.

ing one of the first private universities in the nation to do so. Today, each incoming class is comprised almost equally of men and women.

In 1921, thanks to a gift from Eastman Kodak Company founder George Eastman, the Eastman School of Music opened its doors as one of the first music conservatories affiliated with a university. A year later, the stately Eastman Theatre opened as a performance space for the school's ensembles and other performance groups, and it remains a hallmark of Rochester's cultural scene.

Also in 1921, plans for a new type of medical education—one combining both clinical and academic perspectives in one complex—won the financial support of Eastman, and in 1925, the School of Medicine and Dentistry admitted its first class. Today, the University's

Medical Center—which includes the School of Medicine and Dentistry, the School of Nursing, Strong Memorial Hospital, and, since 1998, the Eastman Dental Center—continues to fulfill its promise as a "model medical school."

In 1925, the University awarded its first doctorate, becoming a true "research" university. By 2000, the University had awarded more than 7,000 Ph.D.s and counted its graduates on the faculty of the nation's top colleges and universities.

Contributing to Rochester's status as the home of imaging technology, the University established the Institute of Optics in 1929. The nation's oldest academic program devoted to the study of optics, the Institute remains the premier center for such research in the world.

In the 1930s, the "academic center" of the University moved to the River Campus about two miles south of downtown Rochester. The University's first permanent home, at the corner of Prince Street and University Avenue, is anchored by the Memorial Art Gallery. Opened in 1913, the gallery is one of only a few university-affiliated art galleries that also serves as a community museum.

In the second half of the 20th century, the University's programs in economics, political science, history, business, and engineering gained national prominence along with those in medicine and music. In 1970, the Laboratory for Laser Energetics was established to study laser fusion as a source of potential energy. Home to the world's largest ultraviolet laser, the lab is one of the world leaders for such study.

As the University entered the 21st century, its dedication to the core missions of teaching, research, clinical care, and community service remained firmly rooted. The 3,715 full-time undergraduates in the College (arts, sciences, and engineering) work closely with faculty in the classroom, in laboratories, and on research projects. The Rochester Curriculum, which emphasizes the flexibility undergraduates need to become well-rounded scholars of the arts, the social sciences, and the natural sciences, has won praise nationwide.

The top-ranked Eastman School has reaffirmed its commitment to the future of cultural appreciation, launching groundbreaking programs to bring music and the appreciation of fine music to audiences that might otherwise not be reached.

At the Medical Center, researchers housed in the Aab Institute for Biomedical Sciences are searching for insights that will lead to a healthier future, focusing work on aging and developmental biology, cancer biology, cardiovascular research, human genetics and molecular pediatric disease, oral biology, and vaccine biology and immunology.

The School of Medicine and Dentistry's programs rank among the best in the country, and the school's "Double Helix" curriculum, which combines patient care and medical science training, has been cited as a national leader in medical education. Since the establishment of the School of Nursing in 1972 (from the original department of nursing), faculty there have pioneered a collaborative approach to nursing education that has been adopted by nursing programs throughout the country.

In 1996, the University's Strong Memorial Hospital and Highland Hospital became partners in Strong Health, a healthcare network that has grown to encompass long-term care facilities and a home care agency. It now serves an 11-county region in upstate New York.

With an operating budget of just over $1 billion and a total employment of more than 15,100 people (including Strong Health), the University has an enormous economic impact on the region.

The University annually brings in well over $200 million from federal and state agencies and from private sources for research, training, and scholarship, a testament to the University's standing as a recognized research institution. A driving engine behind the creation of startup companies in the area, the University has seen dramatic increases in licensing fees and royalty payments for technology developed on campus.

With over 1,000 affiliated physicians (including the faculty of the School of Medicine and Dentistry), the University's patient care network at Strong Health logs more than 530,000 clinic visits and 89,000 emergency room visits each year.

Opened in 1925 as part of "model medical school," Strong Memorial Hospital was one of the first teaching hospitals in the country planned in coordination with an academic program in medical education.

The impact of the University's social and intellectual contributions to the region, the state, and the nation is immeasurable. The University's scholars, scientists, and alumni have included seven Nobel Prize winners, 11 Pulitzer Prize winners, and scores of prominent researchers, artists, educators, performers, and others who have made the world a better place—a tradition that will continue well into the future.

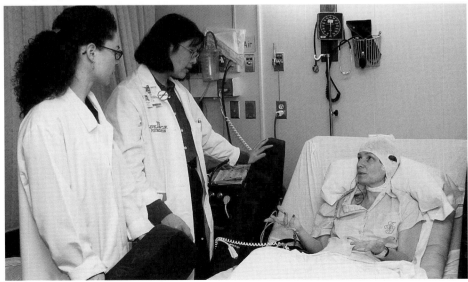

AL SIGL CENTER

Al Sigl Center is a unique, nationally recognized community partnership of independent agencies united to foster the goals of achievement for people with disabilities. The Center is named for Alphonse J. Sigl, a locally renowned radio commentator, who, for thirty years, inspired the community on his daily broadcasts to reach out and help their neighbors.

The Center opened its doors in 1968, with seven Partner Agencies serving 3,400 people with disabilities. In 2000, the Al Sigl Center Partnership of eight agencies served 53,000 children and adults with disabilities and their families.

The Partner Agencies are:
• The Arc of Monroe County—Helping adults with developmental disabilities achieve their highest level of independence.
• Cerebral Palsy Association of the Rochester Area—Helping children and adults with Cerebral Palsy and similar physical challenges achieve life goals.
• Epilepsy Foundation—Providing education, advocacy, and services for people with Epilepsy and similar neurological impairments.
• Mary Cariola Children's Center—Offering educational and residential programs to young people, from infancy to age 21, who have complex, and often, multiple disabilities.
• Medical Motor Service—Providing mobility to medical appointments, therapeutic services, senior centers, partner agency programs, and activities.
• National Multiple Sclerosis Society, Upstate New York Chapter—Helping people with MS maximize abilities and maintain a high level of independence.
• Rochester Hearing and Speech Center—Providing treatment for children and adults with speech, language, or hearing problems.
• Rochester Rehabilitation Center—Providing vocational, physical, and psychiatric rehabilitation

Al Sigl Center brings smiles to thousands of faces each day, as people with disabilities discover and achieve their life goals

programs to put people back to work and active living.

As the Partnership's resource agency, Al Sigl Center is dedicated to meeting the needs of its Partner Agencies by providing shared and dedicated facilities, developing shared business services, and generating community awareness and philanthropic financial support.

With the generous help of Rochester's caring community Al Sigl Center has met the increasing needs of the growing number of people with disabilities and the Partner Agencies who serve them so well. From a single building at the corner of Elmwood and South Avenues, the Center has grown to fill five campuses and numerous day and residential program buildings where Partner Agencies provide therapeutic, educational, vocational, and recreational programs.

The Center's Management Service Organization (MSO) provides cost effective, quality business services in areas such as human resources, risk management, and telecommunications. Efficiencies, cost savings, and best practices improve the Partner Agencies' ability to focus more resources and attention on their mission of providing direct services to children and adults with disabilities.

Al Sigl Center pioneered a compelling community awareness campaign entitled "People with disabilities. See their abilities." At the heart of the campaign are powerful, hard-hitting television public service announcements and print advertisements that encourage viewers to recognize people with disabilities for their abilities as employees, students, and neighbors. With the success of the awareness campaign, the good hearts of the Rochester community will change, and the *"dis"* in disabilities will disappear.

Year after year, thousands of volunteers demonstrate their dedication and commitment to the Al Sigl Center Partnership and the people with disabilities we all serve together, by providing leadership, expertise, and contributions. Loyal volunteers, friends, and supporters enable the Center to continue providing the best services in the best spaces available now and for future generations to come.

The Al Sigl Center Partnership continues Al Sigl's legacy of helping neighbors in need. Everybody knows somebody who's been helped at Al Sigl Center...where thousands of children and adults with disabilities discover and achieve their potential, and live their lives to the fullest.

THE VALLEY CADILLAC CORPORATION

Cadillac has always been the American ideal of unquestioned quality, and Rochester's Valley Cadillac Corporation has lived up to this image for 65 years.

On June 1, 1936 a group of local businessmen came together to form the Valley Cadillac Corporation, acquiring Mabbett Motor Company—a dealership which, like many other businesses of the time, was suffering due to the Depression. Established on 333 East Avenue, the site is now an area landmark.

The principal shareholders and directors were Daniel J. Meagher Sr., a construction contractor and John T. Hanefy, a Rochester banker, along with Dr. James Sibley Watson, Harper Sibley Sr., and Hiram Sibley.

The corporation, which would later be under full control by Meagher and Hanefy, weathered the country's financial and emotional hardships and continued to grow. Meagher, who always strived to guarantee first-rate customer service that would exceed expectations of the selective Cadillac owners, passed away in 1977.

The Meagher name, however, still held its place in the corporation,

Ed Meagher, Jr.

representing the kind of service and satisfaction Daniel had put in place. In 1952, Edward T. Meagher joined his father's company creating a multigenerational business. In 1974, Edward purchased The Valley Cadillac Corporation from the other shareholders.

The Seventies, full of change,

brought even further growth to the company by introducing a third generation. Edward T. Meagher Jr. joined the staff and worked almost every possible position from stocking parts to accounting. Edward Jr. now serves as president of the company, Edward Sr. as chairman, and J. Daniel Meagher, who joined the company in 1992 and is also third generation, as vice president.

These three family members have grown their business on the firm foundation of Daniel Meagher. They have invested in their community, not by just giving good service, but by giving back. Long known for their philanthropic efforts, the family, through The Valley Cadillac Corporation, has donated time, talents and funds to numerous civic and non-profit organizations, including the United Way, National Kidney Foundation, American Cancer Society and other local charitable organizations.

Today's Valley Cadillac Corporation, which has been located on Winton Road South in Rochester since 1976, has received many awards over the years, including Top Sales Leaders–Northeast Region Cadillac Dealerships, the Cadillac Top 100 Gold Medalists and Cadillac Master Dealer, the most prestigious award presented by the brand.

The corporation extends its services past the initial sale, a trait that has made them one of the country's most successful Cadillac dealerships. In fact, Valley Cadillac is the top customer satisfaction dealer for General Motors in Western New York.

Through the changes that time inevitably brings, Valley Cadillac Corporation stands strong, offering quality and service backed by three generations of a hometown family. The Meaghers have steered the company forward without loosing site of that American ideal established so long ago.

The Valley Cadillac Corporation, 3100 Winton Road, South.

VALLEY MANOR APARTMENTS & SENIOR SERVICES

July 2001 marked the 30th anniversary for Valley Manor Apartments. Organized in 1967, Presbyterian Residence Center Corporation opened the doors to Valley Manor as New York State's first full-service retirement community.

When opened, the new facility occupied a property formerly known as Willow Pond. The ornamental pond was situated between two beautiful homes on East Avenue in Rochester and was fed by water from the Erie Canal.

For an appreciation of what Rochester was like in 1971, one can benefit from the best of sources—former City of Rochester Historian and former resident of Valley Manor, Blake McKelvey. Below are excerpts from an article Mr. McKelvey wrote for Valley Manor's *1570 Senior Living Today* in 1996. The article further quotes material from McKelvey's book *Rochester on the Genesee*, published in 1972.

"The city in which Valley Manor was launched in July 1971 was...in turbulent transition to a metropolis. Enjoying a surge of industrial prosperity, it had for two decades been absorbing an influx of untrained job seekers from the southern states and Puerto Rico. That stimulated an outflow of old residents to the suburbs, increasing their share of the county's population from a fourth to almost three-fourths and reducing the city's tax base alarmingly. Recognized by the Census Bureau as the hub of a burgeoning metropolis, Rochester lacked jurisdictional control over its problems, complicated as in other cities by the nationwide civil right controversies.

Yet Rochester was already looking ahead, building for the future. It had suffered and survived the riots of July 1964 as its social agencies, schools and churches rallied to supply needed services.

Fortunately, a sufficient number of the city's migrants to the suburbs retained an identity with Rochester, enabling Lucien Morin, as leader of the county, to reach an agreement with Mayor Thomas P. Ryan, Jr. to share resources under a "Community of Monroe" agree-ment that permitted the city to move ahead with needed construction downtown. There, soaring corporate skyscrapers were proclaiming Rochester's new metropolitan status.

Most Rochesterians still preferred single freestanding houses with gardens attached, and the suburbs beckoned growing families. But as the population aged, and the children graduated and drifted away, an increasing number of senior citizens, retirees, and other survivors found the maintenance of homesteads increasingly burdensome and sought shelter in high rise apartments in the city.

...the Presbyterians planned a resort for seniors that would ultimately supply the full needs of its residents at Valley Manor on East Avenue, a location which provides

Dedication of Schmitt Senior Resource Center, June 1995. From left to right, CEO Michael Walker, board of directors chairman James Atwater, Rochester City Council President Lois Geiss and Rochester Mayor William Johnson at the ribbon cutting.

easy access to the city's cultural and commercial facilities."

Construction of the Valley Manor building began on Friday, October 25, 1969 and, although delayed by a local trades strike and complex legal approvals, was completed for opening in July 1971. However, as early as fall 1967, advertisements for the new apartments at Valley Manor began appearing in the *Democrat and Chronicle* and the *Times–Union.*

The dream was now a reality, and for the next 30 years Valley Manor would grow and continue to lead senior living complexes throughout New York State.

Since its inception, Valley Manor has remained a vibrant community force through the ad-

dition of community programs in home health care, adult day programs and home delivered services through its award-winning Club 24 Senior Living at Home® program.

In 1995, after purchase of the former Dickens Restaurant property, the Schmitt Senior Resource Center was opened, further enhancing Valley Manor's connection and commitment to the Rochester community.

In June 1999, Valley Manor completed a corporate affiliation known as Seniors*first* with Kirkhaven, a nursing and rehabilitation center, to provide a seamless transition of care and support to seniors and their families.

What lies ahead for Valley

Willow Pond, c.1915. Present site of Valley Manor Apartments.

Manor? A new assisted living facility, to be completed in the spring of 2002, is adjacent to Valley Manor and connected to the Schmitt Senior Resource Center. This will provide an additional level of care, complimenting services and programs at Valley Manor and Kirkhaven. In keeping with the times, new apartment styles and upgrades continue to keep Valley Manor at the forefront of accommodations and services to seniors in the Rochester area—the way it all began 30 years ago.

Present day Valley Manor Apartments along tree-lined East Avenue.

WEGMANS FOOD MARKETS, INC.

"Wegmans Food Markets saved my life." So began one magazine article by a journalist who thought she'd been sentenced to living in a "culinary desert" when a career move took her to Ithaca, NY. Her spirits lifted when she discovered she could stuff her pantry with delicacies she'd learned to love through travel abroad by shopping at the nearby Wegmans store. That store, she wrote, made her "chilly year in central New York State not just tolerable, but downright enjoyable."

Funny though it sounds, thousands of Wegmans' customers feel that same affection for their Wegmans store. They often coax out-of-state visitors to come grocery shopping, so they can chuckle when visitors see how much fun a trip to the supermarket can be.

What's going on? Many things that add up to happy shoppers, happy employees, and happy communities.

Shoppers love going to Wegmans because it's not just a grocery errand but a getaway to the global food village. The stores

In the early 1900s, brothers Jack and Walter Wegman sold fresh fruits and vegetables from a horse-drawn cart.

have the charm of an open-air European market, with fresh-baked artisan breads, wheels of cheeses stacked in towers, cases of glistening fresh fish, rainbow-colors of produce from nearby family farms, and ready-to-eat foods with "bon appetit" panache. The jumbo stores save shoppers time, because they can tick off lots of errands at once. Inside the stores are a full-service pharmacy and a bakery that turns out hot-from-the-oven breads, bagels, doughnuts and muffins throughout the day. There's a natural foods department, health and

beauty care products, gifts and cards, a bookstore with magazines and international newspapers, film developing and video rental departments, sushi and espresso bars, gourmet take-out, cooking equipment for the home chef, and cooking stations where home cooks can learn techniques like pan-searing seafood. Kids can hear stories, play computer games, or burn off energy on the climbing gym in the supervised Wkids Play Center for free, while parents shop.

And shoppers love one more thing—the service. Wegmans employees are so pleasant and helpful that shoppers would like to take them home, too!

Employees love Wegmans because it's a great place to work, with benefits and career-building opportunities that lead the industry: The company averages about half the full-time turnover rate of its industry. The company also has been listed on the *Fortune* magazine list of "100 Best Companies to Work for in America" many times.

Communities love Wegmans because the company is an industry leader in "good neighbor" involvement and charitable donations, especially to programs that reduce

Employees gathered in front of one of the first Wegmans stores located at 375 Main Street East in Rochester.

hunger, help young people succeed, and strengthen neighborhoods. Wegmans stores have raised millions of dollars to fight hunger, and the stores donate millions of pounds of food to local food banks. The company pioneered an award-winning work-scholarship program for inner-city youth that has helped hundreds finish high school and develop the work skills they need for success as adults.

Wegmans stores have come a long way since 1916 when a young man named Jack Wegman sold fresh fruits and vegetables in Rochester, NY. His brother Walter joined him a year later, and after five years in business, the brothers bought the Mahatchke Fruit Store and Seel Grocery Company. By 1922, their stores sold canned goods and other grocery items as well as produce.

Wegmans newest stores feature a second-level for Market Café seating. Diners select from hot entrees, soups, gourmet sandwiches, and side dishes. Sushi, old-fashioned subs, specialty coffees, a Chinese buffet, pizza and wings, and a fruit and grain bar are also available.

Robert B. Wegman, chairman (left), Danny Wegman, president (right), Danny's daughters, Colleen (left) and Nicole (right) Wegman.

The Wegman brothers were restless trendsetters, eager to try new ways of doing business that gave them more control over quality, so that they could offer customers the best. By the early 1930s, Wegmans stores were involved in every area of food distribution. The company had its own bakery, coffee roasting business, and in-store, cafeteria-style restaurant. They even made their own candy and killed and processed their own chickens!

When they could no longer find eggs that met their quality standards, Wegmans began its own egg farm in 1967. That egg farm, by the way, is now about one million birds strong. It supplies fresh eggs to all Wegmans stores and developed a remarkable egg that leads all national brands in levels of health-promoting Omega-3 fatty acids.

Today, Wegmans Food Markets is one of the most admired retailers in the food business. It's among the 100 largest privately-owned corporations in the country, with more than 60 stores in the Northeast and over 30,000 employees.

Wegmans also sells a full array of premium-quality products under their own label, from bakery items and meat to canned and fro-

zen foods, and gourmet lines of coffees and teas, extra-virgin olive oils, marinades, sauces and the like.

In 1974, Wegmans ventured into the home improvement business with the acquisition of Bilt-Rite Chase-Pitkin, Inc., a retailer of garden, landscaping, building supplies and lumber, which they continue to operate today as Chase-Pitkin Home and Garden in Rochester, Syracuse, and the Southern Tier of New York State.

One of the most sweeping changes in all of retailing began catching on in the 1930s. Walter Wegman set the company on a "self-service" course before his untimely death in 1936, and his brother Jack continued the direction.

Young Robert Wegman, Walter's son, had worked in the family stores during high school and college, and returned to the company after serving in the Marine Corps in the Pacific theater during World War II. He soon became a store manager, and then, the company-wide champion of self-service. In the early 1950s, the company started pre-packing produce, meat, delicatessen items and bakery goods. "People don't like to be watched while they are picking out things to buy," Robert wisely noted.

With the death of his uncle Jack in 1950, Robert became president of the company at the young age of 32. New suburban communities sprang up and the company moved into them. The earliest expansion efforts took the company to nearby Syracuse and Buffalo.

The company's growth pleased Robert Wegman, but he was always more interested in excellence than in growth for its own sake. "If we happen to become the largest food retailer in the country while maintaining the finest food stores, that would be fine," he said. "But given

a choice, I'd rather continue the Wegman tradition of quality and integrity that hearkens back to my father's time."

Making things easier for shoppers was one of Robert Wegman's single-minded passions. Wegmans stores were the first in the nation to introduce grocery pick-up stations on a large scale, with elaborate conveyors moving orders through tunnels under the floor to the parking lots outside. Robert also wanted to help shoppers cut errand time by offering "one-stop shopping." By the end of the 1950s, shoppers could cash personal checks, buy health and beauty products, household equipment, and some wearing apparel. Some Wegmans stores had "Kiddie Corners" where parents could leave their children while they shopped.

Wegmans stores were first to try many new devices, like automatic doors that whooshed open as shoppers walked across the magic carpet, and "electric eye" checkout stands with cash registers that automatically calculated

change and dispensed the correct amount.

But the most important technology was the Universal Product Code and bar code scanning in the 1970s. Robert Wegman headed the grocery industry finance committee to raise funds to create the Universal Product Code, which he thought would eventually save customers time and money. Wegmans stores were the first chain in New York State and third in North America to install a checkout system with scanning.

Wegmans' distribution facilities have also led the industry in their use of state-of-the-art technology. In the mid-'80s, an automated storage/retrieval system warehouse opened, with "robots" to deliver and retrieve full pallets of product at the touch of a button. New frozen and perishable foods distribution centers were built in the '90s, followed in 2001 by the Meat Depot, a one-of-a-kind facility enabling Wegmans to ship product, usually overnight, to the stores on the same day it's received from suppliers.

Today, Wegmans still pushes the envelope in technology. Its web site saves customers time and money by letting them browse

weekly specials, build a shopping list organized by store layout, and search through a library of recipes. They can also buy gift items such as flowers, sweets, fruit baskets, and gourmet snacks through the web site.

By 1934, Wegmans Food Institute was already teaching housewives how to plan menus for nutrition and economy, how to can foods, and how to make the most of a "good electric refrigerator." By the 1970s, Wegmans had created a consumer affairs department, led by home economist and former journalist Mary Ellen Burris. Burris began writing a column on Wegmans' weekly newspaper ad page that continues to this day. Topics have covered everything customers might need to know, from how to cut a slippery mango without cutting your fingers too, to plain talk about scientific controversies such as feeding animals antibiotics, or irradiating foods.

Today, the consumer affairs staff answers all calls, letters, and email from customers. They produce informative pamphlets, teach shoppers about food safety, and answer questions to help customers—including those with special dietary needs—put tasty, nutritious, economical and easy-to-fix meals on the table. And they oversee food safety and quality assurance initiatives to continually improve products and services.

One of the first actions Robert Wegman took when he became president was to raise all salaries. Within a couple of years, a program of fully-paid health care and other benefits for full-time employees followed. Later, the company added profit-sharing and scholarships—employee benefits that are still unusual in the retail food industry.

Today, many Wegmans employees go to college or graduate school with a Wegmans scholarship. The program costs the company more than $3 million annually. About half of the men and women

Executive chefs with advanced culinary training and restaurant experience are in many Wegmans stores. Their mission is to create convenient fresh market cuisine for customers, to take home or for dining in stores that offer seating.

who are now store managers have worked for Wegmans since high school or college, and many completed their education with Wegmans' help.

The company has also had a tradition of helping communities where stores are located. In addition to a strong partnership with the local United Way, Wegmans stores support many other programs, including community concerts, museum exhibits, and sporting events.

In 1981, Robert Wegman received the Sidney Rabb Award from the Food Marketing Institute, given each year to an individual in the industry for "extraordinary contributions to the food marketing industry and to his community."

Day-to-day leadership of the company turned hands again in 1976, when Robert Wegman became chairman and his son Danny, a Harvard graduate, was named president. By the dawn of the new century, the company had grown

to more than 60 stores in New York State, Pennsylvania, and New Jersey, and it had won dozens of national awards for its outstanding retail operations, its progressive employment programs, and its bold community initiatives. In 1998, Danny Wegman was named 'Supermarket Impresario' by *Self* magazine in their list of the nation's "25 Most Influential Food People."

During the 1990s, a fourth generation of Wegmans became active in the company when Danny's daughters, Colleen and Nicole, came on board after graduating from college.

Like his father, Danny kept raising the bar to make Wegmans stores better places to shop, better places to work, and better neighbors in the community. Danny made the stores better places to eat, too.

The company hired "executive chefs" with advanced culinary training and restaurant experience for some of the stores, and gave them the mission of creating better ready-to-eat foods and ready-to-cook foods.

The company also asked

Wegmans' Pâtisserie is an authentic French pastry shop. The concept was developed in consultation with Chef Pierre Hermé, widely regarded as France's top pastry chef. Hermé has been called "the Picasso of Pastry" by Vogue *magazine's Jeff Steingarten.*

internationally-famed chef/restaurateurs like David Bouley, Cesare Casella, and Mark Strausman to share the secrets of their professional kitchens so that Wegmans could offer prepared foods to rival those of top-ranked restaurants. Wegmans people traveled to Europe and Asia to learn first hand the latest food trends. Those trips led to better food in the stores and new product lines like the "Wegmans Italian Classics" pasta sauces, olive oils and more.

When Wegmans turned to dessert, they recruited France's leading pastry chef, Pierre Hermé, to develop patisseries in some stores. The gleaming marble counters are stocked fresh daily with tortes and tarts that rival the best in Paris.

Beginning in the 1990s, Wegmans shoppers could also eat at the cheerful, in-store Market Café. (Some cafés even had a player piano in the room.) Diners could compose a meal from an eye-popping array of hot and cold prepared foods. If they were on the run, there was hot fresh pizza by the slice, submarine sandwiches made to order, a full salad bar, fresh sushi, or European-style sandwiches, like the grilled chicken with braised raisins and fennel compote on fresh Ciabatta bread.

For a sit-down-and-relax meal, shoppers might go for the poached fillet of sole with shrimp and scallop mouse and lobster sauce, accompanied by the pear and provolone salad with walnut vinaigrette and the wild mushroom and three-cheese risotto. Some Market Cafés even served romantic gourmet feasts for Valentine's Day!

Thus, by the turn of a new century, Wegmans Food Markets had turned "one-stop shopping" into a delicious adventure that could end with a full cart, a great meal, and even a little music from the player piano.

WXXI PUBLIC BROADCASTING COUNCIL

WXXI is an essential, lifelong educational resource for the Greater Rochester Area. WXXI provides programming that stimulates and expands thought, inspires the spirit, opens cultural horizons and promotes understanding of the issues of our diverse community, nation and world.

WXXI began with a dream and a vision—to use the power of broadcasting to educate and enrich the lives of people in the Rochester community. Over the last 35 years, it has remained true to that mission.

Founded in 1958 as the Rochester Area Educational Television Association (RAETA), the station's first few years were dedicated to producing instructional television programs for elementary school students. The studios were located in the old East High School and programs were produced in the gym, with airtime borrowed from commercial stations. In 1959, *Assignment: The World* became the first educational series WXXI produced. More than 40 years later, the program is the longest-running instructional program on television and is broadcast nationwide.

On September 6, 1966, after a five-year quest for a broadcast license, Channel 21 went on the air, broadcasting 50 hours of programming a week. The following year, Congress established the Corporation for Public Broadcasting (CPB) to promote growth of the industry, which resulted in a consistent funding base for the station.

In the late 1960s, Channel 21 expanded its focus on public affairs—broadcasting election previews, the city-school budget hearing, sessions on school desegregation and cultural and public affairs series. In 1969, Public Broadcasting Service (PBS) was chartered as the national distributor of public television programs, and the first episode of *Sesame Street* aired. Also that year, WXXI's tele-

WXXI's first remote production truck.

vision remote production truck went on location for the first time and the station held its first auction, a tradition that still runs deep in Rochester culture today.

Early on, WXXI's programming established it as a community resource that was dedicated to the Rochester area. From Chuck Mangione's *Friends & Love* concert to coverage of the Urban League's Black Family Conference to President Nixon's visit to Rochester, WXXI used its airwaves to inform, inspire, educate and entertain—and continues to uphold those same ideals today.

In the 1970s, volunteers and the support of an increasing number of members became crucial factors of WXXI's success. As programming and community involvement expanded, the need for modern facilities dramatically increased. A successful capital campaign was launched and a new Public Broadcasting Center opened at 280 State Street in 1974.

In the 1970s, WXXI's technology expanded to include more modern equipment for remote broadcasts. In 1974, it stood apart as the only station with a fully equipped color television production truck in the region. Today, WXXI's remote capabilities make it possible for the station to deliver current and

relevant programming, locally and nationally.

Also in 1974, WXXI-FM 91.5 went on the air. Together, WXXI-TV and FM tackled tough issues and provided critically acclaimed local news coverage. One year after it went on the air, FM 91.5 premiered *With Heart & Voice*, a weekly program that is now heard on more than 160 stations throughout the country.

Throughout the 1970s, WXXI's programming continued to address controversial social issues such as women's rights, prison reform and health problems. In the mid-1970s, it started offering college courses for credit and launched the Spanish-language news program *¿Que Pasa Rochester?* which still airs each week.

When WXXI linked to PBS in 1978, it became the first television station in Rochester to utilize satellite transmission. The following year, its radio programming received a boost via a new satellite dish linking FM with National Public Radio's (NPR) nationwide satellite system.

The 1980s marked an increase in viewers, supporters, programming and awards for WXXI. A new antenna, tower and transmitter were installed on Pinnacle Hill, which expanded WXXI-TV's reach by an estimated 50,000 homes. FM 91.5 began broadcasting 24 hours a day, and the nationally distributed *Fascinatin' Rhythm* premiered.

As the number of WXXI listeners grew, the need for another radio station became clear. On July 2, 1984, AM 1370 went on the air as a public affairs, news and jazz station. *1370 Connection*, the station's daily call-in program, premiered. Today, the program still serves as a vital community forum. As AM 1370 launched, FM 91.5 converted to an all-classical music

Groundbreaking at 280 State Street (1973).

WXXI Public Broadcasting at 280 State Street (2000).

format. Today, it remains the only station in Rochester devoted to classical music.

In 1988, WXXI partnered with the Association for the Blind and Visually Impaired (ABVI-Goodwill) to operate Reachout Radio. This closed-circuit radio reading service was established to connect people who are blind, visually impaired or print handicapped, with the written word. Today, more than 200 volunteers read local and national newspapers, magazines and books to more than 3,500 Reachout Radio listeners.

In 1989, RAETA was officially renamed WXXI Public Broadcasting Council. With the addition of a new building at 280 State Street in 1991, all of the station's services were finally moved under one roof and membership surpassed 34,000. Then, despite lobbying efforts, WXXI suffered a 37 percent cut in funding from New York State.

Before long, however, the station rallied and began providing new services. WJSL 90.3 in Houghton, New York, began simulcasting FM 91.5. WXXI started programming Cable City 12 through a partnership with the City of Rochester. In 1996, WXXI launched online services at wxxi.org. Soon after, the only satellite uplink in the Greater Rochester Area was installed. In 1999, Classical 91.5/90.3 and AM 1370 began live audio streaming on wxxi.org, reaching listeners virtually around the globe.

Today, community needs, driven by the mission, continue to foster growth and services at WXXI. The station is preparing for the age of digital broadcasting—the most significant change to hit the broadcast industry since the invention of television. In 2001, construction began on a new digital technical center, which will allow WXXI to simultaneously provide a broader variety of quality programming and integrate computer and Internet technologies with television, making it an interactive experience. With digital technology also comes High Definition Television (HDTV), which will offer sharper and clearer images with CD-quality sound. WXXI looks at digital broadcasting as an opportunity to further pursue its vision of education and enrichment for the Rochester community.

No matter what innovations, initiatives, challenges and opportunities lay ahead, WXXI will continue to bring the Rochester community together...just as it has for 35 years.

ZELLER CORPORATION

In 1958, Henry Zeller moved his family from Jamestown, NY to Rochester. He had taken a job for $150 per week with Horaczek and Hayden to start Rochester Electric Supply. Hank's goal was to provide excellent products and service to industrial customers.

In 1961 Hank was 40 years old. He had worked for many different companies and felt he now had to work for himself to be happy. He was convinced that the way to have a good company was to hire highly qualified people who would provide superior service to their customers. With financial support from a friend, he began Zeller Electric in a rented building next to the railroad tracks. Every time a train went by, it was impossible to hear anyone on the phone so he would have to put the person on hold until the train passed! After a few successful years, however, Zeller Electric moved to a better location and continued to prosper.

But Hank didn't get there alone. He had a benefactor who supported him through college and he valued that opportunity throughout his business and personal life. Education became an

Founder, Hank Zeller.

Chairman of the Board Eric Zeller in the company's demo facility.

underlying tenet and a key to the success of Zeller Electric.

While the company grew from a general line electrical distributor with six employees, technology was changing industry. Zeller Electric saw the future, embracing the introduction of programmable logic controllers in automation controls applications. With this change to his industry, Hank recognized the urgency and once more his deep respect for the power of education came through. Zeller Electric was an innovator in the education of customers in this rapidly changing technology.

In 1986, Hank's son Eric was 40 years old. It was in this year that Eric bought his father's business and became the sole shareholder. The Rochester facility continued to expand with a hands-on technical instruction room, and later a state-of-the-art auditorium and demo area. In 1990 Zeller Electric of Buffalo was founded,

again incorporating a spacious hi-tech customer training facility.

With the growing, evolving technology taking the lead in controls applications, integrating it into value-add projects became a complementary focus for Zeller Electric. With a staff of highly qualified electrical engineers and technicians Zeller Electric partnered with customers to develop and implement scalable solutions for their automation controls challenges.

In 1998 Zeller Electric purchased Vordex Controls (Victor, NY) and Control Digital (Toronto, Canada). The purchase of these two companies provided Zeller with enhanced capabilities in the areas of motion control and machine vision inspection systems. These new additions formed the basis for the start of the Zynergy Solutions division of Zeller. Also in 1998, Zeller Electric of Syracuse was opened with 15,000-square feet, including the signature demo/training facilities. At this time Zeller Corporation was also formed as the parent company of the Zeller Electric branches and Zynergy Solutions.

In 2001, Eric Zeller decided to step down from day to day operations. Gary Haseley was named President and CEO. Ironically, Hank was 40 when Zeller Electric was started; Eric turned 40 when he assumed control; and Gary turned 40 as he assumed the reigns.

Throughout the evolution, growth and diversification of Zeller Electric, founder Hank Zeller's original philosophy of providing the best service possible to every customer has stood the test of time. Hank's original gratitude for his educational opportunity has permeated the success. Both Hank and Eric Zeller personally became benefactors in the college education of aspiring students.

While Hank's generosity extended to students unrelated to his company, Eric's beneficiaries became part of the employees' lives in different ways. He offered to assist a student related to a customer. So as not to appear to have any conflict of interest and to follow through on a personally important commitment, Eric announced to his employees that the company would cease doing business with this customer until this student graduated. He immediately had the complete support of each employee, not to mention their utmost respect! Another beneficiary of Eric's personal generosity is Moses Rodriguez.

Moses began in an Urban League after-school work/study program at Zeller Corporation when he was 14 years old. He worked in the warehouse learning business and personal life lessons until his high school graduation. He used his graduation speech to acknowledge and thank the many co-worker

CEO Gary Haseley.

"mentors" who "adopted" him at Zeller. Eric made certain that the lessons from his program at Zeller would be the foundation for Moses' college education, which he personally underwrites.

With Moses comfortably settled into college, Gary contacted Hillside Children's Center to begin another mentoring relationship for two high school students. Sidney Phinazee and Tykea Shade began working after school at Zeller. Both are currently participating in the business culture with an eye toward college educations.

Gary's own experience as a coop student at General Motors Institute (now Kettering University) was instrumental in his head start to success and he's eager to extend the same opportunity to the next class of future engineers from his alma mater. David Jaques of Ontario, Canada has spent alternating semesters working with Zeller Corp.'s engineers on motion and vision projects, gaining invaluable professional and personal growth experiences. Gary meets regularly with David and closely monitors his educational progress.

When Eric decided to step out of the daily operations, the 65 employees of Zeller Corporation chose to recognize and honor his contributions by establishing the Eric Zeller Scholarship Fund through the Hillside Foundation. It's their hope that the educational

Zeller Corporation's customer training facility.

successes supported by Hank, Eric and Gary will continue to allow contributing, responsible young adults to succeed at home, in school, at work and within the community.

While technology has changed the world, the firm foundation of mission and respect has enabled Zeller Electric to evolve through the decades and into the new century as an integral part of Rochester industry and a true community contributor. Hank Zeller would be proud!

A TIMELINE OF ROCHESTER'S HISTORY

Colonel Nathaniel Rochester, founder of Rochester. Courtesy of Rochester City Historian

1789 Ebenezer (Indian) Allen constructs a sawmill and grist mill on one hundred acres as part of an agreement made between the Senecas and land speculators Oliver Phelps and Nathaniel Gorham when they purchased land east of the Genesee the year before. This westside tract of land was given by the Senecas for the mill site.

1803 Colonel Nathaniel Rochester, William Fitzhugh and Charles Carroll purchase the One Hundred Acre Tract near the Genesee Falls.

1809 Construction of Browns Race at the High Falls begins.

1811 Settlement of the One Hundred Acre Tract begins.

1812 The War of 1812 begins, slowing sales of land.

1814 The end of the War of 1812 stimulates settlement.

1817 One Hundred Acre Tract becomes Rochesterville.

1817 Austin Steward arrives in Rochester, becoming the first black grocer and butcher.

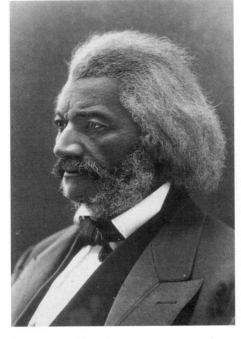

Frederick Douglass. Courtesy of Rochester City Historian

1817 Erie Canal begins construction at Rome, New York.

1821 Monroe County forms from parts of Genesee and Ontario Counties.

1823 First Erie Canal aqueduct over the Genesee opens. Erie Canal finished to Rochester. Immediately successful.

1825 Erie Canal opens from Buffalo to Albany connecting with the Hudson River and New York City ports. Grand opening ceremonies bring Governor DeWitt Clinton to "the Young Lion of the West" as Rochester was known.

1829 On Friday, November 13th, Sam Patch jumps to his death at the Genesee Falls in a dare-devil stunt after having twice jumped Niagara Falls without incident.

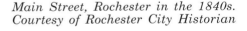

Main Street, Rochester in the 1840s. Courtesy of Rochester City Historian

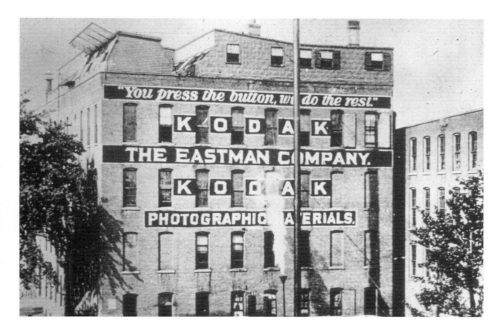

Kodak's headquarters showing famous logo "You Press the button, we do the rest." Courtesy of Rochester City Historian

Selden automobile in 1877. Courtesy of Rochester City Historian

1834 Rochester becomes a city.

1838 Mt. Hope Cemetery laid out.

1842 Second Erie Canal aqueduct opens nearby the first aqueduct. Wider, with less of a tight turn on the east side and it does not leak.

1845 Susan B. Anthony arrives in Rochester with her family.

1847 Frederick Douglass arrives in Rochester and begins the *North Star*, an abolitionist newspaper.

1848 First meeting of Womens Rights at Seneca Falls, New York. Susan B. Anthony is not in attendance though some of her family members are. She attends the second meeting held in Rochester.

1865 The most devastating

Buffalo Street (West Main Street) after the flood of 1865. Courtesy of Rochester City Historian

Susan B. Anthony. Courtesy of Rochester City Historian

Women march to Susan B. Anthony's Mt. Hope Cemetery gravesite carrying placards calling for woman's suffrage. Courtesy of Rochester City Historian

294

flood ever recorded in Rochester destroyed many businesses on the Main Street bridge and downtown. Returning soldiers faced reconstruction.

1884 Establishment of Eastman Dry Plate and Film Company.

1888 Kodak introduces the magical box camera preloaded with film. Eastman adopts Kodak as name along with the slogan "You push the button, we do the rest."

1888 The first twenty acres of land, now Highland Park, accepted for what became the Rochester Parks system.

1889 Famed landscape architect Frederick Law Olmsted arrives in Rochester to design the parks. Identifies Genesee River as focal point of area.

1895 Frederick Douglass dies.

1906 Susan B. Anthony dies.

1928 City Manager form of government adopted.

1932 George Eastman dies.

1934 Centennial of Rochester celebrated.

1950 Chester Carlson and Joseph Wilson unveil the first Xerox machine.

The first flight in Rochester was over Genesee Valley Park. Courtesy of Rochester City Historian

Float celebrates the flower industry in Rochester. Courtesy of Rochester City Historian

Zahner & Son Sausage Store on Front Street. Courtesy of Rochester City Historian

On July 29, 1927 Charles Lindbergh meets with Major Martin O'Neil. Courtesy of Rochester City Historian

1950s GI Bill helps movement to the suburbs and new home construction.

1951 Opening of Mt. Morris Dam south of Rochester ends ravaging floods of the city.

1961 Midtown, the nation's first indoor shopping mall with an underground parking lot, opens.

1964 Racial riots rock the city and launch major urban renewal projects.

1971 Monroe County Sesquicentennial.

1984 City celebrates it's Sesquicentennial.

Opening of the Public Library in the Rundel Memorial Building in 1936. Courtesy of Rochester City Historian

1988 City and County Parks celebrate Centennial.

1991 *Sam Patch* becomes the first tour boat in 75 years to ply the downtown section of the Genesee River, a spur of the Erie Canal.

1994 Rochester's first black mayor William A. Johnson, takes office.

1996 Rochester Public Library opens its expanded complex near the new international headquarters of Bausch & Lomb and the Blue Cross/Blue Shield offices.

2000 Time capsule from 1873 that had been placed in the old City Hall is opened before the end of the century. It is replaced by modern messages to be opened in 2030.

2000 Rochester ends the century with the All America City Award.

2001 Genesee Hospital closed its doors due to declining admissions and increasing costs.

2001 158 fiberglass horses painted by local artists and funded by High Falls Brewery and other sponsors raises hundreds of thousands of dollars for charity. They are scattered throughout the region and are popular works of art.

Soon after the Erie Canal was moved to Genesee Valley Park, the road was built above the aqueduct. The subway was built in the old canal bed under the road and abandoned in 1956. The space is attractive to developers as retail space to connect to the Rochester Public Library and the city's skyway system. Courtesy of the City of Rochester

War Week in downtown Rochester on June 17, 1942. James Farasey, Joe Hausey, Seargent John Evans. Courtesy of Rochester City Historian

Bibliography

Any list of the major historical works on Rochester must include Henry O'Reilly, *Sketches of Rochester; with Incidental Notices of Western New York* (Rochester, 1838); William F. Peck, *Semi-Centennial History of the City of Rochester* (Syracuse, 1884); and Jane Marsh Parker, *Rochester, A Story Historical* (Rochester, 1884). Additional volumes by Peck and by numerous other writers spurred the organization of the Rochester Historical Society in 1888 and the establishment of the City Historian's Office in 1921. As City Historian, Edward R. Foreman launched a series of annual volumes compiled from a long file of addresses delivered over the years at historical gatherings; these now appeared as the Rochester Historical Society *Publications* (1922-1948). As Foreman's successor, Blake McKelvey edited the last ten volumes of that series and launched the new quarterly *Rochester History*, published by the Rochester Public Library, (1939---). He also undertook the research and writing of his four-volume history of the city: *Rochester, The Water Power City: 1812-1854* (Cambridge, 1945); *Rochester: The Flower City: 1855-1890* (Cambridge, 1949); *Rochester: The Quest for Quality: 1890-1925* (Cambridge, 1956); *Rochester: An Emerging Metropolis: 1925-1961* (Rochester, 1961).

Among the numerous articles and books drawn upon in the preparation of this summary account, several deserve special mention: James E. Seaver, *Mary Jemison* (edited with commentary by Charles D. Vail, New York, 1925); Orsamus Turner, *History of the Pioneer Settlement of Phelps and Gorham's Purchase* (Rochester, 1851); Helen Cowan, "Charles Williamson: Genesee Promoter: Friend of Anglo-American Rapproachment," Rochester Historical Society (RHS) *Publications*, XIX, passim; Morley Turpin, "Ebenezer Allan in the Genesee Country," RHS *Publications*, XI:313-338; Blake McKelvey, "Seneca 'Time of Troubles'," *Rochester History*, XIII, No. 3; McKelvey, "Historic Aspects of the Phelps and Gorham Treaty of July 4-8, 1788," *Rochester History*, I, No. 1; McKelvey, "Colonel Nathaniel Rochester," *Rochester History*, XXIV, No. 1; Joseph W. Barnes, "Bridging the Lower Falls," *Rochester History*, XXXVI, No. 1; Barnes, "Obediah Dogberry, Rochester Freethinker" *Rochester History*, XXXVI, No. 3; Adelbert Cronise, "The Beginnings of Modern Spiritualism In and Near Rochester," RHS *Publications*, V:1-22; Whitney R. Cross, *The Burned-over District* (Ithaca, 1950); Leslie A. White, "Extracts from the European Travel Journal of Lewis H. Morgan," RHS *Publications*, XVI: 221-389; McKelvey, "Lights and Shadows in Local Negro History," *Rochester History*, XXI, No. 4; McKelvey, "Rochester's Part in the Civil War," *Rochester History* XXIII, No. 1; McKelvey, "Women's Rights in Rochester: A Century of Progress," *Rochester History*, X, No. 2 & 3; McKelvey, "Walter Rauschenbusch's Rochester," *Rochester History*, XIV, No. 4; McKelvey, "Rochester's Ethnic Transformations," *Rochester History*, XXV, No. 3; Jerry Mangionne, *Mount Allegro* (Cambridge, 1942); Emma Goldman, *Living My Life* (New York, 1931); Carl W. Ackerman, *George Eastman* (Boston, 1930); Clement G. Lanni, *Beat 'Em or Join 'Em* (Rochester, 1931); Henry W. Clune, *Main Street Beat* (New York, 1947) and other books by the same author; Arch Merrill, *Rochester Sketchbook* (Rochester, 1947) and other books; Arthur J. May, *A History of the University of Rochester: 1850-1962* (Rochester, 1977).

Several books of a general interest include: Florence Lee, *Pleasant Valley: An Early History of Monroe County and Region: 1650-1850* (New York, 1970); Jean France and Betsy Brayer, *Of Town & The River: A Rochester Guide* (Rochester, 1977); Blake McKelvey, *Rochester on the Genesee* (Syracuse, 1973); Howard Hosmer, *Monroe County: The Sesqui-Centennial Account of the History of Monroe County, New York: 1821-1971* (Rochester, 1971).

Acknowledgements

I am chiefly indebted, in this summary review of my researches on the history of Rochester, to the city which supported that work over a period of thirty-six years. As City Historian, I produced five books and numerous articles on Rochester's history, and since I have relied heavily on these earlier works for this more generalized account I am indebted to their successive publishers—the Harvard University Press, the Christopher Press, the Syracuse University Press, and the Rochester Public Library.

To give this volume a special anecdotal flavor, I have again consulted the works listed in the bibliography and other resources in the Rochester Public Library. I am grateful to Wayne K. Arnold, head of the Local History Division, for assistance in this research, and to Dr. Joseph Barnes, my successor as City Historian, who had read all of the chapters and supplied many helpful suggestions. I am also grateful to John Phillips, JoAnn Levy, and Margaret C. Tropp of Windsor Publications, Inc., for their painstaking reading of the manuscript as well as Deborah Durell and Paula Schoerner for their editorial assistance. The numerous questions they raised have prompted me to amplify or otherwise clarify many points to make the account more understandable to distant readers. Howard C. Hosmer must not be overlooked for his immense contributions.

I am further indebted to Dr. Barnes for collecting and annotating the rich array of illustrations that illuminate the text. His proficiency in the location and use of historical photographs uniquely qualified him for this service, which has added much to the value of this book. The excellent color photographs taken by Robert Fuschetto in consultation with Dr. Barnes supply an additional bonus. I am also grateful to Thomas T. Mooney and Syl Novelli of the Rochester Area Chamber of Commerce for their counsel and support in the presentation of this volume.

Blake McKelvey

In updating this book, I wish to thank Carol Fede, Shirley Cox-Husted, Ira Srole, Dave Lamb, Harold Hacker, Joe Struble, and Ted Curtis and the Local History Division of the Rochester Public Library.

Ruth Rosenberg-Naparsteck

*I*ndex

301